SEEKING CERTAINTY

THE MISGUIDED QUEST FOR
CONSTITUTIONAL FOUNDATIONS

DANIEL A. FARBER

SUZANNA SHERRY

CHICAGO AND LONDON

Daniel A. Farber is the Henry J. Fletcher Professor of Law at the University of Minnesota. **Suzanna Sherry** is the Cal Turner Professor of Law and Leadership at Vanderbilt University. They are authors of *Beyond All Reason: The Radical Assault on Truth in American Law* (1997) and *A History of the American Constitution* (1990).

The University of Chicago Press, Chicago 60637
The University of Chicago Press, Ltd., London
© 2002 by The University of Chicago
All rights reserved. Published 2002
Printed in the United States of America
11 10 09 08 07 06 05 04 03 02
1 2 3 4 5

ISBN: 0-226-23808-3 (cloth)

Library of Congress Cataloging-in-Publication Data

Farber, Daniel A., 1950–
    Desperately seeking certainty : the misguided quest for constitutional foundations / Daniel A. Farber, Suzanna Sherry.
        p.   cm.
    Includes bibliographical references and index.
        ISBN 0-226-23808-3 (cloth : alk. paper)
        1. Constitutional law—United States—Interpretation and construction.
        2. Constitutional law—United States—Philosophy. I. Sherry, Suzanna. II. Title.

KF4550 .F367 2002
342.73—dc21

                                    2001048006

⊗ The paper used in this publication meets the minimum requirements of the American National Standard for Information Sciences—Permanence of Paper for Printed Library Materials, ANSI Z39.48-1992.

DESPERATELY SEEKING CERTAINTY

DESPERATELY

THE UNIVERSITY OF CHICAGO PRESS

CONTENTS

The book you hold in your hands is not the book we set out to write. Originally, we planned to follow our earlier critique of certain legal theorists on the Left with a companion volume on conservatives. Indeed, our working title for several months was "What's Wrong with the Right?" But scholarship sometimes has a mind of its own. The more we read, the more we came to believe that the most interesting difficulties were not distinctive to conservatives but related to the enterprise of constitutional theory more generally. In particular, we found that some leading constitutional scholars on both the Left and the Right exhibited two troublesome tendencies. They quested after certainty in constitutional law—seeking foundational theories of interpretation to provide simple answers to all constitutional questions and unify all of constitutional doctrine. And in their search for foundations, they proposed ever more novel and less plausible solutions. In consequence, some of the most prominent constitutional theorists of our day reached simple, elegant, and utterly wrong conclusions almost at every turn.

And so we changed our focus from conservatism to constitutional theory. In this book we examine six scholars of varying political inclinations, all of whom fall prey to the perils of foundationalism. In trying to make constitutional interpretation simple, certain, and coherent, they mischaracterize both the Constitution and the judicial enterprise. Both are human creations, and thus both are complex, uncertain, and sometimes inconsistent. Judicial interpretation of the Constitution is a constantly evolving process of accommodation, and it cannot be constrained by artificial theories built from the ground up.

Despite its departure from the original plan, this book is nevertheless a fitting sequel to our earlier work. Both the radical multiculturalist theories we considered in our first book and the more mainstream constitutional scholarship that is the focus of this one are flawed at least in part because they reject pragmatism as an approach to legal decisionmaking. Pragmatist constitutional adjudication is eclectic and uncertain: it takes into account multiple sources, and rarely produces an unequivocal answer. But pragmatist judging does have boundaries—certain types of arguments, such as those that amount to judicial fiat, are illegitimate—and it does rule out some answers and make others more or less persuasive. Uncomfortable with the "neither fish nor fowl" nature of pragmatism, radical and mainstream scholars respond in different ways. The radicals exaggerate the uncertainty and deny that any legal conclusion is logically better than any other. The mainstream scholars whose work we consider in this book reject all uncertainty and fruitlessly seek theories that will eliminate it.

This book, then, is the second in a series designed to critique nonpragmatist approaches. A projected third book, still in the planning stages and by far the hardest to write, will explore the implications of a pragmatist approach to constitutional adjudication. This volume is thus part of a work in progress.

Even as a work in progress, of course, this book benefited from the help of many people, and we are grateful to all of them. We thank Jim Chen, Richard Epstein, Phil Frickey, Barry Friedman, and David McGowan for reading earlier drafts of various chapters and providing helpful comments. Mike Paulsen gave us ideas and insights into some of the conservative scholars we discuss. Katie Moerke, University of Minnesota Law School class of 2001, and Jeremy Kernodle, Vanderbilt University Law School class of 2001, provided excellent research assistance. Tom Sullivan and Kent Syverud, our deans at Minnesota and Vanderbilt, respectively, supported this project financially and intellectually. We also benefited from comments by faculty at workshops at Boalt Hall, the University of Chicago, Duke, the University of Kansas, Loyola (L.A.), Northwestern, the University of Pennsylvania, and the University of Texas. The most important contribution to the book—probably greater than our own—came from Laurie Newbauer, who worked tirelessly to input our changes, correct our errors, and deal with all the technical complications of a project that straddled two universities and two computer networks.

We would also like to thank Robert Bork, Justice Antonin Scalia, Richard Epstein, Akhil Amar, Bruce Ackerman, and Ronald Dworkin (several of whom we have never met). We chose their work as the subject of this book because of its significance and its excellence—it would be no fun to critique second-rate scholars. Their work is thoughtful, influential, and important, and they have made major contributions to constitutional law and constitutional scholarship. And despite our fundamental disagreements with their scholarship, we always learned from it. We hope they will be able to say the same of this book.

Finally, we thank our spouses, Dianne Farber and Paul Edelman, and our children, Joe, Sonia, and Nora Farber, and Hannah and Joshua Edelman, for putting up with us—which is not easy even when we are not trying to write a book.

Please remember that this is a library book, and that it belongs only temporarily to each person who uses it. Be considerate. Do not write in this, or any, library book.

CHAPTER I

OF LAW AND LATKES

An apparently normal, middle-aged woman goes to a psychia-
trist. The psychiatrist asks her why she is there.
"My family sent me," she replies. "They think I'm crazy."
"Why do they think you're crazy?" the psychiatrist asks.
"Because I like potato latkes."*
"That's not crazy," says the doctor. "Why, I like latkes myself."
"That's wonderful! You should come to my house sometime.
I have closets full of them."

This book is about six prominent constitutional scholars who have (figura-
tively, of course) closets full of latkes. Each has taken an interesting and useful idea only to become fixated on it. They have tried to build an entire
constitutional structure from the ground up using very limited materials.
One, for example, looks primarily to the views of the generation that wrote
and ratified the Constitution, another only to its text.

We call this type of approach "foundationalism" because it seeks to
ground all of constitutional law on a single foundation. We believe that
foundationalism is doomed to failure no matter how brilliant the theorist or
how important the foundational idea. Latkes are delicious, but a diet of
nothing but potato pancakes does not make for a healthy individual, and a

---

*Latkes are Jewish potato pancakes, fried in oil and traditionally served at Hanukkah.
Depending on location, they are pronounced "lot-kuhs" or "lot-kees," with the accent
on the first syllable. We include a recipe at the end of the book, just to ensure that even
the most skeptical reader can find something of lasting value in these pages. Of course,
the same joke could be told about almost any food.

diet of a single approach to constitutional interpretation does not produce a healthy constitutional regime.

Indeed, foundationalism often leads to radical results, and the six leading scholars we examine are no exception. The problem is that constitutional law is a messy amalgam of ideas and principles, some of which are in tension with one another. The foundationalist who comes in intending to sweep clean this two-hundred-year-old edifice is likely to suggest some startling changes.

What are the basic ideas and principles of constitutional law, many of which are rejected by the foundationalists? We think that most Americans—including most lawyers—would endorse the following eight propositions about the Constitution:

1. The Constitution is a written document, drafted in 1787 and ratified in 1789, with important amendments soon thereafter adding the Bill of Rights, and other important amendments added in the wake of the Civil War (as well as at other times).

2. The Supreme Court is in charge of enforcing the Constitution. Its job is to follow the law, not to bow to public opinion or to implement the personal values of the justices. In general, interpretation should begin with the meaning the words conveyed to those who wrote and ratified the various parts of it ("the framers" or "the founding generation").

3. The Constitution can only be changed through the formal, cumbersome process of amendment, specified in Article V.

4. The Supreme Court's rulings are law, and must be followed by other judges and government officials as well as by ordinary citizens.

5. Under the Constitution, the federal government has the power to legislate on a broad range of subjects, including health and the environment, workplace conditions and discrimination, drugs, and organized crime.

6. It is unconstitutional for either the federal or state governments to engage in racial segregation or to deliberately discriminate against women or racial or ethnic minorities.

7. The Constitution envisions states not merely as regional offices of the federal government but as possessing their own separate sovereignty. However, both states and the federal government must respect freedom of speech, refrain from unconstitutional searches, respect the right to remain silent, and so forth.

8. It would violate the Constitution—or so most people assume—for the government to assign spouses to people or to dictate their family size, to

require them to get abortions, to deprive them of custody of their children arbitrarily, or to force them to submit to sterilization.

These eight propositions are, we think, little more than common sense, and most people would find no hesitation in affirming all of them. The problem, as legal sophisticates have long realized, is that they are in tension with one another. That is, if given their full scope they would contradict each other. For instance, adherence to original intent is hard to square with rejection of racial segregation, since the same Congress that proposed the Fourteenth Amendment (barring discrimination) also maintained segregated schools in the District of Columbia. This puts the second proposition in tension with the sixth. Protecting family choices—the decision whom to marry or how many children to have—is not mentioned anywhere in the written Constitution, and thus the first three principles conflict with the eighth. And the rules of constitutional law have changed significantly over time without recourse to any formal amendment. Indeed, without such changes, most of the current understanding of government power (such as the federal government's power to protect the environment) would be questionable.

Almost everyone has a quarrel with at least some judicial decisions—either the Court appalls us by recognizing the right to an abortion in the first place or by limiting the right too much, by giving the federal government too much power or too little, by protecting flag burners or by protecting cross burners. We ourselves have serious criticisms of many specific decisions. Yet, however unsatisfactory we may find aspects of the current law, it does fit at least in a general way with the way most people understand the Constitution—it does not, for example, make the federal minimum wage or antidiscrimination laws unconstitutional, nor does it require the government to enact these laws; at the same time, it forbids the government from engaging in racial segregation or censoring books.

Thus current constitutional law is an uneasy compromise between the constitutional law we expect the Supreme Court to give us and the constitutional methods we expect it to use. This vision of constitutional law as an evolving compromise is often described as a "pragmatist" approach. For pragmatists—including, we believe, most past and current Supreme Court justices—each new case presents the need (and the opportunity) to weigh text and history, precedent and policy, principle and consequences. No single factor is dispositive, and the persuasiveness of the result ultimately depends on a blend of statesmanship and workman-like lawyering.

Living with contradictions is not disturbing for most working lawyers, who realize that as a human product, the law often finds itself pulled in several directions by seemingly valid mandates. As one scholar puts it: "Doctrine is destined to stay messy and sometimes illogical, exactly as are the values it is designed to protect and we inconsistent humans who embrace those values."[1] We live with the contradictions through a messy process of accommodation. Case law slowly evolves from the foundation of original intent and text, and over time the rules of constitutional law are modified to fit a changing society without breaking faith with the framers and the text they bequeathed us. The result can be found in any constitutional law textbook today—an enormous body of legal doctrine, full of fine distinctions, balancing tests, and all kinds of other devices annoying to purists.

Not surprisingly, there are those who find this compromise unprincipled. Viewing themselves as Luther-like reformers, they seek to remake a corrupted church from the foundations upward. Like Luther, each claims that a pure vision of the Constitution requires a far-reaching reconceptualization of existing institutions.

Each of the six major figures on whom we focus in this book has recently attempted such a Reformation of American constitutional law. They span the ideological spectrum. Three are conservatives: Antonin Scalia, Robert Bork, and Richard Epstein. Two—Bruce Ackerman and Ronald Dworkin—are liberals, and one (Akhil Amar) is a populist who is liberal on social issues but tough on crime. Some of their conclusions are startling indeed: the Constitution was silently amended by Franklin Roosevelt's New Deal (Ackerman). The federal government is free to engage in racial discrimination (Bork). Constitutional law is in large part a branch of moral philosophy (Dworkin). The Thirteenth Amendment's ban on slavery prohibits child abuse and limits the right to freedom of speech (Amar). The minimum wage is unconstitutional (Epstein). People can be punished for their political positions by being deprived of government jobs (Scalia).

In reaching these remarkable conclusions, all six scholars claim to rely squarely on the true meaning of the Constitution, whether reflected in the text, the original understanding, or simply the correct moral philosophy. They all reject the messy evolutionary process that has created modern constitutional doctrines in favor of what they view as a strictly logical and principled analysis based on indisputable foundations. We sympathize with their desire for logical order and their discomfort with the untidy reality of constitutional doctrine. We too would like a neat theory that reduces constitutional law to a reliable formula, eliminating any need for judicial creativity and making all of constitutional law internally consistent. But we think no such formula exists, and in this book we will show, if nothing else, that none of these six figures has found one.

Most of the book is devoted to demonstrating where each foundationalist scholar goes wrong, and to suggesting that the main problem is not the scholar's ideas, but his fixation on them—in other words, his foundationalism (and where it takes him). Sometimes foundationalism leads to radical—or at least peculiar—results. Chapter 4, on Richard Epstein, and chapter 5, on Akhil Amar, illustrate this tendency. At other times a foundationalist scholar cannot tolerate the results his own theory dictates, and abandons it at key points (as do Robert Bork, discussed in chapter 2, and Antonin Scalia, discussed in chapter 3). Or else he adds so many wrinkles to the theory that it no longer functions as an interpretive blueprint but instead seems merely a rationalization of favored results (both Amar and Bruce Ackerman, discussed in chapter 6, fall prey to this flaw, as does Ronald Dworkin, discussed in chapter 7). The end result, however, is always the same: no single grand theory can successfully guide judges or provide determinate—or even sensible—answers to all constitutional questions. Only an amalgam of theories will do.

Our object is not to suggest that the scholars' ideas are worthless,[2] but to change the focus of constitutional scholarship. We are not the first to criticize these scholars—indeed, several have spawned cottage industries attacking them—but we are the first to draw parallels among the scholars and to place primary blame on their common foundationalism rather than on their individual shortcomings.

Our principal target is not the inevitable flaws in the work of individual scholars but a widespread trend in constitutional scholarship. Our six scholars are both influential and representative of legal academia in general. One leading younger constitutionalist, for example, names among the six books he considers "the most valuable works of constitutional scholarship written in the modern era"—which he claims "will certainly shape and affect all [his] future work"—books by three of our six scholars.[3] For several decades, many of the nation's most prominent constitutional scholars have set the agenda for the development, explanation, and justification of constitutional jurisprudence. And that jurisprudence has turned on grand theories of constitutional law: finding just the right foundation on which to build an entire constitutional edifice.

We, along with a growing number of constitutional scholars, believe that foundationalism—whether originalist, textualist, or some other brand—is a misguided and ultimately futile approach. This book is therefore meant as a multipronged attack on foundationalism, undertaken in the hope that we can persuade constitutional scholars to focus less on devising grand theories and more on solving particular constitutional conundrums.[4]

In particular, constitutional scholarship, on and off the Court, has come to focus more and more on originalism. As one scholar notes, originalism's attractiveness comes in part from the failure of its opponents to provide any alternative: "It takes a theory to beat a theory."[5] We disagree: showing that a type of theory is fatally flawed should be enough to defeat it—and that is what we try to show about foundationalism in the next six chapters. In chapter 8, we give a preview of what we hope is a pragmatic alternative to grand theory, an idea we plan to develop more fully in our next book.

This book is also a broader attack on a phenomenon that has come to pervade legal scholarship—the idea that novelty is the ultimate test of the worth of an idea. It is no coincidence that all our subjects are both leading scholars *and* far off the beaten path in their ideas. Earlier generations of legal scholars built on existing scholarship, often producing work that broke new ground—sometimes brilliantly—without severing all ties to their inherited traditions.[6] Although some constitutional scholars still follow their example, many of the most prominent scholars do not. Indeed, today it sometimes seems that proposing counterintuitive theories is the fastest way up the academic ladder.[7] This perverse incentive is likely to create exactly the scholarship we describe in this book: original, creative, even brilliant, but unfortunately quite obviously wrong. The Constitution(s) described by our six scholars would be virtually unrecognizable to the typical American judge, lawyer, or citizen. And of course, each scholar's Constitution is unrecognizable to the others.

Thus we critique these six prominent constitutional scholars, of varying political and theoretical persuasions, in order to illustrate what we view as the two most important flaws in mainstream constitutional scholarship: foundationalism and a penchant for novelty.[8]

These constitutional scholars may be the last bastion of foundationalism in law. In the late nineteenth century, what has come to be called "classical" legal thought dominated the legal academy. Like our modern constitutional foundationalists, classical legal scholars believed that law was a comprehensive system that could provide unique right answers to every question, and that those answers could be derived from a small number of abstract principles. In most fields of law, the classical scholars' approach has been replaced by a less formalist view of legal analysis. But in constitutional law, it seems, formalism has now regained its appeal. In a sense, these six scholars represent the modern incarnation of Christopher Columbus Langdell and his contemporaries.[9]

We begin with the conservatives. Chapter 2 examines the conventional form of originalism advocated by Robert Bork and other, less well-known, scholars. Bork, who taught at the Yale Law School for many years, was the solicitor general who, in the famous 1973 "Saturday Night Massacre," fired Archibald Cox—the Watergate special prosecutor—after two higher-ranking Justice Department officials resigned rather than do so. Later put on the lower federal bench by President Reagan, Bork's nomination to the Supreme Court in 1987 caused a political uproar; the Senate ultimately rejected him. He is now at the American Enterprise Institute, having resigned his judgeship in the wake of the Senate battle. Justice Antonin Scalia, the subject of chapter 3, taught law at the University of Chicago and the University of Virginia before President Reagan nominated him to a federal court of appeals in 1982 and then to the Supreme Court in 1986. He is the intellectual leader of the right wing of the current Supreme Court, and his version of originalism recognizes and attempts to remedy the defects of Bork's less sophisticated views. Chapter 4 covers the constitutional scholarship of Richard Epstein, who has spent most of his career at the University of Chicago Law School and is justifiably considered one of the most talented legal thinkers in the country. Unlike Bork and Scalia, Epstein makes only a token bow toward the original understanding. He focuses instead on an economic and libertarian approach to the Constitution.

In chapter 5 we begin our discussion of the more liberal scholars with Akhil Amar of the Yale Law School. A generation younger than the other scholars, Amar has already made his mark in legal scholarship with several books and dozens of articles. He, like Scalia, presents a sophisticated version of originalism that pays careful attention to both text and context. Amar's additional emphasis on populism and majority rule leads him to liberal results on most constitutional issues but to a decidedly conservative approach to the rights of criminal defendants. We turn in chapter 6 to another liberal Yale law professor, Bruce Ackerman, who is also an originalist and a populist, but a more subtle one than his younger colleague. His approach to constitutional law distinguishes between two types of politics: ordinary politics and constitutional politics. It is only when Americans are engaged in constitutional politics that their decisions represent the true will of the majority, which then dictates the correct interpretation of the Constitution. Unlike the other scholars, Ackerman does not believe that constitutional politics must produce a text—a written constitutional amendment—to be effective and binding on future generations. He thus lavishes attention on an event largely neglected by the other scholars (and roundly criticized by Epstein): the New Deal. Chapter 7 examines the constitutional thought of one of the premier modern legal philosophers, Ronald Dworkin. Dworkin, who splits his time between Oxford and the New York University Law School, is something of a liberal counterpart to Epstein. Like Epstein, he pays at least lip service to the original understanding, but his primary approach to constitutional interpretation is philosophical. He argues that the Constitution, correctly interpreted, embodies a particular political philosophy—his own.

Dworkin, of course, is not alone in seeing his own philosophy reflected in the Constitution. A close examination of the work of these scholars reveals that, regardless of the specific foundational principle, its application usually seems to produce results that mirror the scholar's political views. Thus Bork and Scalia find that an analysis of text and history yields a conservative interpretation while Amar and Ackerman use other historical evidence to produce liberal interpretations of the same language.

In the last chapter, we return to this and other problems with foundationalism. The key problem is that each foundationalist is engaged in an ultimately futile search for certainty, purity, and consistency: a sort of "unified field" theory of the Constitution. They all have what one academic has wittily called "the endemic disease" of academics—"a hardening of categories that transforms a lower-case theory into an upper-case Grand Theory."[10] But constitutional law is a complex human creation, not an elegant intellectual puzzle. Each theorist, by focusing on only a single aspect of the multifaceted Constitution, reduces its complexity by sacrificing accuracy. The six scholars are much like the blind men and the elephant. Each man feels only a part of the elephant, and thus describe very different things: the trunk feels like a snake, the tusk like a horn, the legs like a tree, and the tail like a broom. But the whole elephant is none of these things—or, rather, is all of them at once—and each man misses the mark in his description. So it is with our six foundationalists, who each ignore all but a favored aspect of the Constitution.

The worst part of it is that they do not even accomplish their aim of producing certainty: the theories are so malleable that a judge adopting any one of them could reach virtually any result. Moreover, the search for a single, certain foundation for constitutional law is not only futile and detrimental to a healthy constitutional regime, but unnecessary. Like the elephant, constitutional law works in practice despite its contradictions in theory.

We close by suggesting the directions that constitutional scholarship might more profitably take. We enjoy constitutional theory—and indeed have written some ourselves—but it is not the most useful form of constitutional scholarship. We like latkes, too, but we don't eat them for every meal.

CHAPTER 2

IN THE BEGINNING: ROBERT BORK AND OTHER ORIGINALISTS

Robert Bork, whose failed nomination to the Supreme Court may have been the Lexington and Concord of the culture wars—the "shot heard round the world"—is perhaps the first and most prominent of the constitutional foundationalists. Bork endorses the simplest form of originalism: he believes that the Constitution should be interpreted to reflect the public intentions of those who drafted and ratified it. But, like all the other scholars we examine, his originalism is unmistakably shaped by his political and moral positions.

Although we begin with Bork, we view him more as a spokesman for originalism than as a serious practitioner of this method of interpretation. His own account of the founders' original intent is superficial and anachronistic. But his work provides an accessible and vivid description of the most basic type of originalism, and he has made a name for himself as a conservative constitutional icon. Thus his theories deserve attention in their own right.

Moreover, regardless of his failings as a constitutional historian, Bork is representative of one prominent strain of constitutional interpretation. Scholars who are less well-known outside of academia but increasingly influential within it not only cite Bork's work, but also carry his simple originalism forward with greater sophistication and more scholarly depth. Thus, although in this chapter we focus primarily on Bork, we also discuss several other scholars with similar theories, including Frank Easterbrook (a U.S. Court of Appeals judge and formerly on the faculty at the University of Chicago Law School), Steven Calabresi of the Northwestern University Law School, and Gary Lawson of the Boston University Law School.

In addition to being a representative of a still-active school of constitutional interpretation, Bork's conventional version of originalism has much in common with the more sophisticated theories of the scholars we discuss in later chapters. Bork, like the others, is a foundationalist in that he seeks to answer all constitutional questions with a single, narrow method of interpretation. One might even view Bork as someone whose foundationalism tripped him up because he took it too seriously—a cautionary example for our other scholars.

There are other commonalities as well. Like several of the other scholars, he wants to constrain judges—indeed, his primary argument in favor of originalism is that it constrains the power of judges to second-guess the popular branches. Moreover, originalism, whether simple or sophisticated, suffers from common flaws that pervade the analysis of all of the originalists in our group (only Epstein and Dworkin make no serious claim to investigate the historical record). Thus, examining Bork's theory exposes difficulties that will recur in the work of other originalist scholars. Finally, because non-lawyers are probably more familiar with Bork than with our other scholars, it is fitting to begin with him.

THE ALLURE (AND IMPOSSIBILITY) OF ORIGINALISM
AS A CONSTRAINT

The role of historical evidence in constitutional law has always been of interest to scholars. Recently, however, the theory that the Constitution should be interpreted solely by looking to its historical meaning has become more prominent. Bork and others argue that the Constitution today can only mean what eighteenth-century readers of its text took it to mean. Thus Lawson speaks of the Constitution's "original public meaning" and says that "other approaches to interpretation are simply wrong."[1] Easterbrook tells us to look at the meaning that "the ratifiers and other sophisticated political actors at the time would have imputed to the text."[2] Calabresi argues that the meaning of the Constitution, and of other legal writings, "depends on their texts, as they were objectively understood by the people who enacted or ratified them."[3] This means, in the words of another originalist, relying on the "ordinary usage" at the time the Constitution was enacted.[4]

Bork, like most of the scholars we examine, is drawn to originalism primarily as a method of constraining judges from imposing their own values on democratic majorities. He insists that following the original understanding of the framers of the Constitution is both possible and desirable, and is indeed the only way to prevent judges from imposing their own political and moral views on the rest of the nation. He denounces most recent Supreme Court doctrine as "political judging,"[5] and maintains that originalism is the only way to avoid such lawlessness:

> This is an anxious problem and one that can be met only by understanding that judges must always be guided by the original understanding of the Constitution's provisions. Once adherence to the original understanding is weakened or abandoned, a judge, perhaps instructed by a revisionist theorist, can reach any result, because the human mind and will, freed of the constraints of history and "the sediment of history which is law," can reach any result. As we have seen, no set of propositions is too preposterous to be espoused by a judge or a law professor who has cast loose from the historical Constitution.[6]

Originalism, on this view, constrains judges more than any alternative method of interpretation.[7] Without such a constraint, moreover, judges "will be able to find no scale, other than [their] own value preferences, upon which to weigh" constitutional claims.[8]

Other originalist scholars also see constitutional interpretation as posing a stark choice between divining the original meaning of the Constitution and purely political decisions by judges. Easterbrook, for example, rejects any method that "does not usefully constrain interpretation."[9] Only originalism, he argues, is logically "capable of supporting a judicial veto" over democratically enacted laws.[10] For him, originalism is derived not so much from fear of runaway judges as from the need to justify judicial review at all—we cannot differentiate judges from politicians, or explain why judges have the power to strike down legislation, without assuming that the Constitution has a single, unchanging, authoritative meaning.[11]

Similarly, Lawson argues that to define unconstitutionality as anything other than "at variance with the Constitution's original public meaning" renders constitutional discourse and adjudication problematic.[12] Like Bork, Lawson believes that there is no other principled way of interpreting the Constitution. Calabresi offers yet another version of the same originalist story: he castigates the Court for enforcing rights "unrooted in text or history," because doing so gives the Court "a major policy-making role" and makes it "an engine of radical social and cultural change."[13] He seeks to find a "vantage point from which to judge the goodness or badness" of judicial interpretations,[14] and he believes that only the original meaning of the Constitution can provide such a perspective. Calabresi's fear is slightly different from Bork's: he is concerned that slim judicial majorities responding to "national majority whims" will force the people of dissenting states to conform.[15]

All these scholars seem alarmed at any hint of judicial discretion, at least in constitutional cases. They thus seek a grand theory that will constrain judges and provide definitive answers to difficult interpretive questions. As we will see, most of the other scholars we examine share this search for a grandly theoretical solution, and several share Bork's specific fears of an imperial judiciary. Each solution is different, but these commonalities lead our scholars to make some similar mistakes.

The first mistake is to view constitutional interpretation as something of a mechanical act. For example, Bork writes that a judge's "first principles are given to him by the document, and he need only reason from these to see that those principles are vindicated in the cases brought before him."[16] In interpreting the Constitution, Bork writes, "[all] that counts is how the words used in the Constitution would have been understood at the time [they were enacted]."[17] He assumes not only that the Constitution has a single, authoritative meaning, but also that modern interpreters can easily discern that meaning. He says the words of the Constitution mean "what the public of that time would have understood the words to mean," and that the answer to such an inquiry is "readily apparent" from the historical record.[18]

Other originalists also seem to view constitutional interpretation as a simple exercise that inevitably leads to a single right answer. They stress repeatedly that constitutional interpretation must depend on fixed rules rather than flexible standards.[19] Easterbrook argues that judicial review cannot be justified unless we believe both "that there [is] one right answer to a problem," and that the judiciary ought to be the source of that right answer.[20] This is no cause for worry, however: judges need not "reach for Augustine" or some other esoteric guidance, because "there is likely to be a simple rule, a bit of law, that can be used in its stead."[21] Calabresi writes of "the written Constitution of 1787, as amended—nothing more and nothing less,"[22] suggesting that it is a simple matter to extract its full meaning. He apparently not only believes that there are simple answers to constitutional questions, he thinks that any American child can recite them: he confidently asserts that "the Constitution's elegant simplicity" embodies exactly what we were taught by "our grade school and high school civics teachers."[23]

These originalists, then, look at judges and see potential tyrants in need of strong restraints. They look at the Constitution and see a simple recipe.[24] And they look at history and find clear directions.

This is a naïve view both of the judicial enterprise and of history. As for judging, these scholars fall prey to the fallacy that there is no middle ground between blind adherence to originalism and purely political decisionmaking. Martha Nussbaum has described the fallacy as a belief that "if not the heavens, then the abyss."[25] But judges do find middle ground, negotiating the treacherous territory between fanatical obedience to the dead hand of the past and unconstrained discretion to implement their own political will. Judging is an act of tightly controlled creativity. Good judicial opinions simultaneously acknowledge our debt to the past and deny that the past can control the present. David Strauss, in an insightful and influential article, has described this process as integral to both the common law and constitutional development.[26]

Original meaning seems to be a particularly problematic response to the presumed need to rein in judges. Originalists necessarily assume that we can ascertain *the* intent of the founding generation. For Bork, this confidence arises mostly because he himself has apparently never looked carefully at the historical record. But even those scholars who have done the research are overly confident of their own historical conclusions. A cursory glance at existing scholarship—or at the other chapters in this book—shows that committed and competent scholars often disagree sharply on the historical meaning of most of the important provisions of the Constitution.

After thorough and careful historical research, scholars disagree on the original meaning of almost every important constitutional provision. Did those who adopted the Establishment Clause of the First Amendment— which states that "Congress shall make no law respecting an establishment of religion"—mean to bar *all* government aid to religion, or only government preference for particular religions? How much protection did the Second Amendment mean to give personal gun ownership by providing: "A well regulated militia, being necessary to the security of a free State, the right of the people to keep and bear Arms, shall not be infringed"? Does the original meaning of the Fourteenth Amendment's Equal Protection Clause prohibit segregated schools? Does the Fourteenth Amendment protect us from *state* violations of the Bill of Rights, or does the Bill of Rights still limit only the *federal* government (as it did when it was written and ratified)? What did the drafters and ratifiers of the Eleventh Amendment mean when they wrote that "[t]he judicial power of the United States shall not be construed to extend to any suit in law or equity, commenced or prosecuted against one of the United States by citizens of another state"? Did they mean that states are immune from suit in federal court only if sued by citizens of another state, or only if the federal court has jurisdiction *because* the plaintiff is a citizen of another state, or in all cases regardless of the citizenship of the plaintiff? On all these questions, different scholars have used the same historical record to reach opposite conclusions.[27] The historical record is not indeterminate, but it rarely points unambiguously to a single answer to questions as complex as these.

The originalist scholars' insistence notwithstanding, history is messy and often open-ended when it comes to answering today's constitutional questions. Perhaps Bork and the others would accuse some historical researchers of being driven by political bias. If so, however, this is only another strike against originalism: it proves that the historical record cannot successfully constrain ideology. Whatever may be said of originalism as a matter of first principle, it seems dubious as a reliable method for answering constitutional questions.

It is not surprising that scholars disagree about the original intent of the Constitution's founders. The originalist methodology is beset with problems. To begin with, how do we define "the framers of the Constitution" whose understanding we are to consult? Was it the fifty-five men who met in Philadelphia to write the Constitution? The many more who met in the various state conventions to ratify it? The voting public of the time? Or, because the voting public was such a small fraction of the population, should we look to the general public? Once we turn to interpreting constitutional amendments, we have similar choices to make among members of Congress, the state legislatures that ratified the amendments, and the public.

Whichever sources we choose, the evidence of the original intent will often be fragmentary, unreliable, and conflicting. Our best record of the Constitutional Convention is James Madison's notes, but it turns out that he recorded only about 10 percent of each day's discussion.[28] The debates in some of the state ratifying conventions were recorded by the ardent Federalist Thomas Lloyd, who was paid by the Federalists to delete all the Anti-Federalist speeches, and who, apparently on his own initiative, significantly revised many of the speeches he did include.[29] Lloyd was also responsible for the *Annals of Congress* in 1789, when the Bill of Rights was debated, and "[f]ar from improving by 1789, Lloyd's technical skills had become dulled by excessive drinking."[30] The *Congressional Globe,* which contains congressional debates during the Reconstruction period of the 1860s (when several important constitutional amendments were drafted), is more reliable, but records of the ratification and public debate at the time are still scant.

Even leaving aside the problem of completeness or reliability, the generations of the 1780s and the 1860s did not always focus on the language—or on the interpretive questions—that are important today. For example, according to Madison's notes, the 1787 convention delegates spent weeks debating how the president should be elected and whether he should be eligible for a second term, but little or no time defining the scope of his powers. The Reconstruction Congress focused not on § 1 of the Fourteenth Amendment—which contains the clauses most relevant today, including both the Due Process Clause and the Equal Protection Clause—but on §§ 2 and 3, which essentially expired within a few years. (Section 2 reduces the representation of states that do not let blacks vote; it was superseded by the Fifteenth Amendment, which flatly prohibits race discrimination in voting. Section 3 prohibits former Confederate officers from holding any federal office.)

Moreover, different framers expressed different views, and many, including Madison, changed their views over time. Just like people today, the framers were often vague or conflicted in their thinking. Thus any perusal of the historical record is bound to yield conflicting expressions of intent. And to make matters worse, some of the evidence suggests that Americans in both the 1780s and the 1860s did not expect their own understanding of the meaning of the constitution to govern future interpretation![31]

The historical obscurities remain great, whether we look at the original "intent" of the Constitution's drafters, or the original "understanding" of their contemporary readers. If we are asking, as a factual matter, what readers of the time believed about its meaning, we are faced with all the gaps and ambiguities of the historical record. If we are asking what a "reasonable" reader of the period would find in the document, without limiting ourselves to what various readers did in fact think, then we have cut free from any tether to the historical record and entered the realm of speculation. Either way, we will find few unambiguous answers to current constitutional questions.

We do not mean to suggest that studying the historical record is either hopeless or useless. If we thought constitutional history irrelevant, we would not have gone to the trouble of writing an earlier book on the subject. It is one thing, however, to find history illuminating, and quite another to try to make it controlling. The difficulty of assessing complex historical evidence may not impeach the legitimacy of originalism as a *theory*, but it does suggest serious problems for it as a practical way of deciding constitutional issues. Most lawyers and judges are neither equipped nor inclined to deal with the complexities and ambiguities of history. Lawyers do not tend to have what one historian has called "[a] historian's fondness for nuance, understatement, texture, and even irony—much less an acceptance of ambiguity."[32] They are not professionally trained to make judgments about the credibility of historical documents or to place those documents in historical context. Historical research requires patience, detachment, and sensitivity, traits that do not come easily to lawyers—however brilliant—who are hungry for evidence about today's constitutional issues.

Bork himself provides a perfect illustration of the perils of lawyers doing history. When it comes to doing the actual historical work of determining the intent of the framers, Bork is too often sloppy, superficial, and sometimes inaccurate. Most of his historical evidence consists of stock citations from the Federalist Papers and Supreme Court cases that appear in every constitutional law casebook for beginning law students. He appears to have read very little else—neither the historical sources nor the professional historians who study them, nor even the original texts themselves. He is seemingly unaware, for example, of the exciting debates in both legal and historical circles over the varying influences on the founding generation, including not only classical liberalism as described by John Locke, but also Whig-inspired civic republicanism and adherence to a theory of natural and inalienable rights. Bruce Ackerman—whom we discuss in chapter 6, and who ironically sometimes falls prey to some of the same pitfalls as Bork—pungently observes that Bork "manages to write a 400-page book in praise of the Framers without ever finding it necessary to cite the standard edition of Madison's Convention Notes or a single page from the *Congressional Globe* containing the debates of the Reconstruction Congresses."[33]

Bork repeatedly ignores or distorts history to reach his own conclusions. In condemning "judicial activism," for example, he ignores the long American endorsement, in theory and in practice dating back to the early 1780s, of judges as guardians of the rights of the people. In urging judges to confine themselves to interpreting the Constitution in accordance with its original meaning, Bork uses the *Dred Scott* case as an example of activist judges run amok. This is a useful rhetorical device but not much of an argument for originalism. *Dred Scott* invalidated the Missouri compromise, held that blacks could never be citizens, and contributed to causing the Civil War. If Bork can derive all these bad consequences from nonoriginalist constitutional interpretation, he has a powerful argument. Unfortunately for Bork, Chief Justice Taney's majority opinion in that much-castigated case (which Bork has apparently not read) relied heavily on original intent, reaching arguably correct conclusions about the framers' desire to protect slavery from con-

gressional interference.[34] Taney may or may not have been a "good originalist," but he does offer a melancholy example of how efforts to base decisions on original intent can misfire.

When the going gets really tough, Bork just gives up and writes the historically troublesome provisions out of the Constitution. He does this both
with the Ninth Amendment—which provides that "[t]he enumeration in
the Constitution of certain rights shall not be construed to deny or disparage
others retained by the people"—and with the clause of the Fourteenth
Amendment that prohibits states from abridging the "privileges or immunities" of citizens of the United States. Bork says that "[t]here is almost no
history that would indicate what the ninth amendment was intended to accomplish,"[35] and that the Privileges or Immunities Clause "has been a mystery since its adoption."[36] He thus likens both clauses to "ink blots" and says
that the courts should ignore them: "For example, if you had an amendment
that says 'Congress shall make no' and then there is an ink blot and you cannot read the rest of it and that is the only copy you have, I do not think the
court can make up what might be under the ink blot."[37]

But neither provision is as historically opaque as Bork would have it.
Many scholars have studied the origins of both the Ninth Amendment and
the Privileges or Immunities Clause, although Bork cites none of this literature. These scholars have found quite a bit of historical evidence about the
meaning of the two clauses. James Madison himself, in introducing the proposed Ninth Amendment to Congress, explained that it was designed to
forestall the sort of narrow interpretation of the Bill of Rights that Bork engages in:

> It has been objected also against a bill of rights, that, by enumerating par-
> ticular exceptions to the grant of power, it would disparage those rights
> which were not placed in that enumeration; and it might follow, by im-
> plication, that those rights which were not singled out, were intended to
> be assigned into the hands of the General Government, and were conse-
> quently insecure. This is one of the most plausible arguments I have ever
> heard urged against the admission of a bill of rights into this system; but,
> I conceive, that it may be guarded against. I have attempted it, as gentle-
> men may see by turning to [the proposed Ninth Amendment].[38]

Madison also expected that judges would enforce the Bill of Rights—including the Ninth Amendment—with a freer hand than Bork imagines. In
brushing off the criticism that bills of rights had been ineffectual in protecting rights against state infringement, he noted that a federal bill of rights

might still prove useful because "independent tribunals of justice will consider themselves in a peculiar manner the guardians of those rights; they will be an impenetrable bulwark against every assumption of power in the legislative or executive."[39]

Madison's vision of the Ninth Amendment as guarding against any interpretation that would construe the Bill of Rights as an exhaustive and complete list of rights also fits the historical context. Even before 1787, both the rhetoric and the reality of judicial review in the emerging United States reflected a strong commitment to unwritten rights—natural or inalienable rights that judges protected from legislative encroachment. One plausible interpretation of the language and history of the Ninth Amendment is that it incorporates that view into the Constitution.[40]

The Privileges or Immunities Clause was also historically tied to protection of individual rights. While the meaning of this clause is not free from ambiguity, it is not strikingly less clear than other parts of the Constitution. Its sponsors invoked broadly libertarian concepts and may well have intended the clause to serve as the counterpart for state government to the Bill of Rights' limits on the federal government.[41] Indeed, Senator John Sherman, one of the primary advocates of the Fourteenth Amendment, explained that the Privileges or Immunities Clause not only incorporated the first eight amendments and made them applicable against the states, but also played the same role as the Ninth Amendment, constitutionalizing unenumerated rights as well. (Others disagreed, illustrating once again that the historical evidence will rarely yield completely clear answers.)[42] Sherman and others cited Justice Bushrod Washington's opinion in *Corfield v. Coryell,* an 1823 case, as exemplifying the privileges and immunities that the Fourteenth Amendment was designed to protect. Washington wrote that the privileges and immunities of citizenship included "[p]rotection by the government; the enjoyment of life and liberty, with the right to acquire and possess property of every kind, and to pursue and obtain happiness and safety."[43] Bork summarily dismisses this evidence of the meaning of the Privileges or Immunities Clause, but does not explain why.

Likening a clause in the Constitution to an ink blot, even if plausible, is a further condemnation of originalism as a method of interpreting *any* part of the Constitution. After all, neither the Ninth Amendment nor the Privileges or Immunities Clause is *actually* obscured by an ink blot; Bork contends only that the language is as opaque today as if it were blotted out. But why is it that we can no longer read these particular phrases? It must be because we are unable to understand the world the founders inhabited. Perhaps they believed in natural rights; perhaps they added meaningless clauses to the Constitution just for rhetorical effect. (The evidence just discussed suggests that the former is more likely.) But in either case, the recognition of the chasm between our world and theirs should make us wary of trying to extract the eighteenth- or nineteenth-century meaning from constitutional language. It is inevitable that we will put a twenty-first-century spin on our interpretation. If time has made some words akin to ink blots, then others have become blurred as well.

Bork is not alone in his failure to acknowledge the breadth of the gap between our world and theirs. Responding to Lawrence Lessig's suggestion that interpretation of the Constitution requires "translation," Calabresi insists that the Constitution need only be applied, not translated: "Our world is not so different or distant from the world of the Founders that 'translation' is needed."[44] The changes that have occurred since 1789, according to Calabresi, have occurred "mostly as a result of the Founding Texts and not despite them," and thus we are "still the same people, the same political community, as the one that ratified the Constitution."[45] But, like Bork, Calabresi fails to take into account such anomalies as the Ninth Amendment and the Privileges or Immunities Clause, both of which invite us to immerse ourselves in a lost tradition, that of natural rights. They are similar, as John Ely once pointed out, to a clause in an old document that makes reference to "ghosts": what are we, who no longer believe in such creatures, to make of that language?[46]

Ultimately, Bork's reduction of these two meaningful clauses to unintelligible ink blots rests not on any historical evidence but on his own view of what the Constitution *must* mean. Because he thinks that judges ought to be mechanically constrained in their interpretation of the Constitution, he cannot accommodate clauses that might intentionally give broader authority to the courts. As he says of originalism itself as an approach to constitutional interpretation: "Even if evidence of what the founders thought about the judicial role were unavailable, we would have to adopt the rule that judges must stick to the original meaning of the Constitution's words. . . . [Even if no framer had endorsed it,] we would have to invent the approach of original understanding in order to save the constitutional design."[47]

This is weak originalism indeed, and the historical case for his own interpretation is even worse than he imagines. For not only is there strong evidence that the Ninth Amendment and the Privileges or Immunities Clause were intended to protect broad unenumerated rights: there is also, as we noted earlier, some evidence that the framers did not intend their own intentions to guide later interpretation. Thus when Bork says that we would have to "invent" originalism if it did not exist, he seems to have no idea that originalism is arguably a modern invention, at least as a full-blown theory of constitutional interpretation.

The historical research of some of the other originalists scholars is less prone to error than Bork's is, for they, unlike him, have done their homework. (Some, like Easterbrook, advocate the general theory of originalism but without often specifying what they think the text or the historical evidence actually tells us in any given case.)[48] Nevertheless, like all historical advocacy their work is necessarily contentious, and even the most thorough pieces of scholarship therefore slight contrary evidence. For example, Calabresi's exhaustive 220-page review of presidential powers relies in part on an argument that the Constitution's list of the powers allocated to each branch is an exclusive list: no branch retains any unenumerated powers. He suggests that the Tenth Amendment bolsters his argument insofar as it states that "the powers not delegated to the United States by the Constitution . . . are reserved to the States respectively, or to the people." But Calabresi neglects to mention that opponents of federal power tried numerous times to insert the word "expressly" before the word "delegated," failing each time. This dispute about the scope of the constitutional delegation might be rather helpful to our attempt to ascertain whether the founding generation thought it was enacting an exclusive list of powers. It may not resolve the question, but as a piece of evidence it is worth examining. That so careful a scholar as Calabresi fails to discuss it suggests the difficulty with using historical analysis so heavily in the service of constitutional interpretation.

BACKING AWAY FROM THE PRECIPICE

Perhaps Bork recognizes deep down that originalism will never be satisfactory, for he occasionally concedes that judges properly engage in "minor, interstitial lawmaking," and that their task is "not mechanical."[49] (These almost pragmatist statements are overwhelmed by the narrow formalism of the rest of his work, but they do exist.) He also candidly admits that there are times when the intent of the framers should not govern. But he gives no guidance on when originalism is appropriate and when it is not, thus leaving judges with much the same leeway his originalist theory was supposed to eliminate. Thus, for example, he thinks that judges can stop "horrible" governmental acts, although he does not specify what provision of the Constitution might give them the power to do so—nor how to define "horrible."[50] Apparently, however, an Oklahoma law requiring the sterilization of any person convicted of two felonies involving "moral turpitude" (excluding embezzlement or tax evasion), which Bork himself describes as "savage," was not horrible enough—he condemns the case in which the Supreme Court struck down just such a law.[51] He writes that "[t]o nullify the Oklahoma legislature's policy on the grounds that it shocks the judge is to embed in the Constitution the judge's notions of public policy."[52]

Perhaps he finds it unnecessary to accommodate the Court's rejection of Oklahoma's mandatory sterilization law because that law was an aberration unlikely to be repeated and therefore unlikely to undermine public support for originalism. His originalism becomes more feeble on issues with greater political salience. He is not willing to use history to overrule doctrines that would make originalism politically unpalatable to the American public. Twice he builds a historical case that would radically change American constitutional law, and twice he backs away from the edge without explanation.

He flinches first on the incorporation doctrine. The Bill of Rights originally applied only to limit the federal government; states were free to do as they liked. The question of "incorporation" asks whether the Fourteenth Amendment "incorporated" the Bill of Rights so that states as well as the federal government are limited by its provisions. There is a great deal of historical controversy on this subject, although the Supreme Court has definitively ruled that most of the Bill of Rights does indeed limit the states. But Bork methodically builds a case against incorporation, rejecting the only two clauses in the Fourteenth Amendment by which incorporation might be accomplished. According to Bork, the Privileges or Immunities Clause, as we have seen, is merely an uninterpretable ink blot, and the Due Process Clause is limited to guaranteeing fair procedures. Thus one might think that his originalist approach would require him to disavow the incorporation doctrine. He never does so, nor does he give any explanation.

Another lapse is his discussion of *Brown v. Board of Education*,[53] in which the Supreme Court declared racially segregated schools unconstitutional. In this he is not alone: Calabresi cavalierly asserts that *Brown* "was warranted on textualist/originalist grounds."[54] Since Calabresi cites Bork's own work in support of this statement,[55] it is appropriate to focus on Bork. As Bork acknowledges, there is powerful evidence that the drafters and ratifiers of the Fourteenth Amendment did not intend to outlaw segregated schools. (One small example of this evidence is the fact that at the time Congress proposed the Fourteenth Amendment, it also rejected a bill outlawing segregated schools in Washington, D.C.) But Bork, unlike a few hardier originalists, refuses to admit that this evidence would doom *Brown* under an originalist approach. Instead, he argues—on the basis of no historical evidence at all—that the framers of the Fourteenth Amendment intended to promote broad racial equality but not to outlaw segregation, thinking that those two goals were consistent. We in the twenty-first century now know that it is not possible to have both segregation and equality, so we have to choose between two inconsistent original intentions.[56]

There are two main flaws in Bork's attempt to save *Brown* from the originalist ax. First, the historical evidence strongly suggests that the nineteenth-century framers intended to protect only civil or legal equality, not social equality.[57] In other words, while they wanted blacks to be able to enter into contracts or to own property, they never expected blacks to become social equals with whites. Indeed, much of the nineteenth-century rhetoric would strike us today as chillingly racist. Representative John Bingham, the father of the Fourteenth Amendment (about whom we will have more to say in chapter 5), reflected the sentiment of the day when he commented on the natural inequality between the races:

> Gentlemen need not trouble themselves . . . about the demagogue cry of "the political equality of the negro." Nobody proposes or dreams of political equality any more than of physical or mental equality. It is as impossible for men to establish equality in these respects as it is for "the Ethiopian to change his skin." Who would say that all men are equal in stature, in weight, and in physical strength; or that all are equal in natural mental force, or in intellectual acquirements?[58]

Other Republican supporters of Reconstruction echoed Bingham's views. Massachusetts senator Henry Wilson stated that "I do not believe in the equality of the African race with the white race, mentally or physically, and I do not think morally."[59] Senator Waitman Willey, representing West Virginia, which seceded from Virginia in order to stay loyal to the Union, said that the black man "is an inferior, he must be inferior, . . . [and] can never be socially equal."[60]

In particular, education was part of *social* equality, and was thus excluded from the rights guaranteed by the Fourteenth Amendment. Bork tries to evade this embarrassing history by lumping together under the rubric of "equality" concepts that the framers thought of as separate things. There was no conflict between segregation and legal equality as defined by many of the framers (which excluded social equality). What had changed by the time of *Brown* was our understanding of legal equality, which had come to include some social as well as civil and political aspects. But that change is inconsistent with the original intent of the Fourteenth Amendment, which makes it illegitimate for Bork.

The second problem with Bork's analysis of *Brown* (as resting on a newly discovered incompatibility between two goals of the framers) is that it offers no guidance to judges and no constraints on judicial decisionmaking. He never explains how courts should choose between two incompatible intents, merely saying that it was "obvious" in *Brown* that the Court should choose equality.[61] But this is a technique with many potential uses, some abhorrent to Bork. Indeed, ironically enough, Justice Blackmun once used an essentially similar argument to uphold affirmative action, which Bork detests.[62] Blackmun conceded that in enacting Title VII, the federal law prohibiting discrimination in employment, Congress "probably thought it was adopting a principle" that would prohibit discrimination in either direction—against or in favor of any particular race. But, argued Blackmun, the "statutory policy" behind Title VII was to bring blacks into full economic equality. Thus, he said, the Court was justified in following the more general policy rather than the specific ban, now that we recognize that we cannot implement both goals.[63] Blackmun's argument for affirmative action applied the same logic as Bork's defense of *Brown*, but to a different ideological end—and of course, Bork and Blackmun would find each other's perspectives repugnant.

And it does not seem to have occurred to Bork that one could use the same strategy to justify his least favorite case, *Roe v. Wade*.[64] It would probably be easy to demonstrate that the founders thought that prohibiting abortion was consistent with, say, political equality for women (an underlying goal of the Nineteenth Amendment) or with prohibiting the legislature from enacting arbitrary and irrational laws (which Bork admits was one underlying purpose of the Fourteenth Amendment). What Bork fails to realize is that it would also be possible to argue that *in today's world,* taking control over reproduction away from women is now inconsistent with one or both of those goals. Who is to say that a judge adopting such an argument would be wrong under Bork's own theory? Bork never provides even the beginning of an answer to that question. Even if this form of argument ultimately fails to persuade in some settings, its availability gives judges great leeway—unless we are supposed to count on the good judgment of the interpreter.

Thus Bork leaves intact *Brown* and the incorporation doctrine only by sacrificing the very point of originalism: a judge following Bork's admonitions about constitutional interpretation would end up with a great deal of discretion to reach the very results that Bork so castigates.

The other originalists are, by and large, more circumspect about their actual constitutional interpretations, so it is difficult to determine whether they too would stop short of fully implementing their theories. Several, however, explicitly indicate that their adherence to originalism is limited by the idea of precedent. Judges should be guided by the original meaning of the Constitution in all future cases, but need not always overrule past cases even if those cases conflict with the true meaning of the Constitution.[65] Often, the decision whether to overrule an existing precedent will turn on its age.

Like Bork's justification of *Brown* and the incorporation doctrine, allowing precedent some unspecified weight gives up the game. Deciding whether a new case is squarely governed by an older case, or whether it is an extension that should instead by governed by the true meaning of Constitution, will require considerable judicial discretion. Similarly, deciding whether an existing case is old enough to warrant the solicitude that prompts these scholars to exempt it from their originalist sweep also requires judicial discretion. And the originalists give little guidance on either of these questions.

RADICAL THEORIES, RADICAL RESULTS

As we have just seen, Bork and the other originalists are sometimes unwilling to let go of some existing constitutional doctrine despite its inconsistency with their theory of interpretation. But at other times, they are willing to follow the theory wherever it leads—and it can lead to some quite radical results.

Not surprisingly, Bork is the perhaps the most radical of the group. His most scholarly suggestions would almost read individual rights out of the Constitution, overturning settled doctrine in a variety of areas. For example, he argues that it is constitutional for public schools in Washington D.C. to be segregated by race and for homeowners to use the courts to enforce racially restrictive covenants in order to prevent blacks from buying their neighbors' homes. (The Supreme Court invalidated the former in 1954 and the latter in 1948.)[66] He hints that the 1964 Civil Rights Act—in which Congress prohibited race and gender discrimination in employment and public accommodations—might be unconstitutional, because it was "social or moral legislation" rather than commercial legislation.[67] (In 1964, the Supreme Court upheld the statute as a regulation of commerce.)[68]

Bork would make even more changes to First Amendment doctrine, stripping most speech of its constitutional protection. First, he has argued that *only* explicitly political speech should be protected by the First Amendment.[69] Although others have argued that political speech should be the focus of First Amendment protection, he is unusual in his enthusiasm for censoring other forms of speech. He titles one of the chapters in his recent book "The Case for Censorship,"[70] and notes approvingly that the period during which movie producers voluntarily adhered to strict standards regulating what could be shown was, "perhaps not coincidentally, the golden age of the movies."[71] Of the Supreme Court's ban on censoring material that has "serious literary, artistic, political, or scientific expression,"[72] he writes that "[i]t is difficult to see merit in the serious value test."[73] So much for James Joyce and D. H. Lawrence, whose works were banned in the days before this test.

Even more radically, Bork laments the increasing protection given to political speech, waxing nostalgic for the days when the government could censor unpopular speech. He finds "no reason whatever" to protect what he considers to be dangerous political ideas.[74]

To understand how radical Bork's suggestions really are, we must look briefly at how the Supreme Court has come to its current doctrines. Free speech has often had a rough ride in the United States; the impulse to government censorship has not always been overcome despite the First Amendment's apparent stance against it. From the Alien and Sedition Acts of 1798 through the suppression of abolitionist speech before and during the Civil War to the McCarthy era of the 1950s, both state and federal governments have abused their power and censored unpopular speech.[75]

The Supreme Court did not originally present much of an obstacle to censorship. In the first few decades of the twentieth century, the Court upheld convictions for the mere distribution of leaflets or adherence to certain unpopular ideas. Justices Holmes and Brandeis dissented in those cases, using stirring language to defend freedom of speech against government censorship.[76] Those dissents form the bedrock of modern free speech doctrine, and are almost universally recognized as some of the most important opinions in our constitutional canon. Bork, however, laments their influence, preferring to keep them as dissenting voices.[77]

What Holmes and Brandeis saw, which Bork does not, is that "the theory of our Constitution" prohibits the government from silencing dissent.[78] By 1943, a majority of the Supreme Court agreed. Justice Jackson, writing for the majority in a case that held that schoolchildren could not be forced to salute the flag, captured the essence of the First Amendment: "If there is any fixed star in our constitutional constellation, it is that no official, high or petty, can prescribe what shall be orthodox in politics, nationalism, or religion, or other matters of opinion or force citizens to confess by word or act their faith therein."[79] In 1969, the Supreme Court formally adopted this speech-protective position, holding that the government could not restrict political speech unless it was intended to cause, and was actually likely to cause, imminent lawless action.[80] The Court has now staunchly adhered to this position for more than thirty years. The Court has also expanded protection for artistic, commercial, and other types of speech, although not quite as much as for political speech. Bork would do away with almost all of this doctrine.

Bork's most recent book is even less scholarly and more radical than his earlier work. In it, he suggests that the entire Enlightenment foundation of the Constitution is misguided. He writes that Enlightenment thinkers "made a serious mistake" in emphasizing the importance of the individual and thus of liberty.[81] He condemns the memorable phrases of the Declaration of Independence, labeling them "pernicious" for the modern era. He says that it is "unfortunate" that the Declaration has had as much influence as it has.[82] If we take too seriously the ideas that "all men are created equal" and that "they are endowed by their Creator with certain inalienable rights," these ideas will "press eventually towards extremes."[83] Indeed, the "unqualified language" of *both* the Bill of Rights and the Declaration of Independence, according to Bork, "feed[s] our national obsession about 'rights.'"[84] These suggestions, coupled with his earlier proposals for doctrinal revisions, illustrate just how far Bork is willing to go in reshaping our constitutional landscape.

The other originalist scholars are less polemical—and not as broad ranging—but their proposals would work equally radical changes. Lawson writes that "the post-New Deal administrative state is unconstitutional, and its validation by the legal system amounts to nothing less than a bloodless constitutional revolution."[85] He thus finds that the government that we have had for the past sixty years is in irreconcilable conflict with our Constitution.[86]

Easterbrook does not make many concrete proposals, but he does suggest that other conservatives are too worried about the potentially radical consequences of their constitutional theory. We must have constitutional rules, not standards, he says, even if they might produce horrible results (he includes "horsewhipping for double parking" and "zoning laws eliminating churches" in his list of unreasonable fears). According to Easterbrook, even Justice Scalia is insufficiently hardened against this "siren song" of a parade of horribles.[87]

And several of the originalists want to undo the underpinnings of the last hundred years of constitutional interpretation. For the past century, the Supreme Court has been attempting to balance the competing interests recognized by the Constitution: federal power, state power, and individual rights. That balance has sometimes tipped in one direction and sometimes in another, and scholars and judges do not always agree on exactly how the scale should be calibrated. But both Gary Lawson and Richard Kay, staunch defenders of originalism for many years, have a simple rule that would eliminate the messy process of accommodating different interests—and incidentally overrule half the Supreme Court's cases.

What Kay and Lawson propose, in independent articles reaching the same conclusion, is a default rule for those cases in which the historical analysis does not produce perfectly clear results. (As we indicated earlier, this category probably includes almost every important constitutional question.) As Lawson puts it: "When the issue is the scope of enumerated national powers (and all national powers are enumerated), resolve doubts against the national government, and when the issue is the scope of specific limitations on national or state powers, resolve doubts in favor of the government."[88] Kay's version is snappier but to the same effect: "Any truly new thing done by the federal government is unauthorized . . . [and] any truly new thing done by a state must be outside of [the] prohibitions [of the Bill of Rights], and must, therefore, be constitutional."[89] In other words, if the question is one of federalism, the federal government nearly always loses; if the question is one of individual rights, the individual nearly always loses. Beyond what little we can glean from history, then, judging becomes a completely mechanical act—and it produces results that would overrule much of the constitutional doctrine developed in the past century.

Originalist theory ultimately calls for radical changes in current constitutional law on the basis of a need to prevent judges from imposing their own values. In the next chapter, we turn to another advocate of constraints on judicial discretion: Antonin Scalia. But Scalia differs from Bork and the other originalists we have discussed in this chapter in two important ways. First, of course, unlike Bork, Justice Scalia is in a position to implement his own proposals—although we will see that he does not do so consistently. And Scalia is a much more sophisticated theorist, recognizing and remedying some of the flaws in Bork's originalism. Nevertheless, Scalia too suffers from the virus of grand theory.

CHAPTER 3

THE FORMALIST CRUSADE OF ANTONIN SCALIA

Unlike the other figures we discuss in this book, Antonin Scalia is in a position not only to talk about constitutional law but also to do something about it. As a Supreme Court justice, he has been an important force—a powerful critic in dissent, and not infrequently the spokesman for the conservative majority. His thinking about originalism would have to be taken seriously if only for that reason. It also deserves to be taken seriously in its own right because, unlike many other originalists, he speaks from experience about the judicial role.

As we will see, Justice Scalia's version of originalism is distinctive in several respects. It is less populist than Bork's initial formulation, more concerned with restricting judicial lawmaking than with the value of popular sovereignty. As a formalist, Scalia is preoccupied with minimizing judicial discretion and making the enterprise of judging as value neutral as possible. Perhaps for that reason, his originalism is somewhat confined in its scope, with more explicit attention being given to precedent and to long-standing traditions as other checks on judicial discretion. In short, unlike Bork, Scalia is seemingly a formalist first and an originalist second: he cares more about constraining the judges than about obeying the framers. One reason may be that he is more aware than its more conventional supporters of the pitfalls of originalism.

We begin with a brief look at some of Justice Scalia's notable constitutional rulings in order to put his originalism in context. We then consider his jurisprudential writings about formalism and originalism. Those writings turn out to be more complex and sophisticated than many academics appreciate. Then we return to his work as a judge, first examining how he uses history in his own opinions and then his nonoriginalist use of precedent and tradition as limitations. In the end, we conclude, his formalism has been a failure on its own terms. It has been no more successful than other methods in purging judicial decisionmaking of value judgments. Both Scalia's theory and his judicial opinions have deeply contradictory strains.

Some of Scalia's scholarly writings have an appealing, almost rueful quality. Just as he has finished a plea for originalism, he admits to doubts about its practical significance. At the end of a defense of formalism, he concedes that the "law of rules" can never be fully realized. But his writings have a darker side as well, a seeming lack of self-awareness about the contradictions within his thinking and the conflicts between his theories and his practice.[1] Between the occasional flashes of humility are long stretches of arid self-righteousness. And while he proclaims that his judicial rulings flow inexorably from the text and original understanding, he often seems willing to allow the proclamation to substitute for the performance.

In some respects, Scalia is the most intriguing of our subjects. His judicial opinions and at least some of his theoretical writings seem little different from those of Bork and other conventional originalists, forcefully asserting a straightforward version of originalism. But some of his other writings strike a different note, admitting to the flaws of originalism and the weaknesses of some of its traditional rationales. These writings, however, seem also to make a strategic case for maintaining originalism as a public stance, despite its admitted weaknesses. Thus, although Scalia's dominant tone is not unlike Bork's, the most thought-provoking passages are more nuanced and raise questions about how his more Bork-like pronouncements are really intended. We do not believe that Scalia has successfully resolved these internal tensions in his thinking, and indeed, his most recent theoretical writings seem to have reverted to a more simplistic version of originalism.[2] At times, however, Scalia exhibits an awareness of the limits of grand theory that is absent in our other subjects. In the end, though, he seems to have suppressed these flashes of self-awareness, or at least refused to think seriously about their implications.

As we will see, there is a gap between Scalia's theory and his actual practice.[3] Since we are not ourselves formalists (or originalists, for that matter), we can hardly claim that Justice Scalia's failure to make a success of his originalist brand of formalism demonstrates a fatal flaw in his judicial opinions. Those opinions must stand or fall on the merits of the individual arguments in each case, rather than on his failure to successfully comply with the dictates of an unworkable methodology. However, the failure of his judicial opinions to correspond to his theory is an indictment of the theory itself—and particularly of the theory's failed promise to reform judicial practice. He has made a valiant effort to implement a jurisprudence based solely on text, rules, and history. His failure to make such a barebones jurisprudence operational has a simple moral: it cannot be done.

THE CONSTITUTION ACCORDING TO SCALIA

Before we examine Scalia's theory of constitutional law and his jurisprudential writings, it is helpful to have an overall sense of the direction in which his ideas have taken him. Though he is no revolutionary, he does seek profound changes. From Justice Scalia's perspective, much of the core of current constitutional doctrine is in principle erroneous. If the Supreme Court had ruled correctly in the first place, the states would not be bound by the Bill of Rights; the national government would have much less regulatory power; and free speech would be limited to the common law rights of 1790. Like the "old" Bork (but unlike the "new" one), Justice Scalia recognizes the impracticality of rooting out all of those existing precedents (though as we will see later he is sometimes reluctant to extend them). In short, for Scalia as for Bork, American society has already fallen away from much of the true constitutional order. Scalia appears willing to live with the most well establlished of these erroneous rulings. But where the fall into constitutional sin is not irremediable, Scalia continues to advocate constitutional rulings that deemphasize individual liberty from state regulation, narrow the power of the federal government, and expand the power of the executive branch.

Although we disagree with some of those rulings, our purpose here is not to critique his constitutional views but merely to describe some of the most notable ones for the benefit of readers who are not constitutional lawyers. Although space allows us to discuss only a handful of opinions, we believe they aptly illustrate not only Scalia's views of the Constitution, but also the boldness and clarity of his analysis. For Scalia, one feels, there are no hard constitutional issues, only judges who fail to grasp the essential theorems of our constitutional system.

OF SOVEREIGN STATES AND IMPERIAL PRESIDENTS

Justice Scalia's view on federalism has two parts. First, he believes that the power of the federal government has expanded beyond the intended limits.

Thus he joined the majority in *United States v. Lopez*,[4] limiting congressional power to regulate private conduct under the Commerce Clause for the first time since the Great Depression. (We discuss *Lopez* more fully in chapter 4.) Second, he believes that the states possess inherent sovereignty and are largely immune from federal authority. This view of state immunity is a cornerstone of one of his important recent opinions, *Printz v. United States*.[5]

Printz involved the 1993 Brady Act, a federal law banning the sale of guns to minors, felons, and drug users. Pending the establishment of a national system of background checks, the Brady Act required local police to make a "reasonable effort"[6] to determine whether a proposed gun sale would be illegal. In a 5-4 decision, the Supreme Court struck down this seemingly innocuous provision as a violation of state sovereignty. According to Justice Scalia's majority opinion, the "Federal Government may not compel the States to implement, by legislation or executive action, federal regulatory programs."[7] Justice Scalia argued that such "commandeering" of state officials violates the state's inherent duty to "represent and remain accountable to its own citizens" rather than to those of other states. According to Justice Scalia, the "Framers explicitly chose a Constitution that confers upon Congress the power to regulate individuals, not States."[8] Notably, he could point to no specific ban on commandeering in the text of the Constitution, nor (as we will see later) to any specific evidence that the framers meant to deprive the federal government of this power.

Printz also provided Scalia with the opportunity to air his views about the separation of powers. The federalism holding in *Printz* was not unexpected, for the power of the federal government to make use of state officials had been sharply contested in an earlier decision, *New York v. United States*.[9] A more startling, and often overlooked, part of *Printz* held that the Brady Act violated the rights of the president, not just those of the states (though the president at the time in fact supported the statute). Article II of the Constitution, according to Justice Scalia, provides that only the president (and his underlings) shall "take Care that the Laws be faithfully executed." The Brady Act transferred this authority to thousands of local law enforcement officials "who are left to implement the program without meaningful Presidential control (if indeed meaningful Presidential control is possible without the power to appoint and remove.)"[10] Pointing to the "well known" desire of the framers for "unity in the Federal Executive—to ensure both vigor and accountability," Justice Scalia concluded that this "unity would be shattered, and the power of the President would be subject to reduction, if Congress could act as effectively without the President as with him, by simply re-quiring state officers to execute its laws."[11] As one commentator observed, this "unprecedented argument" potentially "threatens the legitimacy of many administrative agencies."[12]

This part of the rationale in *Printz* may be unprecedented, but it is not surprising, for the sanctity of presidential power is central to Scalia's consti-tutional vision. Accordingly, he has devoted much attention to the separa-tion of powers, an issue that seems to evoke more fervor on his part than protecting the rights of states or individuals.

Scalia's best-known opinion on the separation of powers is his dissent in a case concerning the constitutional status of the independent counsel. The majority opinion, written by no less a conservative and stalwart defender of presidential authority than Chief Justice Rehnquist, upheld the constitu-tionality of the independent counsel. Justice Scalia penned a lone dissent, reasoning simply that law enforcement is part of the executive power, the executive power is vested in the president by the opening sentence of Ar-ticle II, and the statute deprives the president of exclusive control of that power. (Note that by this reasoning, independent administrative agencies such as the Federal Communications Commission and the Securities and Exchange Commission are also unconstitutional, since they also engage in regulatory enforcement actions.) Justice Scalia objected most strenuously to the Court's balancing test, which examined whether the statute impaired the central functioning of the executive branch. This "ad hoc approach to constitutional adjudication," he said, "has real attraction, being guaranteed to produce a result, in every case, that will make a majority of the Court happy with the law." "If to describe this case is not to decide it," he said, "the concept of a government of separate and coordinate powers no longer has meaning."[13]

Scalia's view of executive authority has led him to some unusual reason-ing. Just as he found executive power subtly infringed by the Brady Act, he has also found other surprising infringements. For example, in *Lujan v. De-fenders of Wildlife*,[14] Congress had authorized any citizen to challenge gov-ernment violations of the Endangered Species Act. Writing for a six-justice majority, Scalia held the statute unconstitutional to the extent that it autho-rized suit by individuals who were not themselves harmed by the govern-ment's action. Although controversial, this rationale is not an unexpected reading of the Constitution's description of the powers of the judiciary un-der Article III. More startling was Justice Scalia's view that the statute implicated Article II of the Constitution by invading presidential power: "To permit Congress to convert the undifferentiated public interest in executive officers' compliance with the law into an 'individual right' vindicable in the courts is to permit Congress to transfer from the President to the courts the Chief Executive's most important constitutional duty, to 'take care that the Laws be faithfully executed.'"

There is a certain irony to Justice Scalia's invocation of the Take Care Clause. Citizen-suit laws and the independent counsel law are not relevant to situations in which a president is seeking to enforce the law over congressional efforts to interfere. Rather, these statutes are designed for situations in which the president or his delegates prefer *not* to faithfully execute a law, finding it disagreeable to bring law enforcement actions against members of his own administration or to comply with a legal dictate regarding endangered species. A cynic might say that Justice Scalia had rewritten the clause to require the president to "take care that the Law be *fitfully* executed."[15]

As these examples show, Justice Scalia's opinions are as notable for their methods as for their results. Rather than viewing the structure of government as a complex matter, resting on text, practicality, and evolution over time, he views federalism and separation of powers questions as simple logical deductions from a few constitutional axioms such as the Take Care Clause. In this respect, his reasoning epitomizes foundationalism.

DELIMITING INDIVIDUAL RIGHTS

Cases involving individual rights are a central part of the Supreme Court's agenda, and Justice Scalia has had occasion to make notable pronouncements in more cases than we can reasonably describe here. He has been an outspoken judicial opponent of abortion rights and affirmative action laws, a supporter of expanded protection for property rights, and a staunch supporter of free speech (as shown by his famous opinion striking down a ban on cross-burning.)[16] We content ourselves here with a few illustrations of his constitutional vision, chosen not just as examples of his substantive views but also as reflecting his core conceptions of the Court's function. Note how strongly Scalia's positions are fortified by his conception of the judicial role—a conception that stresses the need for sharply defined rules and eschews any hint of value judgments by the judiciary.

Employment Division v. Smith[17] is now the seminal authority on the meaning of the Free Exercise Clause of the Constitution. The issue before the Court was whether religious use of peyote by Native Americans could be banned by the state. The state law in question did not single out religion, but evenhandedly banned any use of peyote whatsoever. In some earlier cases, however, the Court had required the state to show a compelling interest to justify applying such general bans to religious practices. *Smith* purported not to overrule those previous cases but rejected the general principle on which they had appeared to rest. With a few limited exceptions, the Court held, the states are normally free to apply general laws even if the result is to make illegal a practice central to a particular religion. A contrary approach, Justice Scalia said for the majority, "would be courting anarchy" and "open the prospect of constitutionally required religious exemptions from civic obligations of almost every conceivable kind." Thus the need for uniform clear rules outweighed concern about religious freedom.

Some of the greatest controversies in constitutional law in recent years have involved protection for individual rights that are not specifically listed in the Constitution, such as abortion. Justice Scalia has staunchly opposed such protection of unenumerated rights. When the Court reaffirmed major portions of *Roe v. Wade* in 1992, he foresaw the end of the independent judiciary:

> As long as this Court thought (and the people thought) that we Justices were doing essentially lawyers' work up here—reading text and discerning our society's traditional understanding of that text—the public pretty much left us alone. Texts and traditions are facts to study, not convictions to demonstrate about. But if in reality our process of constitutional adjudication consists primarily of making *value judgments* . . . a free and intelligent people's attitude towards us can be expected to be (*ought* to be) quite different. The people know that their value judgments are quite as good as those taught in any law school—maybe better. . . . Value judgments, after all, should be voted on, not dictated; and if our Constitution has somehow accidentally committed them to the Supreme Court, at least we can have a sort of plebiscite each time a new nominee to that body is put forward.[18]

Justice Scalia has continued to lament what he sees as a judicial imposition of values in the abortion context. In his dissent in the most recent abortion case, he suggests that the Court invalidated a state's restriction on abortion by "precisely the process" he had condemned in the earlier cases: "a democratic vote by nine lawyers, not on the question whether the text of the Constitution has anything to say about this subject (it obviously does not); nor even on the question (also appropriate for lawyers) whether the legal traditions of the American people would have sustained such a limitation upon abortion (they obviously would); but upon the pure policy question whether this limitation upon abortion is 'undue'—i.e., goes too far."[19]

It would take more space than we have available here for a full exploration of the substance of Justice Scalia's constitutional views. Certainly, our brief descriptions should not be taken as full elaborations of his arguments, let alone as refutations. But the small sample we have presented here should give the reader some sense of the overall direction of his rulings. What is significant is not simply their generally conservative bent, but the stark line that Scalia draws between his own judicial practices and those of most of his colleagues. Scalia's rulings are not ad hoc reactions to particular legal issues; they are embedded in a coherent conception of the judicial role. In the next section, we examine Justice Scalia's vision of judging.

SCALIA'S VISION OF LAW

Justice Scalia has an enviable flair for polemic, which makes him a formidable opponent in debate and a forceful advocate on the Court. But polemic lends itself to oversimplification, with the result that his views can readily be caricatured, or simply misread, as an unsophisticated return to a mechanical view of the judicial function. As we will see, however, his originalism is part of a sophisticated vision of the judicial role that combines some of the aspirations of nineteenth-century formalism with some of the insights of twentieth-century legal realism.

THE REVIVAL OF FORMALISM

Justice Scalia's view of jurisprudence harkens back to an earlier era of American law, though he is not alone in his desire to resurrect that approach. The golden age of formalism followed the Civil War. It was later characterized, perhaps too simplistically, as having been an effort to make law into a deductive structure like Euclidean geometry. The current view of nineteenth-century formalism was cogently expressed by Grant Gilmore in a classic essay on American legal history:

> The post–Civil War judicial product seems to start from the assumption that the law is a closed, logical system. Judges do not make law: they merely declare the law which, in some Platonic sense, already exists. The judicial function has nothing to do with the adaptation of rules of law to changing conditions; it is restricted to the discovery of what the true

rules of law are and indeed always have been. Past error can be exposed and in that way minor corrections can be made, but the truth, once arrived at, is immutable and eternal.[20]

Legal realists such as Justices Oliver Wendell Holmes and Benjamin Cardozo led the campaign against this variety of formalism, with enough success to render the term "formalism" something of an insult in legal debate. But this victory may turn out to have been merely temporary.[21]

Although far more sophisticated than the classical formalists, Scalia shares their passion for order and logic. He has campaigned tirelessly against the use of legislative history in statutory interpretation, advocating in its place more firmly text-based methods of interpretation. In constitutional law, he has attacked current judicial methodologies in favor of reliance on original intent. Throughout, he has expressed a passion for clarity, logic, and stability in law.[22]

Consider first Scalia's desire for consistency, which he views as the first of all legal virtues, the "very foundation of the rule of law."[23] Consistency is even more important in the work of judges than it is for legislators and administrators:

> Besides its centrality to the rule of law in general, consistency has a special role to play in judge-made law. . . . The only checks on the arbitrariness of federal judges are the insistence upon consistency and the application of the teachings of the mother of consistency, logic. . . . [C]ourts apply to each case a system of abstract and entirely fictional categories developed in earlier cases, which are designed, if logically applied, to produce "fair" or textually faithful results.[24]

Because of his desire for clarity, certainty, and consistency, Justice Scalia has mixed feelings about the common law. He is uneasy about the common law process in which law grows, "not through the pronouncement of general principles, but case-by-case, deliberately, incrementally, one-step-at-a-time." But this process is inherently inconsistent with the ideal judicial role, according to Scalia: only by announcing and following clear rules can judicial decisions be respected, and only so can they provide certainty, limit future judicial discretion, and provide uniformity.[25] Indeed, he maintains, judges who do not provide abstract rules but instead rely on the totality of the circumstances are "not so much pronouncing the law in the normal sense as engaging in the less exalted function of fact-finding."[26]

No wonder another leading formalist was recently moved to ask whether the common law qualifies as law.[27] Indeed, Scalia himself seems to view the common law with some suspicion, and regrets that it receives so much attention in law schools. Because law school begins by studying the common law, he says, the students'

> image of the great judge—the Holmes, the Cardozo—is the man (or woman) who has the intelligence to discern the best rule of law for the case at hand and then the skill to perform the broken-field running through earlier cases that leaves him free to impose that rule: distinguishing one prior case on the left, straight-arming another one on the right, high-stepping away from another precedent about to tackle him from the rear, until (bravo!) he reaches the goal—good law.[28]

Justice Scalia's thought is not, however, merely a reincarnation of nineteenth-century formalism. Unlike the earlier formalists, he is seemingly aware that formalism can never be fully realized. Indeed, there is some evidence that he views it instead as a sort of noble myth to which judges ought to give their allegiance even if it is not wholly true. Recall his discomfort with the common law method and his preference for abstract principles. "Without such a system of binding abstractions," he argues, "it would be extraordinarily difficult" to maintain consistency so as to produce equality among litigants. Then the key comment: "That is why, by the way, I never thought Oliver Wendell Holmes and the legal realists did us a favor by pointing out that all these legal fictions were fictions: Those judges wise enough to be trusted with the secret already knew it."[29]

What is most notable about this last remark is the assumption that it is better for judges to adhere to certain myths despite their fictional nature, while maintaining a wise silence about the truth. In a perceptive essay on Scalia's theory of interpretation, Gordon Wood explains that "[t]he real source of the judicial problem that troubles Justice Scalia lies in our demystification of the law, which is an aspect of the general demystification of all authority that has taken place in the twentieth century."[30] Thus, jurisprudential criticisms of formalism to some extent miss the point of Scalia's position. Whether formalism is in some ultimate sense the best philosophical theory of law may be somewhat beside the point for Scalia. His mission is law reform, or at least reforming judicial practices, rather than philosophy. He is less concerned with perfecting legal theory than with changing the legal culture in which judges operate—less concerned with the true nature of law than with the myths by which judges should live.[31]

Thus at the root of his formalism is, paradoxically, at least as much a pragmatic effort at institutional change as a deeply principled theoretical stance. Scalia's core pragmatism allows him to dodge some of the pitfalls that trip up true believers such as Bork. It also, however, leaves his rhetoric ungrounded in fundamental principle, making his fervent denunciation of judicial opponents seem inflated and self-righteous rather than principled.

THE SKEPTICAL ORIGINALIST

There is reason to believe that Scalia sees originalism in somewhat the same way, as a creed that judges should endorse, but that cannot correspond fully to reality. In a lecture entitled "Originalism: The Lesser Evil," he presents more or less the standard defenses of originalism, but ends on a different and more interesting note—one that reflects an ambivalence toward the claims of originalism. In the concluding portion of the lecture, Scalia paints a portrait of the "faint-hearted originalist," using as an example a state law "providing public lashing, or branding of the right hand" as punishment. He doubts that any federal judge—including himself—would sustain such a law, regardless of the historical evidence, and "any espousal of originalism as a practical theory of exegesis must somehow come to terms with that reality."[32]

Because originalism is such "strong medicine," Scalia adds, often even those who espouse it cannot take originalism in its pure form. Thus a "faint-hearted originalist" might ascribe to the framers an intent to allow some degree of evolution, leaving "really no difference between the faint-hearted originalist and the moderate nonoriginalist, except that the former finds it comforting to make up (out of whole cloth) an original evolutionary intent, and the latter thinks that superfluous." Indeed, he says, "most originalists are faint-hearted and most nonoriginalists are moderate . . . which accounts for the fact that the sharp divergence between the two philosophies does not produce an equivalently sharp divergence in judicial opinions."[33] This is a notably faint-hearted defense of originalism by one who is often considered one of its most strenuous advocates.

Indeed, although Scalia rejects the "living Constitution" in principle, he seems to regard it as inevitable in practice. Originalism will, in practical effect, have an evolutionary component, not only because some of its adherents are faint of heart, but also because of the difficulty of applying the methodology. Later in the same lecture, Scalia concedes that the original intent will often be hard to establish from the historical record. (On this point, he seems far more realistic than Bork.) Hence "[t]he inevitable tendency of judges to think that the law is what they would like it to be will . . . cause most errors in judicial historiography to be made in the direction of projecting upon the age of 1789 current, modern values—so that as applied, even as applied in the best of faith, originalism will (as the historical record shows) end up as something of a compromise."[34]

Scalia closes the lecture with a very interesting observation that raises some question about the ultimate significance of his attachment to originalism: "Having made that endorsement [of originalism], I hasten to confess that in a crunch I may prove a faint-hearted originalist. I cannot imagine myself, any more than any other federal judge, upholding a statute that imposes the punishment of flogging. But then I cannot imagine such a case's arising either."[35] So Scalia the judge, it seems, may not turn out to be quite so much the originalist as Scalia the theoretician, which may come as something of a surprise to those familiar with the fervently originalist rhetoric of his opinions.

In any event, Scalia said, he doubted that many cases will present "the stark choice between giving evolutionary content (not yet required by stare decisis) and not giving evolutionary content to particular constitutional provisions." Instead, most will "be able to be framed in the terms that, even if the provision in question has an evolutionary content, there is inadequate indication that any evolution in social attitudes has occurred." To "conclude this largely theoretical talk on a note of reality," he says, the "real dispute" is not between originalist and nonoriginalists. Rather the significant dispute takes place *within* all three groups: (a) nonoriginalists, who embrace evolution for its own sake; (b) faint-hearted originalists, who believe evolution was intended by the framers; and (c) originalist purists, who accept the idea of evolutionary law only for the sake of argument. This debate is not over the theory of constitutional interpretation, but only over the "nature and degree of evidence necessary to demonstrate that constitutional evolution has occurred."[36] The theoretical dispute over whether the Constitution is "living" or frozen in time turns out to be irrelevant. The real issue is how quickly to keep pace with social values. This, again, will come as a surprise to the reader of his judicial opinions.

Thus Scalia the theorist seems a bit dubious about the direct relevance of the originalism debate to judicial practice. He does not seem terribly regretful about his inability to uphold a statute requiring flogging, and the drift of originalism toward current values is also something he seems to view with some complacency. This being the case, one might wonder why Scalia thinks it important to insist so strongly on originalism.

The answer is suggested by Justice Scalia's writings about the connection between originalism and judicial discretion. He does not actually expect originalism to extinguish the human element of judging. Most succinctly he says, he has "never claimed that originalism inoculates against willfulness; only that (unlike aspirationism) it does not cater to it."[37] In reality, Justice Scalia recognizes, it is impractical to wring all elements of discretion out of the process. Consider an excerpt from his closing comments in an essay about formalism:

> I have not said that legal determinations that do not reflect a general rule can be entirely avoided. We will have totality of the circumstances tests and balancing modes of analysis with us forever—and for my sins, I will probably write some of the opinions that use them. All I urge is that those modes of analysis be avoided where possible; that the Rule of Law, the law of rules, be extended as far as the nature of the question allows; and that, *to foster a correct attitude toward the matter,* we appellate judges bear in mind that when we have finally reached the point where we can do no more than consult the totality of the circumstances, we are acting more as fact-finders than as expositors of the law.[38]

The key moment in this otherwise unexceptionable passage is the italicized reference to "attitude." For Scalia, formalism (the "law of rules") is not a completely accurate description of even the ideal judge, but it does describe an attitude judges should cultivate. Similarly, originalism seems to be valuable because it produces a desirable mindset among judges.[39]

The reference to "attitudes" here is a recurrent theme in Scalia's thinking. Much of his objection to recent jurisprudence seems attitudinal. Speaking of the past few decades of legal thought in his response to historian Gordon Wood, he writes that "[t]here has been a change in kind, I think, not just in degree, when the willful judge no longer has to go about his business in the dark—when it is publicly proclaimed, and taught in the law schools, that judges *ought* to make the statutes and the Constitution say what they think best." In his commentary, Wood had said that "[u]ltimately there seems to be no easy way to limit the judges' interpretative power except by changing the attitude of judges themselves (in effect, changing the judicial culture, which is what I suppose Justice Scalia's essay is trying to do)" or by appointing judges with congenial attitudes. Much of Scalia's writing can best be understood in this vein, as an effort at cultural change rather than legal philosophy.[40]

ORIGINALISM AND DEMOCRACY

Compared to some other originalists such as Bork, Scalia seems to place relatively little emphasis on the argument that we must follow the original intent because that intent represents the views of the Sovereign People. Scalia does view democracy as being at odds with an active role for judges in making value judgments: "All of this [common law judging] would be an unqualified good, were it not for a trend in government that has developed in recent centuries, called democracy." But Scalia is only a lukewarm democrat. Consider, for instance, his view of the judicial role in private law: "development of the bulk of private law by judges (a natural aristocracy, as Madison accurately portrayed them)" is arguably "a desirable limitation upon popular democracy."[41]

In short, his originalism is driven at least as much by his formalism as by any devotion to doing the will of We the People. Scalia's main priority is properly confining the role of judges—as he says in his response to Professor Wood: "I am sure that we can induce judges, as we have induced presidents and generals, to stay within their proper governmental sphere." Note in this regard that one of his main arguments for originalism is that it counters the tendency of judges to be swayed by their personal predilections, which he calls the "principal weakness of the system."[42]

Strangely enough, Scalia's objection to nonoriginalism seems to be not that it is antimajoritarian, but rather that it may become too responsive to contemporary public opinion. Although the Warren Court was able to pursue unpopular values, he says, this was only because the new approach was a surprise: after the public catches on to nonoriginalism, judges will be selected largely because they share popular values. Just prior to that remark, he says that "increasingly, the 'individual rights' favored by the courts tend to be the same 'individual rights' favored by popular majoritarian legislation[.] Women's rights, for example; racial minority rights; homosexual rights; abortion rights; rights against political favoritism[.]" But, he says, a "democratic society does not, by and large, need constitutional guarantees to insure that its laws will reflect 'current values,'" because "[e]lections take care of that quite well."[43]

In contrast, according to Justice Scalia, the purpose of constitutional protections for individual rights is "precisely to prevent the law from reflecting certain changes in original values that the society adopting the Constitution thinks fundamentally undesirable." With specific regard to the Bill of Rights, the provisions were intended to codify existing legal rights and protect them against future change. For example, in analyzing what is a "cruel and unusual" punishment, we are to consult the concept of cruelty as it existed in 1790, not that of today. The 1790 concept must be understood on the basis of the undisputed paradigm cases of the period such as the assumption that hanging is not "cruel." Other punishments would be forbidden if they violated the 1790 concept of cruelty, even if today's majority does not consider them so. The whole point of the Constitution is thus to bind later generations to the moral values of the founders.[44] Thus for Scalia the trouble with judicial activism is apparently not that it is antimajoritarian but that it is antimajoritarian in the wrong way. By admitting that it is enforcing its own value judgments, the Court risks the loss of its power to curb the majority in the name of the eternal values endorsed by the framers.

Taken as a whole, Justice Scalia's jurisprudential thought is both engaging and disturbing. It is engaging because of his candid admission of the gap between his originalist rhetoric and the realities of law. As much as he emphasizes the importance of rules, he realizes that they cannot always govern; as much as he emphasizes originalism, he recognizes that theoretical positions about originalism are usually remote from the disputes in actual cases.

His candid recognition of the gap between rhetoric and reality is also disturbing. Judicial candor is a basic norm of our legal system, yet Justice Scalia seems to suggest that judges (at least the best judges) should consciously adopt rhetoric that they themselves know is simplistic if not misleading, so as to foster the right attitude toward legal issues. Perhaps for this reason, Scalia's opinions are far more polemical and blustering than these candid jurisprudential works.

Indeed, while formalism on its surface celebrates the importance of logical validity in legal decisions, Scalia's version ironically—in what one might almost call a postmodernist move—posits that this logic can only be supported by a rhetorical stance that itself evades logic. Similarly, while claiming to be a type of judging peculiarly suited for a democracy, his formalism is also sharply antidemocratic in its elitism. Wise judges have secrets that they must not share with ordinary judges; the values of 1789 must be preferred over the values of today's society; the public must not be allowed to realize that formalism is only a partial truth lest they politicize the appointments process. Perhaps, in the end, this stance was too uncomfortable to be maintained: in his latest writing about interpretation, much of the candor is gone, submerged in an overdrawn polemic about the evils of applying common law methods to statutory and constitutional issues.[45] These recent writings even gain rhetorical force through their silent abandonment of the sophistication of his earlier work.

LEGAL HISTORY AS OPEN-FIELD RUNNING

We have seen that what Justice Scalia most cares about is "following the rules laid down," not heeding the voice of We the People. But how successfully has originalism operated in his own opinions as a check against what he calls "judicial willfulness"? As we will see, Scalia's use of history bears a striking resemblance to the picture he draws of the common law judge's approach to precedent. The striking image of the broken-field runner, dodging arguments that threaten to bar his preferred result, seems to apply as much to his own use of historical materials as it does to common law judges' use of precedent. Rather than guiding him to a conclusion, the historical record often seems to function as a source of potential obstacles to be overcome.

We do not intend to evaluate whether, in the end, Scalia's rulings are compatible with the historical record. To be meaningful, any such investigation would have to cover a broad range of his opinions, not the handful we have room here to discuss. Moreover, such an investigation would be beside the point, because historical accuracy is a by-product rather than a central goal of Scalia's program. Whether case outcomes happen to coincide with the original intent is secondary under Scalia's theory of judging, which is more focused on the process of decisionmaking than on the ultimate outcome. The important thing is supposed to be the constraint created by the judge's attention to original intent. What is notably absent from Scalia's major opinions is any sense that his rulings were initially motivated by any study of the historical record.[46] Rather than trying to derive his rulings from history, Scalia is mostly content to show that they do not clearly violate the original understanding. But the historical record is seldom crystal clear, and a judge who is only interested in determining whether his preferred result is blocked by unambiguous historical evidence is unlikely to find himself seriously restrained from reaching his preferred results.

DEFENDING THE NEW FEDERALISM

Justice Scalia's most important opinion on federalism is *Printz,* the ruling (discussed earlier) that struck down the Brady Act. Recall that Scalia posited an absolute rule against federal mandates to state officials. Justice Stevens's dissent pointed to historical evidence that the framers assumed, contrary to

Justice Scalia, that state officials would be assigned to carry out federal laws.[47] Indeed, in another dissent, Justice Souter found the historical record decisive, but on the opposite side of Scalia. Admitting to having found the case harder than he originally anticipated—and perhaps himself placing more weight on history than he should have—Souter said "it is The Federalist that finally determines my position." He pointed to language in Federalist No. 27, in which Hamilton states that "the Legislatures, Courts and Magistrates of the respective members will be incorporated into the operations of the national government, as far as its just and constitutional authority extends; and will be rendered auxiliary to the enforcement of its laws." Of course, the framers did not anticipate the exact circumstances of the Brady Act, their language was not utterly unambiguous, and a few excerpts from the Federalist Papers are not necessarily decisive. Still, as evidence of original intent goes, this is clearer than usual and seemingly pertinent to the specific issue before the Court.[48] An originalist who started out with no particular predisposition about the merits of the constitutional issue presumably would find this evidence strong indeed.

In response, Justice Scalia attempted to explain away this contrary evidence. He argued that some passages were meant to endorse only voluntary enforcement of federal laws by the states, while other passages, if read correctly, referred to something other than commandeering. It is not our purpose to determine whose reading of these passages is correct. As one perceptive commentator puts it, however, "all of this interpretive work (some of it quite creative) does no more than attempt to rebut the contention that the Framers' original intent clearly supports the constitutionality of conscription; it does not purport to provide affirmative evidence supporting the contrary proposition."[49]

The question of the "correct" original understanding, if there was one, of the commandeering question would go far beyond the scope of this book. For present purposes, we are agnostic about whether Justice Scalia's ruling in *Printz* was consistent with the original understanding. But the historical evidence is certainly not strong enough to invalidate the Brady Bill under an approach that stresses judicial restraint in order to minimize judicial discretion. And it is obvious that research into the original understanding had little to do with the genesis of the opinion. Scalia's opinion relies primarily on general conceptions about state sovereignty rather than on concrete historical evidence. The treatment of specific historical evidence resembles to a remarkable extent the "open-field running" that Scalia attributes to the creative common law judge. Perhaps he successfully evades being tackled by Madison and Hamilton, but the opinion provides little evidence that he was notably guided or constrained by the historical record.

As we saw earlier, the concept of presidential supremacy is central to Justice Scalia's view of the separation of powers. To support this vision he has in general been content to rely on historical evidence that the framers intended a unified, vigorous executive branch. Precisely how the framers understood the authority of the president is a much-mooted question. Justice Scalia has never provided a detailed historical analysis. The closest he has come has been a sketch of the evidence that "might have been used" to support the argument for broad presidential power:

> [T]he traditional English understanding of executive power, or, to be more precise, royal prerogatives, was fairly well known to the founding generation, since they appear repeatedly in the text of the Constitution in formulations very similar to those found in Blackstone. It can further be argued that when those prerogatives were to be reallocated in whole or part to other branches of government, or were to be limited in some other way, the Constitution generally did so expressly. One could reasonably infer, therefore, that what was not expressly reassigned would— at least absent patent incompatibility with republican principles—remain with the executive.[50]

Thus, Scalia seems to suggest, George III may have provided the model for the presidency. Perhaps so, but as Scalia also admitted, the historical record is also replete with evidence that "many in the founding generation" were still repelled by the notion of using the English monarchy as a guidepost for executive power.[51] Scalia's failure to do any real historical spade work on an issue so central to his constitutional vision may indicate the shallowness of his concern for original intent.

Indeed, Scalia's historical conclusions are at odds with mainstream historical scholarship. The conventional wisdom on the subject of executive power has been aptly expressed by conservative legal scholar Henry Monaghan, himself a staunch originalist. According to Monaghan, the "transformation of the Constitution of 1789 is seen nowhere more clearly than in the modern Presidency." As Monaghan says, "[t]here is no need to labor the familiar: the President today plays a dominant role in the national government completely beyond the understanding in 1789." This conventional wisdom is not without support in the historical record. For instance, today presidential dominance in foreign affairs is axiomatic, but only a few years after the founding, no less a figure than James Madison argued that making treaties was primarily a legislative rather than executive function; indeed, he bitingly accused those taking the contrary view of attributing to the president the powers held by the English monarch.[52]

Our purpose, once again, is not to show that Scalia is necessarily wrong in his conclusions, but to probe his own methods of using history. Notably, the closest he has ever come to providing a historical defense of his own vision of executive power is to sketch an argument that "might be made" on its behalf. Perhaps this is an argument that not only "might be made" but can actually be made successfully. Possibly the conventional wisdom is wrong, and the framers did have a coherent vision of a powerful presidency. What is clear, however, is that Scalia did not await the success of the historical analysis before taking his stand on the true meaning of Article II.

FENDING OFF RELIGIOUS MINORITIES

Given Justice Scalia's general position as an advocate of original intent, it is ironic that inconsistency with the framers' intent has been one of the major grounds of criticism of his *Smith* opinion, which held that states need not exempt religious practices from general prohibitions. Scalia's opinion in *Smith* focuses on the need for bright lines and says nothing about the original understanding. In her dissent in a later case, Justice O'Connor mustered significant historical evidence against *Smith*, drawing on the work of earlier legal scholars. For instance, several state constitutions protected religious exercise except when it harmed specific state interests. In New York, the exception was for "acts of licentiousness" and "practices inconsistent with the peace or safety of this State." In Maryland, it was any disturbance of "the good order, peace or safety of the State," infringement of "the laws of morality," or injury to "others, in their natural, civil, or religious rights." The Northwest Ordinance provided that no person "demeaning himself in a peaceable and orderly manner" shall be "molested on account of his mode of worship or religious sentiments."[53]

Justice O'Connor devoted particular attention to James Madison's views because of his central role in the adoption of the First Amendment. In the debates over the Virginia Declaration of Rights, Madison's proposed language endorsed the "full and free exercise" of religion, "unless under color of religion the preservation of equal liberty, and the existence of the State be manifestly endangered." Later, in supporting a "Bill for Establishing Religious Freedom" drafted by Jefferson, Madison drafted his famous "Memorial and Remonstrance against Religious Assessments," in which he argued that free exercise entails a "duty towards the Creator." Madison maintained therefore "that in matters of Religion, no man's right is abridged by the institution of Civil Society, and that Religion is wholly exempt from its cognizance." Similarly, Jefferson held that the federal government was constitutionally forbidden "from intermeddling with religious institutions, their doctrines, discipline, or exercises." Justice O'Connor also observed that the "practice of the Colonies and early States bears out the conclusion that, at the time the Bill of Rights was ratified, it was accepted that government should, when possible, accommodate religious practice."[54]

As Justice Scalia pointed out in reply, Justice O'Connor's arguments are not ironclad. The state constitutions typically applied only to government actions taken "for," "in respect of," or "on account of" religion, a description that may not apply to neutral laws of general application. Moreover, the exceptions about preserving "good order" and so forth could be read broadly, since "peace" and "order" in eighteenth-century usage were often taken to encompass the obligation to obey general laws. Nor are the religious exemptions granted by legislatures decisive, since they do not show that the legislators felt constitutionally *obligated* to provide the exemptions. As usual, then, the historical record does not speak with unmistakable clarity to the point in dispute today.[55]

Thus O'Connor's evidence may not be decisive. Indeed, in the end, Scalia's position might turn out to have equal or even better historical support. But what is most notable is that Justice Scalia did not even turn to the historical evidence until after the *Smith* doctrine was challenged. When he did, his only concern was to defend the doctrine against historical attack, to finish his open-field run across the historical record without being tackled. He made no effort to show, then or earlier, that the original understanding affirmatively supported the *Smith* rule.

THE ROLE OF POST-ORIGINAL UNDERSTANDINGS

Although originalism plays a central role in Justice Scalia's jurisprudence, his practice as a judge also recognizes the importance of two kinds of post-enactment history. First, in large areas of the law, the judge is bound by well-established precedents that preclude reliance on original intent. Second, in addition to original intent, the judge is bound by entrenched American traditions, some of which may not have played any particular role in the framing of specific constitutional provisions. Not only is Scalia perhaps a "faint-hearted" originalist, but his originalism has two large gaps, where events after the founding are explicitly allowed into play. How Scalia views the relationship between "tradition" and originalism is, as we will see, a mystery that he has never attempted to explain. If he is untroubled by this question, it may be because he sees tradition and originalism as alternative means to the same end: expunging judicial discretion.

Despite its centrality in his thinking about judicial review, originalism plays a limited role in some of Justice Scalia's most notable opinions. For instance, he does not apply it to the First Amendment, an area in which he has been a staunch supporter of free speech. He defends his First Amendment decisions as applications of "long-standing and well-accepted principles (not out of accord with the general practices of our people, whether or not they were constitutionally required as an original matter) that are effectively irreversible."[56] He defends this use of precedent despite its potential conflict with the original intent:

> Originalism, like any other theory of interpretation put into practice in an ongoing system of law, must accommodate the doctrine of *stare decisis*; it cannot remake the world anew. It is of no more consequence at this point whether the Alien and Sedition Acts of 1798 were in accord with the original understanding of the First Amendment than it is whether *Marbury v. Madison* was decided correctly.[57]

Thus, Scalia says, "originalism will make a difference," "not in the rolling back of accepted old principles of constitutional law but in the rejection of usurpatious new ones." As examples of novel constitutional rights, he cites rulings that invalidated "statewide laws denying special protection to homosexuals," excessive jury awards, exclusion from government contracts because of party affiliation, and single-sex state schools.[58]

There is an appealing pragmatism in Scalia's candid concession that existing constitutional rights, warranted or not, are here to stay. But the line between existing and new rights is problematic in ways that Scalia does not appear to recognize. The Court almost always claims to be following the logic of earlier rulings rather than creating new rights out of whole cloth. It is very difficult to discern any principled distinction between what Scalia considers a novel right and what he considers an established one. Of the four cases on his list of novel rights, two were admittedly not covered by clear-cut existing precedents (though this does not necessarily mean they were wrongly decided). But the single-sex school decision was a straightforward application of a host of earlier rulings disfavoring gender discrimination, and the government contracting case was only a small extension of previous cases involving political patronage. (Those rulings in turn derived from earlier decisions on the free speech rights of public employees.) Thus, the "novelty" of these "usurpatious" decisions seems to exist mostly in the eye of the beholder.

In contrast, Justice Scalia's decision in the cross-burning case was widely seen as a significant expansion of precedent. Language in previous decisions seemed to suggest that "fighting words" were wholly outside the protection of the First Amendment, but Justice Scalia held that even as to fighting words, the government cannot draw distinctions based on objections to the ideas expressed by the insults. Thus the case was an expansion of existing precedent (which is again not to say that the expansion was unwarranted). It is also hard to imagine that the framers of the Bill of Rights understood it to protect activities such as cross-burning. But Justice Scalia apparently did not consider the case to involve a novel right, only a principled application of current law.[59] The distinction between new rights and novel applications of old rights seems elusive and subject to manipulation, particularly since Scalia has never even attempted to explain why he draws the line where he does.

Perhaps the answer is that the single-sex school involved a long-standing traditional practice, whereas cross-burning has not been blessed with a similar history of acceptance. If so, then to truly understand Scalia's view of precedent, we must also consider his position on the role of tradition in constitutional law.

TRADITION

One of the most puzzling aspects of Justice Scalia's jurisprudence is his attitude toward tradition. If the meaning of the Constitution is dictated by how it was understood when it was enacted, it is hard to see why later historical practice has probative value. What difference does it make what people thought in 1950, or 1850 for that matter, when what we care about is what they thought in 1789? And yet, not only does Scalia consider this evidence relevant, he often seems to find it dispositive.[60]

Justice Scalia's dissent in the patronage contracting cases is a good illustration of his use of tradition. In previous cases, the Court had held that hiring or firing employees based on their party affiliation violated their First Amendment rights. In two 1996 cases, the Court applied this rule to government contractors. Justice Scalia's dissent was joined only by Justice Thomas. Scalia protested that "like rewarding one's allies, the correlative act of refusing to reward one's opponents . . . is an American political tradition as old as the Republic."[61] In his view, this history was dispositive:

> If that long and unbroken tradition of our people does not decide these cases, then what does? The constitutional text is assuredly as susceptible of one meaning as of the other; in that circumstance, what constitutes a "law abridging the freedom of speech" is either a matter of history or else it is a matter of opinion. Why are not libel laws such an "abridgement"? The only satisfactory answer is that they never were. What secret knowledge, one must wonder, is breathed into lawyers when they become Justices of this Court, that enables them to discern that a practice which the text of the Constitution does not clearly proscribe, and which our people have *regarded* as constitutional for 200 years, is in fact unconstitutional?[62]

Although he admitted that the practice of patronage is controversial and has in fact been made illegal in many settings, Justice Scalia insisted that "[t]he relevant and inescapable point is this: No court ever held, and indeed no one ever thought, prior to our decisions [in two earlier cases], that patronage contracting could violate *the First Amendment*."[63]

More generally, Scalia insisted, when a "practice not expressly prohibited by the text of the Bill of Rights bears the endorsement of a long tradition of open, widespread, and unchallenged use that dates back to the beginning of the Republic, we have no proper basis for striking it down." Rather than subjecting such practices to current constitutional doctrines, "such traditions are themselves the stuff out of which the Court's principles are to be formed"—the "very points of reference by which the legitimacy or illegitimacy of *other* practices is to be figured out."[64]

Justice Scalia closed his dissent in this seemingly mundane case in apocalyptic terms, perhaps because of other unsettling cases that were decided at about the same time. After reiterating that "[f]avoritism such as this happens all the time in American political life, and no one has ever thought that it violated—of all things—the First Amendment to the Constitution of the United States," he added a cry of despair about the state of constitutional law: "The Court must be living in another world. Day by day, case by case, it is busy designing a Constitution for a country I do not recognize."[65]

Apart from its possible rhetorical excess—the band of judicial activists at whom Scalia was aiming his spear in this particular case included, among others, Chief Justice Rehnquist—Scalia's dissent probably also overstates the facts. Patronage hiring in the current sense would not have been endorsed by the framers for two reasons: First, they considered the use of government patronage to strengthen political power to be a dangerous form of corruption. Second, political parties in the modern sense had not yet arisen and would have been considered undesirable factions of the kind the Constitution was designed to control. And, as the majority pointed out, patronage contracting has been controversial for more than a century and has been subjected to numerous legal restrictions. Thus it is not a tradition in the sense of having an unquestioned status as beneficial and appropriate. What may be part of our traditions is not the practice itself but (perhaps) the assumption that, for better or worse, the practice was not governed by the First Amendment—in other words, what seems crucial here is not whether the practice itself is an accepted part of our tradition, but whether the constitutional interpretation is part of that tradition.[66]

Scalia is not alone—nor, in our view, wrong—in finding tradition relevant to constitutional law.[67] He is unusual, however, in two regards. First, he defines tradition very narrowly: it is the tradition of patronage contracting, not the tradition of unbridled public discourse, that counts in the independent contractor case. Second, the tradition is unbreakable, regardless of how inconsistent with later judicial holding or social values. By this test, for instance, gender discrimination seems an impeccable constitutional tradition, since until recently there were no serious constitutional challenges to laws disfavoring women.

The axiom that Scalia endorses, as we understand it, seems to be that constitutional interpretations that have been universally accepted for sufficiently long periods of time are binding on the Court. He has not, however, explained the basis for this axiom. For the record, we think that the arguments for tradition have a grain of truth, though we question whether they ought to create an absolute presumption of validity.[68] So far as we are aware, however, Justice Scalia has never explained which of these arguments, if any, underlies his endorsement of tradition. At least some theories supporting tradition seem at odds with originalism or formalism, or inconsistent with other Scalia rulings. Moreover, the arguments have different implications about when the rule should apply—for example, under some but not others, it is critical that a tradition stretch back to the nation's founding. It is unfortunate that Scalia has been content to posit the rule without ever feeling the need to explain it.

A more serious problem is the difficulty in applying this rule. Interpreting traditions involves many of the same problems as interpreting original intent. We are apt to find ambiguities in the historical record if we look carefully enough. It seems unlikely, for instance, that no one had *ever* attacked firing an employee for taking a political position as a violation of free speech; the argument seems too obvious to have been wholly overlooked for two centuries. Another problem is the relationship between tradition and precedent. It is unclear when precedents become powerful enough to stand as counterweights to other traditions. Until the mid-twentieth century, as Scalia points out, libel would have been clearly understood to be outside the protection of the First Amendment, but a host of Supreme Court cases beginning with the landmark 1964 decision in *New York Times v. Sullivan* are now to the contrary. Yet Scalia has shown no inclination to overrule that line of cases. Similarly, laws against flag-burning seem venerable, and it is doubtful that until recently anyone would have questioned their validity under the First Amendment, but Scalia has felt bound to apply current First Amendment principles even to such traditionally proscribed practices as burning the flag. Yet, as the patronage contracting cases show, Scalia is not always willing to bow to precedents inconsistent with earlier traditions— some twenty years later, he was still protesting the decision to apply the First Amendment to patronage in the first place.[69]

There is a final irony to Justice Scalia's dissent in the patronage contracting cases. He begins the dissent with the charge that "this Court's Constitution-making process can be called 'reasoned adjudication' only in the most formalistic sense." Later, he echoes the charge of a lower court judge that "the issue that the Court today disposes of like some textbook exercise in logic 'raises profound questions of political science that exceed judicial competence to answer.'"[70] This complaint about "formalistic" decisions and "exercises in logic," it should be recalled, comes from the Court's foremost advocate of formalism!

THE FAILURE OF SCALIAN ORIGINALISM

The prime directive of originalism is to decide constitutional issues in line with the most probable reading of the original understanding. This formulation is not free from difficulty, as we have already seen. Still, it at least directs the judge's attention to a single source of authority: the historical record preceding the enactment of the provision in question. Because he has failed to grapple seriously with the historical record in most of his important decisions, however, it seems doubtful that an engagement with history has motivated Scalia's key decisions.

In this sense, it is questionable whether Scalia can properly be considered an originalist at all in his judicial method, and some of his more theoretical writings seem to reflect an awareness of the practical limitations of originalism. Instead of originalism, he has tended in practice to invoke entrenched interpretations of constitutional provisions by either the Court itself or by long-standing public consensus. Thus he can invoke four possible sources of authority: (1) the constitutional text; (2) preenactment history; (3) post-enactment practices; and (4) judicial precedents. But with each additional source of authority, he gains an additional degree of freedom, weakening the constraints of formalism. A formalist who has four different methodologies among which to choose is hardly distinguishable from a nonformalist, because it is impossible to be fully consistent about such methodological choices across cases. Indeed, in his theoretical writings, Scalia seems to have at least a glimmering that his brand of originalist formalism may be an impossible dream that can never be fully realized.

What is important is that, whatever Justice Scalia himself may think, his constitutional stance is not, to any greater extent than that of any other judge, forced upon him by objective sources of law. His own vision of American society also plays a role. If he fears that the Court is "busy designing a Constitution for a country I do not recognize," his own quest—like those of the other theorists we discuss—is to find a Constitution for another country, one he can recognize as his own.[71] What *that* country would look like is something we can only infer, based on hints in his judicial decisions rather than his theories. In contrast, our next subject has devoted much effort to a systematic explanation of his vision for America.

CHAPTER 4

RICHARD EPSTEIN AND THE INCREDIBLE SHRINKING GOVERNMENT

During the past two decades, many Americans have come to believe that government regulation has gone too far, that the federal government has become too powerful, and that we need to "get the government off the backs of the people." The Reagan presidency was at least in part dedicated to implementing that viewpoint, which continues to be politically influential. Although the policy perspective is commonplace, it was less obvious—even to most of its advocates—that the Reagan platform was *constitutionally* mandated. It took Richard Epstein, a brilliant libertarian scholar at the University of Chicago Law School, to make that case. He has argued that most government regulations violate the Constitution's Takings Clause and its companion, the Contracts Clause.

The power of the federal government is especially limited, in Epstein's view. He gives a very narrow reading to the specific federal powers listed in the Constitution. The Supreme Court has expansively interpreted the Commerce Clause—which gives Congress power over interstate commerce—to embrace the entire economy. Epstein's view of the Commerce Clause is far narrower. Only actual transfers across state lines are subject to federal regulation: "the Ford Motor Company did not manufacture goods in interstate commerce, but the Northern Pacific Railroad shipped them in interstate commerce." Epstein concludes his discussion of federal power in no uncertain terms: "The affirmative scope of the commerce power should be limited to . . . interstate transportation, navigation and sales, and the activities closely incident to them. All else should be left to the states."[1] Leaving "burning issues" to the states—such as labor unions and farm policy in the depression— "reduces the risk of misguided policies with nationwide impact."[2]

A striking illustration of Epstein's view of governmental—especially federal—power is provided in his book about employment discrimination. He argues that the federal laws against private racial and sex discrimination are unconstitutional on two grounds. First, "[t]here is no question that the 1964 Civil Rights Act falls within the scope of the commerce power as it is currently understood, and none that it falls *outside* that power as it was originally written and understood." Thus antidiscrimination laws are no affair of the federal government. Second, antidiscrimination laws are outside the authority of any level of government because they violate the rights of owners and employers who wish to discriminate. Individual rights are "necessarily infringed by a statutory command that denies the owner of property the rights to the exclusive use possession and use of his own land," which is "exactly what an antidiscrimination statute does by requiring the employer to hire a given worker against his will." Except as a transitional measure to overcome the effects of prior state segregation statutes, the case for federal laws against racial discrimination "looks very weak indeed" to Epstein.[3] Indeed, he has argued, broad acceptance of government regulatory power was a crucial factor in the creation of Jim Crow, which would have been avoided in a more virtuous, property-oriented regime.[4]

An anonymous critic once quipped that what Epstein really wants is to shorten the First Amendment to its initial five words: "Congress shall make no law." Although Epstein's views are more complex—for instance, he does see some role for environmental regulation—his version of the Constitution would eliminate most of the laws passed during and since the New Deal. (In contrast, as we will see, the main mission of one of our other theorists, Bruce Ackerman, is to rescue the New Deal from Epstein's challenge.) Though he is not alone in taking this position as a matter of policy or even in his interpretation of the Constitution,[5] he has been the most formidable advocate for this constitutional vision. We will begin by examining his argument that economic regulation violates individual constitutional rights, and then consider the argument that most federal economic regulation violates the principles of federalism. Despite the temptation to approach Epstein as merely a clever academic debater, it would be a mistake to dismiss his views as purely ivory tower. As we will see, the Supreme Court, while never coming close to adopting his vision outright, has gradually moved in his direction.

Like the other scholars we discuss, Epstein elevates a single value above all others, around which he constructs an elaborate constitutional theory. For Bork, the value is popular rule (limited only by mandates adopted by supermajorities). For Scalia, the value is a certain style of logical, value-free judicial decision. For Epstein, it is distrust of government: "in praising the good that can come from government discretion, we should never forget the evils it has wrought."[6] So great is his fear of abuse of the political process that he wishes to remove as much as possible from its scope.

Fear of government power is not illegitimate—that is, after all, why we have individual rights—but for Epstein this fear has become the dominant motivation. Because disputes about fairness and redistribution can be abused by special interests, Epstein would remove them from politics almost entirely. Because federal economic regulation can be unwise, he seeks to eliminate it as much as possible. As with the others, Epstein's obsession with a single value leads him astray. It causes him to ignore the basic historical fact that the Constitution was designed to *strengthen*, not to eliminate, federal government power. This obsession leaves no room in his constitutional scheme for competing values. It leaves his scheme utterly out of touch with the existing legal regime with all its compromises and complexities. What it does give him, however, are intellectually elegant, if misleadingly simple, answers to hard questions.

Of all the "grand theories" discussed in this book, Epstein's is in some sense the grandest because of his ambition to cover all of public and private law in one unified framework. For this reason, it has a certain intellectual grandeur that makes the other theories look ad hoc and shabby by contrast. Epstein also seeks, somewhat paradoxically, to ground his theory in common sense and practicality. Some readers may be taken aback by his own summary of his thinking:

> If you keep your common sense and intellectual bearings both, then you can learn [from] a lesson taught me by one of my own teachers at Columbia University, the late Ernest Nagel, who taught that it was more important to be right than to be clever, and that in most moral or legal disputes the right answer will be simple and straightforward. It is the thinkers with all the razzmatazz who are likely to get it wrong. So do not give up on your common sense; try to refine, improve and systematize it. That is all that we can ask of ourselves. That is what we must ask of ourselves.[7]

We applaud this call for common sense over cleverness. The paradox, however, is that all of the thinkers who are our focus in this book would probably do the same, though we consider their work to be characterized more by brilliance than by soundness. Where they go wrong—and none more brilliantly or thoroughly than Epstein—is in the assumption that common sense is ultimately complete and coherent, so that we can expect to find that the "right answer will be simple and straightforward," if only we use our common sense as the basis for the right theory. But common sense cannot provide the axioms needed for such a theory. Common sense is an unruly collection of hunches, experience, sentiments, and both formal and informal reasoning. What it can best offer are not starting points for grand theory but a sense of reality, and it is in abandoning reality in favor of theoretical consistency that constitutional theorists so often go astray.

Like Epstein, most of the theorists in this book believe our world is upside down. The more realistic among them realize that not everything can be righted overnight; like Epstein they ask us only to place our new furniture on what we now consider to be the room's ceiling rather than the floor. Even so, theirs is a quixotic venture. However messy and philosophically disoriented it may be, the floor is where we actually live.

ENDING GOVERNMENT REGULATION

Although Epstein argues that special limits apply to the federal government, he believes the powers of *all* levels of government should be sharply limited. He considers nearly all existing regulations to be unconstitutional "takings" of private property. Since this area of constitutional law is likely to be unfamiliar to many readers, we begin with some background materials. Then we turn to Epstein's brilliantly unconventional analysis.

THE TAKINGS CLAUSE: CURRENT LAW AND HISTORICAL SCHOLARSHIP

Epstein rests his analysis on the Takings Clause: "Nor shall private property be taken for public use without just compensation." The most obvious application is to government seizure of land for roads and other projects. In Justice Holmes's famous opinion in *Pennsylvania Coal v. Mahon*,[8] however, the U.S. Supreme Court held that a taking could also exist if the government "went too far" in regulating private property. In *Mahon,* the Court struck down a Pennsylvania law that effectively destroyed the economic value of certain mining rights. Until 1975, however, the Court rarely decided takings cases.

In the past twenty-five years, the Court has applied the takings clause to a variety of government regulations. For instance, the federal government was required to pay a developer for public access to a marina that the developer had connected with a public waterway.[9] The Court also found a taking when New York required landlords to give their tenants access to cable television. The reason was that a cable box would "take" some of the space on the roof.[10] Later, in *Lucas v. South Carolina Coastal Council*,[11] the Court found a taking when a beach preservation law prevented an owner from making any use whatsoever of his land on a fragile beach. Fears arose in some quarters, and hopes in others, that the Court would make aggressive use of the Takings Clause to attack government regulation. So far, such a judicial campaign has not emerged. There is no doubt, however, that the Takings Clause has taken on renewed importance.

In light of its renewed legal significance, the history of the Takings Clause has recently attracted increased attention from legal historians. Their findings, while not completely unambiguous, lend little support to Epstein's thesis about the sweeping nature of the clause. Their work exemplifies the gap between bold pronouncements about the original understanding and the complex, nuanced, sometimes tedious work of actual historical research.

The relevant history falls into three periods: pre-Revolutionary colonial practices, the post-Revolutionary period leading up to the drafting of the Takings Clause itself, and early interpretations of takings provisions in the federal Constitution and in state constitutions. None of this history provides much support for aggressive application of the Takings Clause to government regulations. Indeed, a fair reading of the history leaves some doubt about whether the framers understood it to apply to government regulations at all, as opposed to government actions taking title to or physical possession of property. As we will see later, this history forces Epstein to reconceptualize originalism in order to make his case. (One of our originalist friends complained bitterly about the dullness of the following historical summary. Alas, that's the trouble with history: full of complexity and detail!)

To begin with the pre-Revolutionary history, the issue of compensation for takings arose most often in the eighteenth century in connection with highway construction. Colonial practice varied, depending mostly on the structure of local society (the sort of factor that greatly interests historians but is hard to fit into an originalist analysis). John Hart recently surveyed the historical evidence and found two distinct sets of practices. In the major southern colonies (Virginia, South Carolina, and Georgia), landowners were not compensated for the use of their property for highways. Government mostly took place at the county level, and disgruntled landowners had little political recourse. In the New England colonies of Massachusetts, Connecticut, Rhode Island, and New Hampshire, local governments used compensation to assuage the anger of local landowners who might otherwise have disrupted close-knit communities. Other colonies fell between these two extremes. New York and Pennsylvania moved toward compensation requirements, whereas New Jersey moved in the opposite direction.

According to Hart, the availability of compensation had little to do with concepts of individual rights: "[I]t is in the colonies exhibiting entrenched oligarchies founded on real property—Virginia, Maryland, South Carolina—that we find the most resolute resistance to paying compensation for highway land. If privatistic, possessive individualism can account for paying compensation for highway land, then these colonies could have been expected to enact compensation provisions." Instead, he concluded that "[t]he reason why the New England colonies . . . consistently supported compensation to individuals for highway land is that the town fathers viewed compensation for highway land as one of the many mechanisms employed to maintain cohesion in their communities. The mundane imperatives of communitarian governance, seem to have supplied the most fertile soil for highway compensation in the colonial period." Notably, in neither group of colonies did Hart find "much evidence that the assemblies originally approached the question of highway compensation as a matter of constitutional rights."[12]

William Treanor picks up the story after the Revolution, tracing the developments leading up to the Fifth Amendment.[13] Vermont's 1777 Declaration of Rights contains a lengthy preamble stressing the necessity for security in land titles, prompted by the failure of New York courts to recognize New Hampshire titles to land claimed by New York. Vermont broke new ground with the proposition that "private property ought to be subservient to public uses, when necessity requires it; nevertheless, whenever any particular man's property is taken for the use of the public, the owner ought to receive an equivalent in money." The framers of the Massachusetts constitution of 1780 soon followed suit. And the Northwest Ordinance provided in 1787 that "should the public exigencies make it necessary for the common preservation to take any persons property, or to demand his particular services, full compensation shall be made for the same . . . ." The provision about demanding services could be a reference to the practice of "impressing" sailors and soldiers (that is, kidnapping people and forcing them into military service). The provision about property may also have been aimed at military requisitions, but concern about the security of land titles may also have played a role.

In the initial version of the Bill of Rights proposed by Madison, the Takings Clause read: "No person shall be . . . obliged to relinquish his property, where it may be necessary for public use, without a just compensation." The reference to relinquishment of property suggests a transfer, not merely a restriction on property use. Madison's own understanding of the clause seems unclear. Late in his life, he remarked that "whatever may be the intrinsic character of that description of property [slaves], it is one known to the constitution, and, as such could not be constitutionally taken away without just compensation." Madison's view that abolition would be a "taking" seems to broaden the clause to the extent of including destruction of title rather than merely transfer to the government. On the other hand, in opposing some of Hamilton's economic plans, he seemed to concede that "indirect" violations of property rights did not require compensation.[14]

Government regulation was widespread in early America, covering such matters as land use, price controls for essential commodities, and regulation of professions. Treanor contends that prior to the Civil War, state courts usually required compensation only when the government physically took or physically invaded property. He maintains that compensation was not required for consequential damages from activities that did not involve physical invasions or appropriations of property but that had physical consequences, such as subsidence caused by a road-building project.

Treanor's conclusion has been contested by Kris Kobach. He points to several categories of nonacquisitive takings that were recognized by state courts (and on occasion by federal courts). The most notable examples were government activities resulting in physical interference with the water rights of downstream owners or destruction of access rights by closing streets or highways. Although viewing these cases as establishing a broad principle of compensation for government harm to property rights, Kobach acknowledges two limits: only vested rights in existing uses of land were protected, and only direct rather than consequential injuries were compensable, following the causation requirements of tort law of the time.[15] The most important takings disputes today involve the right to develop land, rather than to continue existing uses. The right to develop was not, however, a "vested" right that would be protected under Kobach's view of the original understanding.

This history, even on Kobach's reading, falls short of establishing a basis for the aggressive restrictions on government regulation favored by Epstein. Despite the Supreme Court's growing interest in property rights, the Court remains generally deferential toward economic regulations. Thus neither standard historical research nor legal precedent supports Epstein. Without support in these conventional legal sources, how does Epstein justify his sweeping conclusions, such as the view that civil rights laws are unconstitutional takings?

GETTING TO "NO": EPSTEIN'S THEORY OF TAKINGS

Epstein's is the most intellectually ambitious of all the theories we consider in this book. He seeks to provide a comprehensive analysis of the entire legal system, not just constitutional law. Before trying to explain how Epstein connects his theory with the Constitution, it is useful to begin with a brief overview of that theory, which is in two parts.

The first part of the theory defines the term "taking of private property." Epstein classifies as a taking of property any government action that would be unlawful on the part of an individual, judged by the traditional standards of the common law. Jones has no right to tell his neighbor Smith whether to use her property for residential or commercial purposes, how much to pay her workers, or which workers to hire. If no single neighbor has the right to take these actions, Epstein reasons, then all of Smith's neighbors collectively have no greater rights. Thus zoning, minimum wage, and discrimination laws are all "takings of property." So are taxes, obviously: Jones certainly doesn't have the right to demand 10 percent of his neighbor's income or 5 percent of the value of her property, and all the Joneses of the world in unison have no greater power collectively than the sum of their individual powers. Two hundred and forty million times zero is still zero.

Except for government actions that enforce common law rules about property, then, virtually everything the government does is a "taking of property," as defined by Epstein. If the government were forbidden absolutely to take private property, the result of this definition of "takings" would be to outlaw most government, which could not operate without the ability to collect taxes and engage in many other activities beyond the common law authority of any individual.[16] But Epstein considers himself a moderate because, unlike more extreme libertarians, he does see *some* legitimate scope for government regulation.

This brings us to the second part of Epstein's theory, in which he adopts a definition of just compensation broad enough to allow some but not all government activities. Obviously, a cash payment can constitute just compensation; indeed, this is the normal form of compensation when the government takes land for use in a project. But Epstein argues that compensation does not need to take this form. Just compensation is also present when a government action satisfies a somewhat complicated principle of

proportionality. This principle requires that each individual be able to anticipate, before the fact, expected benefits from the government's actions pro-
portionate to the cost imposed on that individual. Thus, if it is to withstand
challenge, the regulation's expected effects cannot include redistributing
wealth away from anyone identifiable in advance—rather than receiving
just compensation, such a person would anticipate only unjust financial
loss. (The progressive income tax is a particularly obvious example.) Epstein
fears that the threat of such negative effects on wealth would be a socially
wasteful and disruptive jockeying for political power.

Note that this proportionality principle has two prongs. First, the government's action must increase social wealth, so that there is a surplus to
share. Thus laws must pass a test based on economic efficiency. This means
that society as a whole is wealthier. But depending on how the surplus is distributed, some individuals might know in advance that the government's
action will make them relatively poorer and others richer. The second prong
blocks such outcomes—the surplus must be divided in such a way that the
net result of the government's action is to leave the proportional distribution
of wealth untouched. In short, government actions must satisfy two criteria:
they must increase social wealth, and they must be distributionally neutral.
In principle, Epstein views these as empirical questions, and one can imagine a cautious, empirically based version of his approach. But in practice,
Epstein rarely seems to need any empirical evidence or sophisticated economic models, nor is he willing to trust democratic governments to answer
these questions.[17]

Epstein states that "[o]ne important implication of this general theory is
that it proscribes both as a matter of constitutional and political theory all
coerced transfer systems, including those designed to aid the poor and the
needy." He recognizes, of course, that it is impossible to root out at least
some existing institutions such as social security. (In fairness, it should also
be noted that Epstein's opposition to government transfer programs is not
based on an opposition to the transfers themselves. He is a fervent supporter
of the moral duty to engage in private charity, but he is opposed to government compulsion.) But the implications stretch beyond transfer programs.
"It will be said that my position invalidates much of the twentieth-century
legislation," Epstein observes, "and so it does." He goes on to eliminate any
doubts on this score: "[t]he New Deal *is* inconsistent with the principles of
limited government and with the constitutional provisions designed to secure that end."[18]

Epstein devotes much energy and ingenuity to establishing the economic and philosophical bases for this position and elaborating its implications. He devotes relatively less attention to establishing the constitutional basis for this reading of the Takings Clause. Nevertheless, he clearly sees it as firmly rooted in the text and original understanding of the Constitution. He views the Constitution as embodying an underlying theory of the state: one in which people have natural rights, including property rights, that are not created by the state, and the role of the government is to protect those individual rights. Thus, like the other originalists we consider, his reading of history is heavily colored by his own constitutional vision. The first part of his theory, then, establishes the basic rights of property as being essentially those recognized in the common law. The second part of the theory delineates the appropriate role of government. Although he does not exactly follow Locke's views about property, the general treatment has, as Epstein emphasizes, a Lockean foundation. This may make him more of an intellectual purist than the framers, who also drew on non-Lockean thought.[19] As to the text, Epstein believes that the term "property" and the connected term "taking" have well-understood legal meanings, which have not noticeably changed since Blackstone's days. And the term "just compensation" is equally straightforward, he argues: it is simply whatever compensation is required by justice (more specifically, by the best available theory of justice).[20]

Thus Epstein views his theory as in part based on the "internal intellectual integrity of the constitutional provision," "treated as a self-contained intellectual proposition." This part of Epstein's argument is reminiscent of the constitutional methodology of liberals such as Ronald Dworkin: he is trying to provide the best possible moral and political theory to make sense of the Constitution.[21]

Undoubtedly, there is a great deal one might quarrel with here. One can, for example, criticize the way the theory is worked out, particularly Epstein's overly confident empirical judgments. He also overemphasizes the clarity of the constitutional text and the significance of Lockean thought among the framers. But the theory does have considerable intellectual appeal because it cuts the Gordion knot of takings law.

The intellectual puzzle about takings, which has left so many commentators at sea, is the circularity between property rights and legislation. If property is determined by state law, which is always subject to change, then it is hard to see how a change in laws governing property can be a taking. Thus government regulation becomes tied into the definition of property in a way that makes it very hard to separate the two. Yet the law is clear that some regulations do constitute takings. Epstein breaks out of the circularity by defining property rights in terms of the common law, but then deploys the concept of just compensation broadly in order to uphold some intrusions on traditional rights.

Epstein's theory also avoids the line-drawing problems that plague other theories of takings. Unlike others, he does not need to draw lines between acquisition of title versus interference with possession, or physical versus use regulations, or total versus partial destruction of value. These lines are all somewhat arbitrary and awkward to apply. In this sense, Epstein's solution is more intellectually satisfying. Unfortunately, this elegant solution to the Takings Clause comes at the price of playing havoc with the framers' other goal: not only protecting individual property rights, but promoting vigorous government.

One price of this brilliant solution is a strangely ahistorical view of property.[22] Even within the common law itself, property rules have fluctuated, as has the autonomy of the owner.[23] Property rights have always been conditioned by regulation, in the framers' time as well as our own. As one economic historian explains it, "[t]he ideas of laissez faire were not widely known in colonial times." Instead, "[r]egulation was the right of government and its duty," before the American Revolution as well as after.[24] There is no reason to think that the framers *intended* to overturn the commonplace regulations of their time.

Epstein's response to the historical record is not to disown originalism but to change the focus of the historical inquiry from specific intention to broad principle. He concedes that the framers may have mistakenly thought that the takings principle was compatible with many government regulations. But, he maintains, this was a mistake on their part, and it is the principle rather than the mistaken applications that they wrote into the Constitution.[25] (Compare Bork's defense of the desegregation decisions on the similar ground that the framers mistakenly thought school segregation compatible with racial equality.) If the result is a legal regime that looks nothing like what they had in mind, so much the worse for them, one gathers.

Epstein's theory of takings is brilliantly designed, but it is also designed for some other world, one in which neither we nor the framers have ever lived. Even before the American Revolution, governments regulated land use, licensed peddlers and taverns, controlled prices for bread, and engaged in other economic regulations. No wonder Madison, in Federalist No. 10, referred to the "principal task of modern legislation" as the regulation of the "various and interfering interests" of land owners, manufacturers, merchants, creditors, and debtors.[26]

Thus the great irony of Epstein's view is that it is squarely in conflict with what Justice Scalia has called "the traditions of our people." Whatever may be said of Scalia's theory of tradition in other contexts, it is surely a serious flaw, in a theory that purports to be devoted to protecting property, that it would overturn the past two centuries of traditional understandings regarding the scope of property rights. As an illustration of the willingness of legal scholars to put intellectual elegance above workability, we can hardly better Epstein's willingness to overthrow vast areas of our legal regime in order to achieve intellectual tidiness in the arcane area of takings law.

RESURRECTING FEDERALISM

According to Epstein, most existing regulations are beyond the power of any level of government because they are unconstitutional takings of private property. But he sees the federal government as particularly dangerous, and therefore in need of additional limitations. If a state overregulates, it is likely to harm its own economy, which provides a natural check on excessive regulation. The federal government is much less subject to this check because the national economy is more self-contained than state economies even in this era of globalization. Epstein argues that the framers rigorously limited federal power to sharply defined spheres in order to prevent regulatory overreaching. Thus, in his view, modern regulations such as federal antidiscrimination laws are doubly unconstitutional: not only do they violate property rights, but they transgress the special limits on federal authority as well.

FEDERAL POWER AND CONSERVATIVE CONSTITUTIONAL THEORY

Epstein's federalism theory is less distinctive than his theory of takings, though equally bold. It builds on the work of other conservative theorists and dovetails with some recent judicial views. His call for renewed limits on federal power is shared by others, as we will see in this section. But it is his effort to specify the precise boundaries of that power that is most distinctive.

In the 1980s, conservative theorists began to take a vigorous stance in defense of the states. In light of later developments, the work of two scholars besides Epstein himself deserves particular mention. First, Raoul Berger continued his campaign on behalf of unadulterated originalism with a book on federalism[27] that in many ways anticipates the views later expressed by Justice Thomas on several key points: that the states predated the federal government and retained their separate sovereign existence after ratification,[28] that the Commerce Clause extends only to trade across state lines,[29] and that the Supreme Court's Commerce Clause doctrines are ripe for reevaluation.[30] The second of these efforts to rethink federalism took a markedly less radical tone. In a thoughtful review of Berger's book, Michael McConnell attempted to make the intellectual case for reviving federalism.[31] He stressed the potential practical benefits of federalism, invoking sophisticated economic theory, but he gave even more emphasis to the role of federalism in protecting individual rights and preserving local self-rule.

Federalism has also received new attention from the courts. Until recently, disputes about federalism in the courts related mostly to whether Congress could regulate the activities of state officials, as opposed to its regulation of individuals and businesses. (In chapter 3, we saw that Justice Scalia has been a leader in the area of state immunity from regulation.) But the broader concerns voiced by Epstein and his allies are beginning to find an audience on the Supreme Court.

In *United States v. Lopez,*[32] the Court held for the first time since the depression that Congress had exceeded its power to regulate private activity under the Commerce Clause, striking down a federal ban on the possession of guns in the vicinity of schools. With *Lopez,* the new judicial federalism broke out of the limited area of state government immunity and began to realize some of its broader potential.[33] Although most of the judges in the majority were cautious, Epstein seems to have found a disciple in Justice Thomas. Like Epstein, Thomas argues that modern Commerce Clause jurisprudence is almost wholly illegitimate. His analysis in *Lopez* rests on two premises. First, commerce consists only of sales transactions and transportation in connection with those transactions.[34] Second, most areas of life should be subject only to state regulation:

> The exchanges during the ratification campaign reveal the relatively limited reach of the Commerce Clause and of federal power generally. The Founding Fathers confirmed that most areas of life (even many matters that would have substantial effects on commerce) would remain outside the reach of the Federal Government. Such affairs would continue to be under the exclusive control of the States. . . . [D]espite being well aware that agriculture, manufacturing, and other matters substantially affected commerce, the founding generation did not cede authority over all these activities to Congress. Hamilton, for instance, acknowledged that the Federal Government could not regulate agriculture and like concerns.[35]

Justice Thomas's history seems valid, at least up to a point. The framers seemingly did not expect the federal government to legislate about manufacturing and agriculture under the Commerce Clause. Yet it is difficult to assess the import of some of these sources. McConnell points out that this argument may "confuse the founders' expectations about how the nation would be governed under the Constitution with the founders' understanding of the meaning of the Constitution." As McConnell explains:

> For example, did the founders expect agriculture to become an important element in national commercial life? I agree . . . that they did not. Hamilton, no advocate of "states' rights," wrote that "the supervision of agriculture and of other concerns of a similar nature . . . which are proper to be provided for by local legislation, can never be desirable cares of a general jurisdiction." Does it follow that the Congress of 150 years later acted illegitimately when it concluded that regulation of agriculture was a "necessary and proper" means for curing national economic depression? . . . [T]he founders' expectations about agriculture are interesting and important, but cannot take precedence over the constitutional standard.[36]

If we look to the text of the Constitution, rather than to the framers' possible expectations, the answer is less clear than Thomas and Epstein seem to assume. First, the word "commerce" was sometimes used broadly during this period to encompass all commercial matters, not just trade or transportation. Second, the Commerce Clause speaks of commerce "among" rather than "between" the states. The preposition "among" was often used broadly to refer to activities by members of a group whether or not those activities involved interactions between members of the group.[37] Third, the federal government's other economic powers, such as the bankruptcy and patent clauses, reach situations of national economic significance even if a specific transaction is purely local.

Rather than look for the specific interpretation of the Commerce Clause, we might consider instead more general conceptions of federalism, but here again the evidence is unclear. The framers' general intentions regarding federalism are much disputed. Those taking a more favorable view of federal power have also identified support in the historical record for their position. One recent historian refers to the Convention as a "rally of nationalists."[38] Another eminent historian observes that the Anti-Federalists "had no doubt that it was precisely an absorption of all the states under one unified government that the Constitution intended, and they therefore offered this

prospect of an inevitable consolidation as the strongest and most scientifi-
cally based objection to the new system."[39]

The difficulty of ascertaining the original understanding here is heightened by the enormous changes that have taken place in the economy. It is
hard to know what the framers would have thought about the local character of agriculture if they had known that farmers would sell most of their
products on the interstate or foreign market, that farming would involve the
purchase of seeds, fertilizer, and expensive machinery produced nationally,
and that much farming would be conducted by national or even multinational corporations. Faced with the practical problems of their time, the
framers had no reason to speculate about the application of constitutional
provisions under hypothetical future conditions.[40]

Apart from a halfhearted attempt to deny that the American economy
has changed in any relevant respect since 1787, Epstein's contribution to
the historical debate is rather thin, consisting primarily of the same cursory
look at the constitutional text and contemporary usage offered by Raoul
Berger and later by Justice Thomas. What makes his work most interesting,
however, is his effort to define more precisely the extent of federal jurisdiction. As we will see, if indeed he is right about the original understanding of
the Commerce Clause, his analysis makes it entirely understandable why
the Court has chosen a different path. By his account the true meaning of the
Commerce Clause seems utterly unworkable in the modern world.[41]

REDRAWING THE PERIMETER OF FEDERAL POWER

Epstein's disenchantment with federal regulatory power is difficult to over-
state. Indeed, at one point he speculates that it might have been better if we
did not have the commerce power at all. "Perhaps the ideal form of the commerce clause should have been negative," he says, offering as suggested revision a statement that "No state shall have any power to pass legislation
that interferes with the freedom of commerce among the several states."
(Instead of having a federal government, we might have an institution more
like the World Trade Organization.) He admits that "[t]here are of course
certain difficulties to this proposal"—for example, he says, it would cause
some difficulties in railroad regulation—but the "mischief of excessive federal action" is "far greater."[42] The latter risk seems to arise only because of
the Supreme Court's misinterpretation of the Commerce Clause, since if
correctly understood à la Epstein, the clause would have precious little significance anyway.

Like some other conservatives, Epstein believes that the post-1937 understanding of the Commerce Clause is unsupportable, but he goes farther by suggesting that even the pre-1937 understanding was probably too broad. He begins with an obscure 1870 case. The Court's decision in *The Daniel Ball*[43] upheld the federal government's power to inspect any ship in navigable waters, even when the particular ship did not cross state lines (though it was carrying goods that did cross state lines). The Court was impressed by the absurdity of allowing companies to escape federal regulation by transferring goods to a different ship in the middle of a river or lake, so that neither ship actually crossed over a state boundary. But Epstein thinks the Court was too hasty to jump to this conclusion—after all, each of the two states could have conducted its own inspection.[44] (One shudders to imagine the corresponding inspection and safety regulations for the airline industry, in which safety requirements would depend on whether a plane was being flown across state lines on a particular day.)

Epstein stops short of explicitly rejecting the result in *The Daniel Ball,* although it is not clear that he regards the case as correctly decided. What is clear is that he regards the case as the beginning of a long and unfortunate slide down a slippery slope.

The next step in this decline was to hold that the government could regulate charges for local trips on interstate railroads, forbidding the railroad from charging more for short hauls than for longer interstate hauls. Here, "as a matter of first principle, one could forcefully insist that the proper answer should have been no." Then things went from bad to worse: the Court went on to uphold a federal law that prevented state commissions from pushing local rates below interstate rates (which would have left the interstate shippers subsidizing local traffic). Still, despite these seemingly overexpansive interpretations of the Commerce Clause, a "stable stopping point" was available: federal jurisdiction over transportation facilities that handle interstate commerce, even as to their intrastate shipments.[45]

Thus, by 1937, federal power over interstate transportation facilities had already reached a point giving Epstein grounds for unease. The same is true of federal power to control what items are shipped over state lines. He applauds the Court's rejection of a federal law against interstate shipment of goods made with child labor, but worries that the Court too easily accepted a federal law banning interstate sale of lottery tickets.[46] Combined, these lines of cases went to the very limits of congressional power, if indeed they did not go too far: "[t]he line between state police power and the commerce clause had shifted, and there is reason to think that some of the shifts had already placed too many matters on the federal side of the line." Indeed, Ep-

stein is not the only observer to question the pre–New Deal Court's effectiveness in restraining federal power, though he seems alone in worrying
that the pre–New Deal government of Coolidge and Hoover had already become a dangerous leviathan.[47]

At least one bastion remained: the line between manufacture and pro-
duction on the one hand and commerce on the other. Because Epstein
places such great importance on this line, he regards *United States v. E.C.
Knight*[48] as a hard case. In that case, the defendant acquired several other
sugar companies in order to obtain a nationwide monopoly over the manufacture and sale of sugar. The Court held that since the merger only involved
manufacturing facilities, it was outside of Congress's power under the Commerce Clause, even though the purpose and effect was also to gain a monopoly over sales in interstate commerce. Again, Epstein withholds a final
verdict, but his four pages of discussion suggest that he finds this a difficult
case, although he would readily accept a ban on cartels that directly allocate
interstate sales.[49]

Alas, during the New Deal, these distinctions were swept away, leaving
no significant barrier to federal regulatory power. The fatal blow came with
NLRB v. Jones & Laughlin Steel Corp.,[50] which upheld Congress's power to regulate labor conditions in the steel industry. For Epstein, this was virtually
the death knell for the Constitution.

THE MAGINOT LINE OF FEDERALISM

One of the most striking things about Epstein's discussion is the odd boundaries that mark the differences between easy cases and hard ones. A single
ship traveling from New York to New Jersey is an easy case, but if two ships
meet by agreement at the "state line" in order to exchange goods, that's a
hard case. Banning goods produced by child labor is an easy case, but banning lottery tickets is a hard case. A ban on the use of cartels to destroy interstate competition is an easy case, but banning the use of mergers for the
same purpose is hard. Indeed, Epstein himself seems to find understandable
the Court's repeated unwillingness to abide by artificial boundaries to the
commerce power. His argument is less that these boundaries made any
sense than that they were necessary, lest "the basic structure . . . be lost in a
series of small accretions, each one palatable on its own."[51]

As an aside, Epstein's recognition that some cases remain "hard" even
under his theory[52] is probably typical of most of the scholars who are our focus in this book, certainly of those who are most reflective about their theories. When we say they are engaged in a search for certainty, this does not

mean they expect certainty about the results in every individual case. What they do seek, however, is certainty in the form of a single foundational constitutional value and a predefined formula for analyzing every issue. In short, their quest for certainty is a search for a constitutional litmus test; this is no less a quest for certainty because even litmus paper is sometimes hard to read.

The cases these theorists find hard are usually quite simple under existing doctrine; their "difficulty" often reflects flaws in the theoretical framework. Thus the merger case is particularly telling because it reveals much of what is wrong with Epstein's analysis. A multistate or multinational corporation is in some sense nothing but a forum for agreements about how to conduct economic transactions across and within states. A major car company is nothing but a means of moving raw materials and partially finished goods around to various locations nationally and internationally and to coordinate their assembly and sale across and outside the United States. Trying to separate its local from its interstate activities would be as pointless as trying to separate the two sets of activities for a major air carrier.

Some of Epstein's easy cases seem equally puzzling. If a steel strike in Ohio prevents steel from being produced for shipment to Michigan, resulting in a shutdown of the national car industry, why is it so obvious (as Epstein believes it is) that this is a matter of concern only to the Ohio legislature? If the steel company cannot ship its steel because the truck drivers go on strike, Epstein would find federal jurisdiction, but not if the factory workers who load the trucks go on strike. It seems little wonder that the Court was unable to maintain boundaries that seem to have so little connection with common sense.

Perhaps Epstein is willing to maintain these lines because he sees little harm in striking down federal laws anyway. For instance, he says, because many people assume that laws against child labor are good, they are reluctant to find constitutional barriers to such laws. In contrast, because he is skeptical of child labor laws, he is happy to allow them to be tested at the state level rather than give them carte blanche at the federal level.

Although Epstein approves of the use of the Commerce Clause when it "facilitates national markets by preventing state balkanization," he opposes it when it goes too far "to impose national uniformity which frustrates, rather than facilitates markets." Thus he views the major New Deal legislation as "long-standing social disasters that could not long have survived with their present vigor solely at the state level."[53] Not surprisingly, he feels little discomfort about invalidating laws even on the basis of narrow or illogical distinctions.

Ideally, Epstein thinks, "[t]he affirmative scope of the commerce power should be limited to . . . interstate transportation, navigation and sales, and the activities closely incident to them." But he is "hesitant to require dismantling of large portions of the modern federal government, given the enormous reliance interests that have been created." "We had our chance with the commerce clause," he laments, "and we have lost it." Still, at the very least, he hopes to foster uneasiness about the modern state of affairs, so as to prevent further expansion. In conclusion, he says, "[t]here is a powerful tension between the legacy of the past fifty years and the original constitutional understanding. It is a tension that we must face, even if we cannot resolve it."[54]

Like the other conservative thinkers we have examined, Epstein seems to face something of a dilemma. The original understanding of the Constitution beckons us, but is beyond our reach. We have created institutions that we cannot feasibly undo. Even worse, the public shows no apparent interest in undoing most of them. As Epstein remarks, for example, "[a]t present there is no political sentiment anywhere for a revival of the constitutional doctrine, as it relates to either race or sex, for striking down the Civil Rights Act." Epstein also recognizes that people have relied in important ways on current law. But this creates a conundrum.[55] True, we might try to draw a line, preserving the status quo but allowing little new federal legislation. But once what Epstein calls the basic structure has been irrevocably lost, there may be little to be gained by insisting on preserving isolated remnants. And we do so at the sacrifice of consistency, leaving in place federal legislation that is indistinguishable in principle from new legislation we would strike down.

Even if lawyers can be brought to understand the need for such a patchwork, can the public be expected to understand that the Social Security system, federal labor and antidiscrimination laws, and so forth are only anomalies? When 99 percent of the legal regime consists of anomalies, how long can they be expected to remain "exceptions"?[56]

In short, even assuming that Scalia, Bork, and Epstein are right about the content and authority of the original understanding, there is a sense in which for all practical purposes the constitutional order simply changed in the course of the twentieth century, as much so as if there had been a formal amendment. This conundrum will occupy us in a later chapter, but note that it arises only if we assume that originalism defines the "normal" interpretation of the Constitution—only then do we need some way to validate the "abnormal" events of the past sixty years. As we will see in chapter 6, Bruce Ackerman has made an ingenious effort to do so. Despite their varying views of the New Deal, Epstein and Ackerman actually have a good deal in common. They both view the New Deal as a decisive break from the original constitutional understanding. And they are both skeptical of the everyday workings of government, viewing ordinary politics as more a playground for special interests than a forum for public deliberation.

Before turning to Ackerman, however, we first consider a more optimistic vision of politics. Akhil Amar, the subject of our next chapter, is a striking contrast to Epstein. Even more than Bork, he stresses the primacy of majority rule over individual rights. Indeed, his faith in ordinary politics is so great that he would be willing to allow constitutional amendments by referendum. In his unbridled populism, he is the polar opposite of Epstein, whose great contribution is to remind us of the frequent imperfections of government and its ability to threaten liberty.

CHAPTER 5

AKHIL AMAR AND THE
PEOPLE'S COURT

If the last three chapters give the impression that the dangers of foundationalism are a particular hazard for conservative thinkers, the next three will dispel that illusion. Some prominent liberal scholars engage in a similar search for a grand theory to constrain judges, often motivated by similar worries about the legitimacy of judicial review.

Akhil Amar of the Yale Law School is the first of our liberal foundationalists. Like the other scholars we examine, he has both an interpretive strategy and a substantive agenda. Most of the positions he takes are commonplace articles of faith among liberal academics: he supports affirmative action and thinks the government should be allowed to restrict hate speech, for example.[1] Occasionally he sides with conservatives, as when he would abandon the exclusionary rule—which keeps reliable but illegally seized evidence out of court—as a remedy for Fourth Amendment violations.[2] None of these positions are particularly extraordinary, although his reasoning is often dazzlingly innovative. (For example, he argues that the government can regulate hate speech because the speech violates the *Thirteenth* Amendment—which bans slavery.)

It is his reasoning—his constitutional theory—that ultimately gets him into trouble. He interprets the Constitution to allow freewheeling majority rule, including a right to amend the Constitution without following the rules laid down in Article V.[3] He finds in the Thirteenth Amendment's abolition of slavery not only a right to be free from hate speech—which is surprising enough—but also protection against child abuse.[4] Colorado's antigay referendum violates the clause prohibiting bills of attainder (a bill of attainder is essentially a legislative verdict of criminal guilt).[5] The Fifteenth

Amendment, which prohibits racial restrictions on the "right to vote," includes the right to "vote" on juries.[6]

Amar, who is one of the leading constitutional scholars of his generation, calls the interpretive approach that leads to these striking results "intratextualism" or "documentarianism."[7] This turns out to be a cross of sorts between textualism and originalism. But he almost always qualifies his commitment to any single interpretive methodology. The result is to complicate considerably any criticism of his arguments.

Amar says, for example, that he is "a constitutionalist, a textualist, and a populist."[8] Text is not "all that constitutionalism is, but . . . one important part of constitutionalism is [the] text, both in ordinary language and in legal language."[9] And, he says, he shares Justice Scalia's "commitment to constitutional text, history, and structure, and his suspicion of 'free-form' constitutionalism."[10] Elsewhere, he notes that he "place[s] heavy, if not exclusive, reliance on constitutional text, history, and structure."[11] He urges us to be "willing to measure [our] accounts [of the meaning of the Bill of Rights] against the text itself in order to see which ones best fit the precise words that eventually became the Supreme Law of the Land."[12] Nevertheless, he says that "[s]ometimes plain-meaning textual arguments in the end must yield to the weight of other proper constitutional arguments—from history, structure, precedent, practicality, and so on."[13] And he admits that when a documentarian interpretation conflicts with "deeply entrenched and widely accepted practices," sometimes "a documentarian must acknowledge that it is too late to go back."[14] (Like Bork, Amar does not tell us how to identify those times when it is appropriate to stray from the path of pure documentarianism.)

As two of his critics have noted, all this gives his work "more hedges than an English garden."[15] Moreover, as we will see, a substantive commitment to popular sovereignty underlies and shapes his use of the various interpretive tools. Despite Amar's complex stance regarding his preferred methodology, however, it remains basic to understanding his often startling constitutional views.

INTRATEXTUALISM

Amar has described himself as an "intratextualist." An intratextualist, he writes, "tries to read a word or phrase that appears in the Constitution in light of another passage in the Constitution featuring the same (or a very similar) word or phrase."[16] Thus, for example, Chief Justice John Marshall used intratextualism in his exegesis of the Necessary and Proper Clause in

McCulloch v. Maryland.[17] The case upheld the establishment of a national bank, concluding that it fell within the clause giving Congress authority to "make all laws which shall be necessary and proper for carrying into execution" Congress's enumerated powers. Marshall compared the word "necessary," standing alone in that clause, with the nearby clause prohibiting states from taxing imports except where "absolutely necessary" for executing inspection laws.[18] Marshall also compared "necessary" to the use of "needful" in Article IV, § 3, which gives Congress the power to "make all needful rules and regulations respecting" United States territories and other property.

Marshall made these intratextual moves in the context of an opinion that is famous for its eclectic approach to constitutional interpretation. We have even considered teaching an entire course on constitutional interpretation out of *McCulloch* alone, since Marshall resorted to textual, intratextual, historical, structural, and pragmatic arguments to buttress his conclusion that Congress had power to establish a national bank. It is hard to quarrel with including intratextualism in the arsenal of interpretive tools—but as Amar himself notes, intratextualism used in this way is neither controversial nor innovative.[19]

What Amar adds is what critics have labeled "strong intratextualism" (to distinguish it from Marshall's "weak intratextualism"). They describe Amar's strong intratextualism as "an approach using inferences drawn from parallel provisions to trump localized arguments based on text, history, and precedent."[20] And given that most existing constitutional doctrine is in fact based on text, history, and precedent, strong intratextualism will be of value primarily when it provides a radically new interpretation. Amar explicitly prefers textual analysis to precedent, noting that "the document has tended to outshine the doctrine."[21] Thus it should not be surprising that Amar has sometimes been described as a "radical destabilizer"[22] whose approach "stands at odds . . . with the settled practice of constitutional interpreters" and would "destabilize interpretive practice."[23]

So, for example, Amar suggests that the word "speech" in the First Amendment should be read in tandem with the Speech and Debate Clause in Article I, § 6. The latter clause protects federal legislators by providing that "for any speech or debate in either House, they shall not be questioned in any other place." Amar draws dramatic conclusions from this juxtaposition, arguing for a rethinking of modern First Amendment doctrine—including stripping some speech of any constitutional protection at all, and abandoning the long-standing presumption that restrictions based on the content of speech are invalid. Noticing that the word "speech" appears in both clauses is clever, but it cannot bear the weight Amar puts on it.

To begin, observe that Amar has already taken us a step further than Marshall's weak intratextualism, since the two occurrences of the word "speech" appear in passages that were enacted by different groups of people several years apart. Moreover, it seems at least questionable to equate the protections given legislators with the protections given the general citizenry, since they serve different roles in the constitutional scheme. Nevertheless, Amar's strong intratextualism—combined with his focus on populism, to which we turn in the next section—allows him to use the Speech and Debate Clause to interpret the First Amendment.

Since the Speech and Debate Clause is solely about political discourse, Amar says, he would focus the First Amendment's protections on speech that is "at its core, about democracy," stripping both commercial speech and campaign expenditures of their current status as protected speech.[24] The current protections afforded both commercial speech and campaign expenditures, as well as the absence of any government obligation to subsidize poor people's speech, means, according to Amar, that existing First Amendment doctrine turns on the ability to pay. And ability to pay for one's opportunities to speak should be irrelevant, he contends, because on the floor of the Senate wealth does not matter: "even if some Senators are rich and others poor, every Senator is entitled to be part of the great debate." He thus criticizes as constitutionally wrong the current regime, in which "Ross Perot, Steve Forbes, and Bill Gates get to talk more than the rest of us put together if they own more than the rest of us put together."[25]

One problem with Amar's reasoning is his insufficiently supported assumptions: his assumption that campaign expenditures have nothing to do with democracy is controversial, to put it mildly. And whatever the antipopulist impact of campaign expenditures, protecting commercial speech, at least, seems quite populist insofar as it allows consumers to receive comparative information: the case that established modern commercial speech jurisprudence struck down a state law prohibiting pharmacies from price advertising. The most substantial problems with Amar's theory, however, go deeper than weak premises and lie instead in the core principles of his intratextualism.

Other scholars have reached the same conclusions as Amar about commercial speech and campaign finance legislation. Indeed, the Court's decision in *Buckley v. Valeo*[26]—which equated campaign expenditures with speech—is one of the most frequently criticized First Amendment cases.[27] Other scholars have also argued that the government should be required to subsidize the exercise of constitutional rights.[28] But all of these scholars have felt forced to defend their conclusions on multifaceted grounds, often stressing the dangerous or antidemocratic consequences of current doctrine. Amar's intratextualism makes an attack on the Court's First Amendment jurisprudence seem more like a simple syllogism: since we would not allow a certain situation on the floor of either house of Congress, we cannot allow it in our public discourse either. And yet the syllogism stems from the initially undefended move of equating the two clauses. Dazzling us with the novel results of his intratextualism, Amar has directed our eyes away from its weak beginnings.

Continuing with his Speech and Debate Clause analogy, Amar further argues that Congress can surely regulate the content—although not the viewpoint—of speeches on the floor, "reserving Tuesday for a campaign-finance debate and Wednesday for a discussion of nuclear proliferation."[29] Since the scope of the First Amendment is to be interpreted in light of the protections afforded congressional speeches, this means that "content-based discriminations are not themselves (even presumptive) violations of the freedom of speech."[30] But careful scrutiny of content-based restrictions on speech is a core aspect of modern First Amendment jurisprudence; indeed, the content distinction has been described as "the modern Supreme Court's closest approach to articulating a unified First Amendment doctrine."[31] Thus Amar's approach would jettison a central tenet of First Amendment doctrine. Significantly, abandoning the content distinction would likely allow the regulation of hate speech—a result that is contrary to current doctrine but that conveniently corresponds to Amar's own views.[32] He seems not to notice, however, that his theory might lead to results even he would disapprove: for example, because the Senate can discipline one of its members for using impolite language toward another member, would the government be permitted to regulate the media's use of harsh language in criticizing senators?

If Amar's analysis of the First Amendment rests on treating two uses of the same word similarly, another example of his intratextualism shows that even *different* phrases can be treated similarly. One of the conundrums of constitutional law is how to analyze race discrimination by the federal government. In *Bolling v. Sharpe*,[33] a companion case to *Brown v. Board of Education*,[34] the Supreme Court invalidated segregated schools in the District of

Columbia. Although the result must surely be correct, the Court's reasoning has not generally been considered satisfactory.

The problem is this: the Equal Protection Clause of the Fourteenth Amendment limits only the states, not the federal government, and the Fifth Amendment (which restricts the federal government) contains a Due Process Clause but not an Equal Protection Clause. Thus there is no language in the Constitution that seems to prohibit the federal government from discriminating on the basis of race. This should not be so surprising. The generation that embedded protections for slavery and the slave trade into the Constitution was unlikely to be concerned about race discrimination, while the later generation that added the Fourteenth Amendment after the Civil War was not concerned about limiting the power of the federal government. Nevertheless, after striking down segregated schools in the states, the Court could hardly uphold segregated schools in the nation's capital. The Court reasoned that the Fifth Amendment's Due Process Clause "incorporated" the Fourteenth Amendment's Equal Protection Clause. Never mind that the Fourteenth Amendment was enacted more than eighty years after the Fifth, or that the country had in the intervening time been through a Civil War triggered partly by racial concerns. Again, the result in *Bolling* must be right, but only pragmatic arguments can truly support it: we have seen that because it cannot be supported historically, Bork rejects the result in *Bolling*.

So far as we know, Amar is the only constitutional scholar who has ever tried to defend the Court's reasoning on *textual* grounds. Again, his arguments are clever but implausible. He makes two separate intratextualist arguments. First, he suggests, considering the Constitution as a whole leads us to conclude that in matters of race discrimination the states and the federal government must be treated alike. This is because there are two clauses that do place identical textual limits on both entities: Article I, § 9 prohibits Congress from passing bills of attainder or ex post facto laws or from granting titles of nobility. Article I, § 10 prohibits the states from doing the same three things. And, he concludes, race discrimination is both a bill of attainder and a title of nobility because it elevates some people (light-skinned people) and targets others (dark-skinned people) for disfavored treatment simply because of who they are. So far as the historical record shows, not one framer or ratifier of the original 1787 Constitution, the Bill of Rights, the Reconstruction amendments, or any other part of the Constitution imagined that the Bill of Attainder and Titles of Nobility Clauses have anything to do with race discrimination. One might construct an argument that those clauses *should* be interpreted to bar race discrimination, or that they exemplify some broader principles that might apply as well to race discrimination,[35] but it would not be either a textualist or an originalist argument, and thus would not fit within Amar's general framework for constitutional interpretation.

Amar's second intratextualist defense of *Bolling* is even more creative. Intratextualism, he argues, tells us to read the Fourteenth Amendment, which adds an Equal Protection Clause to its Due Process Clause, as identical to the Fifth Amendment with its lonely Due Process Clause. Recall Amar's praise of John Marshall's contrast between "necessary" standing alone and "absolutely necessary." How do we know that the differences between the Fifth and Fourteenth Amendments shouldn't be treated the same way? Because, Amar says, the Fourteenth Amendment should be "read as declaratory, glossing earlier words [in the Fifth Amendment] and making explicit what these words only implied." Of course, Amar admits—as he has to, given the historical evidence—that "none of the [Fifth] Amendment's drafters or ratifiers in the 1780s and 1790s" thought it "contain[ed] an equality component."[36] He is arguing that the Fourteenth Amendment made explicit what the drafters and ratifiers of the Fifth Amendment *did not* think it implied.

Thus, Amar argues that a purely textual analysis requires us to treat *similarly* two clauses enacted more than eighty years apart and containing different language—although the same textual analysis also, in the case of *McCulloch*, requires us to treat *differently* two clauses enacted at the same time but containing different language.

He is equally inconsistent in his treatment of similar language. We have already seen, in the case of "speech," that Amar believes that similar phrases should be treated alike despite the passage of time between their enactments. But Amar also suggests that sometimes *similar* phrases should be treated *differently*. Article II, § 1 provides that Congress shall choose the day for presidential elections, and that that day must be the same "throughout the United States." Article I, § 8 gives Congress the power to lay duties, imposts, and taxes, which must be uniform "throughout the United States." Should these two identical phrases—enacted at the same time—be interpreted similarly? No, according to Amar. The Article II phrase can only refer to states, not territories, since citizens in the territories are not entitled to vote for any electoral college members. But the Article I phrase should nevertheless be interpreted to include territories as well.[37] (He never tells us how we should define the similar language in the Preamble, which refers to "We the People of the United States.")

This attentiveness to the specific wording of the Constitution is one of Amar's strengths, but he uses it unpredictably. For example, he places great significance on the subtle observation that in the Bill of Rights much of the time the words "the people" appear alone, but in the Fourth Amendment, both "the people" and "persons" are used.[38] But despite his careful distinction between "the people" and "persons," he is willing to treat as synonymous the use of "rights," "freedoms," "privileges," and "immunities," where the first two appear in the Bill of Rights and the latter two in the Fourteenth Amendment.[39] While that might or might not make sense as a historical matter, it is hardly mandated by the text itself, and legal scholars have often been at great pains to distinguish these concepts.

To the extent that intratextualism is designed to mandate some conclusions and preclude others, then, it is too weakly specified and too easily manipulable. Indeed, Amar himself recognizes that "intratextualism may lead to readings that are too clever by half—cabalistic overreadings conjuring up patterns that were not specifically intended and that are upon deep reflection not truly sound but merely cute." Indeed, he admits, "intratextualism can become a mechanical exercise that blunts good judgment and leads to outlandish outcomes."[40] And, of course, intratextualist maneuvers cannot be performed in a vacuum. Although one piece of text might be compared with another, the first still must be interpreted somehow; it would be completely circular to interpret the First Amendment by reference to the Speech and Debate Clause and then turn around and interpret the Speech and Debate Clause by looking to the First Amendment.

Thus Amar needs a context in which to exercise—and to limit—his interpretive strategy. He must be able to distinguish between deep patterns and random fortuities, to determine when linguistic similarities should lead to similar interpretations and when they should not, and to identify which linguistic differences should be relied upon and which ignored. This is where his substantive commitment to popular sovereignty—primarily deployed as a historical argument about the intent of the framers—becomes important.

He situates his textual analysis within a framework of what he believes to be the founding generation's commitment to popular sovereignty. Although it is never completely clear whether the textual (or intratextual) analysis drives the historical conclusions or the historical conclusions inform the textual analysis, Amar clearly relies on a symbiotic relationship

between the two; if he is wrong about popular sovereignty, his entire constitutional structure collapses. In this he is much like the other scholars on
whom we focus in this book, resting his conclusions on a single foundation.
And like the others, the foundation he has chosen is historically shaky.

POPULAR SOVEREIGNTY

According to Amar, the Constitution (including the Bill of Rights) is *about*
popular sovereignty. The "central pillar" of the republican government established by the founders is self-rule by a majority of the people. Every word
in the Constitution and the Bill of Rights should be read with that notion in
the foreground. Thus he can draw a distinction between "persons" and "the
people," because the latter refers to the collective sovereign people rather
than to individuals; this in turn allows him to argue that the use of the
phrase "the people" throughout the Bill of Rights indicates that most of the
rights are collective, majority rights.

This constitutes his most counterintuitve move: to argue that the Bill of
Rights was designed—at least primarily—not to protect individual minority
rights against majority tyranny, but to safeguard the majority's rights against
legislative unfaithfulness and corruption. The Bill of Rights, like the structure of the Constitution itself, is designed to ensure popular sovereignty, not
to limit it. In making this argument, Amar does highlight some neglected
connections between the Bill of Rights and early conceptions of local self-
rule. But, once again, he attempts to build too grand a structure on too small
a foundation.

Of the twin evils that Madison worried about—majority tyranny and
legislative perfidy (or "agency costs" of a representative government)—
Amar argues that the latter alone was truly important to the founding generation. He is careful to note that the language of the Bill of Rights is broad
enough to encompass individual rights, but he argues that such was not its
core purpose. Sometimes he almost seems to suggest that protecting individuals from majority tyranny was not a purpose at all, except in Madison's
own mind. He points to the rejection of Madison's proposed limits on state
governments as evidence that the rest of the founders were mostly worried
about a possibly corruptible federal government, not about majority tyranny.
He suggests that the main reason that the Fifth Amendment Takings Clause—
which, like Epstein, Amar identifies as sounding in individual rights rather
than in majority control over the legislature—did not meet the same fate is
that it was seductively packaged with other more favored populist provisions.

Because of this preference for popular sovereignty over individual rights, his reading of the constitutional text—whether alone or in conjunction with other parts of the text—can lead him to conclusions that are unusual, to say the least. For example, his view of the constitutional provisions governing criminal procedure is that they are largely about promoting "truth and the protection of innocence."[41] This is an easy conclusion for Amar. His emphasis on government excess rather than individual autonomy allows him to argue that while the innocent need protection from overbearing government prosecutors acting against the will of the community, the guilty need not be insulated from prosecutors acting in accordance with community will. And juries, as representatives of the populace, can generally distinguish between the innocent and the guilty.[42] His focus on innocence is in great tension with much current criminal procedure doctrine, which focuses as much on the procedural rights of the guilty as it does on the effectiveness of the sorting process. And even in Amar's populist system, he overlooks several arguments in favor of protecting procedural rights of the guilty as well as the innocent.[43] Enforcing procedural rules also ensures that the system does not deteriorate into a search-and-destroy mission: almost everyone is guilty of *something,* and if Amar has his way, only saints will have rights.

Amar's strained interpretation of the criminal procedure amendments leads him to downplay the individual protections they afford to both the guilty and the innocent. In examining the Fifth Amendment's privilege against self-incrimination, for example, he focuses individually on each of the words or phrases in that clause: no person shall be *compelled* in *any criminal case,* to be a *witness* against himself. He argues for restricted readings of each of the words and phrases and ultimately suggests that the privilege limits only the introduction in court of judicially compelled testimony, not the compulsion itself (so that one may be forced to testify as a witness at another's trial as long as the testimony is not subsequently introduced at one's own criminal trial). Nor does it prohibit being forced to produce papers—except, he says without explanation, "possibly [one's] intimate personal papers."[44]

His focus on populism leads him to a similarly creative interpretation of the Fifteenth Amendment. That Amendment, ratified in 1870, provides that "[t]he right of citizens of the United States to vote shall not be denied or abridged by the United States or by any State on account of race, color, or previous condition of servitude." Amar concludes that this language protects not only the right to vote, but the right to serve on juries ("Jurors *vote*," and "[t]he Amendment is not limited to voting *for* office") and the right to serve in the military ("[i]n Republican theory, those who vote traditionally bear arms, and those who bear arms vote").[45]

In fact, the linkage of voting and jury service may well be historically inaccurate: a recent careful study argues that nineteenth-century Americans viewed jury service and voting as distinct, with different social significance.[46] Amar does not provide the historical evidence he would need to support his thesis, but relies instead on mere assertions.

As for the "Republican theory" that Amar uses to justify bringing military service into the meaning of the Fifteenth Amendment, the problem is that the theory is never fully translated into American practice. Amar relies on the notion that "civic republicanism" animated the eighteenth-century founders, and reads the Fifteenth Amendment together with the Second (which refers to the right to bear arms).[47] Not only have historians suggested that Amar and others have overstated the case for a "civic republican" influence on the founding generation, but it seems that generation was quite willing to limit arms-bearing even by qualified voters.[48] Again, rather than supporting his own historical assertions with evidence, Amar simply bypasses the historical controversy.[49] His argument is audacious and original, but it simply cannot survive careful scrutiny.

Amar's interpretation of the Fifteenth Amendment, then, illustrates the trouble with textualism: language is complex and subtle, and the meaning of words is often opaque or ambiguous. Meanings also change over time. Historical context can provide some illumination, but is not itself free from doubt. Textualism—even when combined with originalism—thus must be tempered by judgment: we must be able to sit back and evaluate the results produced by a textualist analysis and essentially ask if they make sense. (Does it make sense that the right to "vote" includes the right to carry a gun, or that the Thirteenth Amendment outlaws hate speech?) Unfortunately, textualism (whether intra- or other), by purporting to provide clear answers to all constitutional conundrums, tends to downplay the role of judgment and common sense—and thus often leads to tenuous conclusions.

Amar does try to include historical context in his textualism, but that context is colored by his attachment to popular sovereignty. Amar's view of the whole Bill of Rights as protection *of* the majority rather than *against* the majority may be summed up by one of his discussions of the Ninth and Tenth Amendments and the Preamble:

We have been taught to look at the Constitution through the wrong end of the telescope. We have been told that the Bill of Rights was designed to inhibit majority tyranny and limit popular passion; and so we have missed the many ways in which it was also structured to enhance majority rule and promote popular sovereignty. . . . What we miss is how all these references to "the People" are embodiments of the Constitution's unitary structure and overarching spirit of popular sovereignty—of the people's right to "ordain" and "establish," and their "reserved" and "retained" rights to alter or abolish, their Constitution.[50]

In his book on the Bill of Rights, Amar states that the "primary target" of each amendment is "attenuated representation, not overweening majoritarianism."[51] "In the end," he writes, "individual rights in our system are, and should be, the products of ultimately majoritarian processes."[52] This is an interesting and often illuminating perspective. Where Amar goes wrong is in taking it as gospel. For example, his embrace of populism leads him to interpret the Constitution to allow amendment by referendum.

And in the end, Amar's historical understanding, while impressively broad, lacks depth. Populism was probably not the dominant theme of the founding generation. From a historical standpoint, it is questionable to suggest that the founding generation—especially the Federalist members of it, who prevailed—sought to place their entire trust in the citizenry. In fact, the most plausible interpretation of the historical evidence is that many (if not most) of the drafters and ratifiers of the Constitution profoundly mistrusted the people, and structured the Constitution to put as little power as possible in the hands of the masses.[53] The election of senators by state legislatures and the election of the president by the electoral college are two of the more obvious devices they used to create a filtered or mediated democracy, which prevented the voting public from having a direct effect on the government. Of course, we have a much more direct form of democracy now: the Seventeenth Amendment put the election of senators in the hands of the voters, and members of the electoral college now simply vote the will of the electorate rather than exercising their own judgment—but Amar is talking about the eighteenth century, not the twenty-first.

Indeed, many of the founders believed, as Connecticut convention delegate Roger Sherman put it, that "the people . . . should have as little to do as may be about the Government."[54] Massachusetts delegate Elbridge Gerry noted: "The evils we experience flow from the excess of democracy . . . . He had . . . been too republican heretofore: he was still however republican, but had been taught by experience the danger of the levelling spirit."[55] Virginian Edmund Randolph defended his original draft proposal—the very first draft of what became the Constitution—by cataloging the problems with the state constitutions and the Articles of Confederation. He complained that they created too much democracy: "Our chief danger arises from the democratic parts of our constitutions. It is a maxim which I hold incontrovertible, that the powers of government exercised by the people swallow up the other branches. None of the constitutions have provided sufficient checks against democracy."[56] And James Madison himself advocated an aristocratic Senate in order to "protect the people [against] the transient impressions into which they themselves might be led."[57] Madison also complained to Jefferson about the products of the populist state legislatures:

> The mutability of the laws of the States is found to be a serious evil. The injustice of them has been so frequent and so flagrant as to alarm the most stedfast friends of Republicanism. I am persuaded I do not err in saying that the evils issuing from these sources contributed more to that uneasiness which produced the Convention, and prepared the public mind for a general reform, than those which accrued to our national character and interest from the inadequacy of the Confederation to its immediate objects.[58]

These similar statements came from men with varying views on the Constitution: Madison and Sherman were staunch supporters, Randolph refused to sign it but later changed his mind and urged Virginia to ratify it, and Gerry not only refused to sign it but publicly opposed it.

The ratification debates show both that Americans were aware of the antidemocratic aspects of the Constitution—but ratified it anyway—and that even some Anti-Federalists shared the Federalist fear of the masses. An essay by "Montezuma" in the *Philadelphia Independent Gazetteer* attacked the proposed constitution by purporting to offer an aristocratic defense of it:

> We the Aristocratic party of the United States, lamenting the many inconveniencies to which the late confederation subjected the *well-born*, the *better kind* of people bringing them down to the level of *rabble*, and holding in utter detestation, that frontispiece to every bill of rights— "that all men are born equal," beg leave (for the purpose of drawing a line between such as we think were *ordained* to govern, and such as were *made* to bear the weight of government without having any share in its administration) to submit to *our friends* in the first class for this in-

spection, the following defence of our *monarchical, aristocratical democracy.*[59]

Although this attack on the Constitution as aristocratic was a common theme among some Anti-Federalists, others were more wary of popular sovereignty. "Agrippa" wrote that it was "as necessary to defend an individual against the majority in a republick as against the king in a monarchy,"[60] and a Maryland "Farmer" suggested that in democratic governments, "the tyranny of the legislative is most to be dreaded."[61] The letters of "The Federal Farmer," widely distributed in pamphlet form, expressed concern about taking power from "the solid interest of the community" and placing it "in the hands of men destitute of property, of principle, or of attachment to the society and government."[62]

Amar has thus mistaken the eighteenth-century founders for modern democrats, misunderstanding their notion of popular sovereignty in the process. As G. Edward White has pointed out, the eighteenth-century American innovation of placing sovereignty *in* the people is not the same as Amar's popular sovereignty, much less majority rule. Amar claims to be trying to "realign the dominant legal narrative about Creation . . . with the dominant historical narrative (as evidenced in history books written about history by history professors)."[63] He cites Gordon Wood in passing—correctly calling his work "pathbreaking"—but White points out that Amar has really misunderstood the teachings of Wood and other modern historians:

> Wood has shown that alongside the evils of monarchic tyranny and corruption that American republicans identified were another set of evils, and that the form of government created by the Constitution was designed to respond to those as well as to the former set. The other evils were *democratic* tyranny and corruption, the expected results of interactions between demagogues and the untutored masses. Wood has argued that the proponents of the Constitution, while understanding the importance of a theoretical relocation of sovereignty in "the people," held, in the main, a skeptical view of the capacity of the people as a whole to govern themselves, and believed that the best hope for tempering the excesses of unbridled democracy was the principle of representation, as embodied in the structure of federated constitutional republicanism.[64]

Amar, on the other hand, seems to disagree with this consensus of historians, concluding that the founding generation was intent upon giving more rather than less power to the people. While this would be intriguing if supported by any evidence, his argument suffers from circularity: his primary evidence for this controversial conclusion is the constitutional text itself, which he is supposedly using the historical conclusions to illuminate and interpret. (He also sometimes uses individual historical incidents—a sort of history by anecdote.) Unfortunately, people who think texts speak for themselves often turn out to have strong presuppositions about what those texts will say, and Amar is no exception.

Amar's account, which places majoritarianism at the center and rights at the periphery, also leaves little room for an equally influential strand of eighteenth-century thought, that of natural rights.[65] Many Americans of that era passionately believed that their most important liberties were natural and inalienable. For these Americans, written bills of rights were merely declaratory, reaffirming the existence of rights but not creating them. Documents ranging from the Declaration of Independence and the Virginia Declaration of Rights to the state constitutions of the 1770s and 1780s bear traces of this commitment to unwritten, natural, *individual* rights. Further historical evidence of the American attachment to natural rights can be found in judicial opinions, both state and federal, from the 1780s through the middle of the nineteenth century. In case after case, judges enforced unwritten natural rights, striking down legislation despite the absence of relevant provisions in the written constitutions.[66] Like Bork, who cannot fathom the Ninth Amendment because he does not understand the eighteenth-century faith in natural rights, Amar neglects this strand of the founders' views because it does not fit his vision of popular sovereignty.

In short, Amar's history is too often lawyers' history: it ignores what one scholar has called "the existence of competing historical strands, of uncertainty, of vagueness—in other words, the often disorderly and unruly nature of constitution-making and of the Founders' own understandings."[67] Amar's history is too simplistic, too neat, and for that reason alone it is unlikely to be fully accurate. Even if popular sovereignty as Amar defines it was one strand of the founders' vision—and most historians doubt that—it was not the only one or even the primary one. Amar succumbs to the temptation to think that, in contrast to the pervasive confusion and conflicts among modern thinkers, the past was a golden age of coherence and clarity.

If Amar is mistaken about the centrality of popular sovereignty, his intratextualism also fails. He can no longer use the historical context as a background against which to sort out textual ambiguities or distinguish among permissible readings of the language. Without such a device, intratextualism itself as an interpretive strategy has no anchor. Moreover, the many interpretations that rely on the centrality of popular sovereignty—such as almost his entire view of criminal procedure—become suspect.

ENTER JOHN BINGHAM ON A WHITE HORSE

After spending half a book concluding that the Bill of Rights was not meant to protect individual rights, Amar springs a final surprise: he argues that the Fourteenth Amendment literally changed everything. The "overall theme" of his book on the Bill of Rights is that "[o]nly after the Fourteenth Amendment did Madison's vision of strong national protection of minorities against majoritarian oppression become the dominant strand of American constitutionalism."[68] While popular sovereignty animates the Bill of Rights, individual rights animate the Reconstruction Amendments. Thus according to Amar our modern vision of individual rights comes not from the eighteenth-century founders—who were thoroughgoing republicans with little or no use for individual safeguards against majority tyranny—but from the nineteenth-century founders:

> [T]he 1789 Bill [of Rights] tightly knit together citizens' rights and states' rights; but the 1866 amendment unraveled this fabric, vesting citizens with rights *against* states. The original Bill also focused centrally on empowering the people collectively against government agents following their own agenda. The Fourteenth Amendment, by contrast, focused on protecting minorities against even responsive, representative, majoritarian government.[69]

The conclusions he draws from his view of nineteenth-century constitutional history are as idiosyncratic as those he draws from his view of the eighteenth-century events. As in his discussion of the first era, Amar overlooks contrary evidence: citing Madison or Hamilton or Wilson indiscriminately for the intent of the eighteenth-century framers and Bingham, Howard, Stevens, and others for the intent of the nineteenth-century framers, without explaining that they sometimes differed in their views.   ·

Amar's version of Reconstruction history seems to miss the forest for the trees. One example is his treatment of the Thirteenth Amendment's ban on slavery. He concludes, by careful analysis of text and history, that the Thirteenth Amendment extends its protections to all "slaves," including children, even if they are offspring of their master, even if they do not have African roots (this is the most doubtful conclusion but he supports it well), even if they are not used for financial profit, and even if they are enslaved de facto rather than de jure. From this series of cautious steps beyond the Amendment's core condemnation of chattel slavery, Amar takes a huge leap: a father who beats his son violates the Thirteenth Amendment.[70] We doubt any nineteenth-century abolitionist could even have begun to understand this reasoning; certainly, Amar provides no evidence that anyone thought the Thirteenth Amendment of its own force outlawed domestic abuse.

He also interprets the Thirteenth Amendment as guaranteeing a right to welfare. It is worth quoting the Amendment itself here: "Neither slavery nor involuntary servitude, except as a punishment for crime whereof the party shall have been duly convicted, shall exist within the United States, or any place subject to their jurisdiction." Amar looks at the text of the Amendment and reasons that we have not really abolished slavery unless we "guarantee each American a certain stake in society."[71] Thus, he reads the Thirteenth Amendment with the same sweep with which Epstein reads the Takings Clause, though to opposite political ends. Unlike Epstein, however, he does not provide an elaborate analytic superstructure to support his policy views.

Amar's view of the historical and textual relationship between the eighteenth-century Constitution and the Reconstruction amendments, besides producing results such as his freestyle interpretation of the Thirteenth Amendment, leads him to two conclusions. The first is that perhaps we give "too much credit to James Madison and not enough to John Bingham" and that we "celebrat[e] Thomas Jefferson and Patrick Henry but sligh[t] Harriet Beecher Stowe and Frederick Douglass."[72] Proposing greater relative credit for the nineteenth-century Reconstruction authors is not a novel suggestion, but once again Amar seems to overdo it.[73] His claim rests largely on the conclusion that the original Bill of Rights was mostly about majority will, not minority rights—a conclusion that, as we have seen, is historically doubtful.

His second insight, relating to the doctrinal implications of his revisionist Reconstruction history, is equally vulnerable to historical critique and suffers from additional problems as well. As we saw in chapter 2, one of the most controversial constitutional disputes, now definitively settled by the Supreme Court, was about the extent to which the Fourteenth Amendment Due Process Clause "incorporated" the provisions of the Bill of Rights and thus made them applicable to states as well as to the federal government. After several decades of debate, the Court finally settled on a doctrine of "selective incorporation, " under which the Due Process Clause is held to incorporate all the "fundamental" provisions of the Bill of Rights. (It turns out that almost all of them are indeed fundamental. One of the few that is not is the requirement that criminal juries consist of twelve persons.)[74]

Amar suggests that his portrayal of the interrelationship between the Bill of Rights and the Reconstruction Amendments requires a change in this settled doctrine. In this he is even more radical than Justice Scalia, who says that even if the incorporation doctrine is wrong, it is now too late to change it. But Amar plunges ahead: instead of selective incorporation, he believes that the Due Process Clause should be interpreted to require a doctrine he calls "refined incorporation," under which only personal rights, not collective rights, are incorporated against the states by the Fourteenth Amendment. "Instead of asking whether a given provision is fundamental [or not], as [Justice] Brennan suggests, we must ask whether it is a personal privilege—that is, a private right—of individual citizens, rather than a right of states or the public at large."[75] The "refinement" process also means that some rights change their character as they pass through the Reconstruction amendments.

Of course, Amar's theory that the Fourteenth Amendment "refines" the Bill of Rights necessarily depends on his earlier interpretation of the Bill of Rights as primarily majoritarian. If the original Bill of Rights was *not* primarily about community or majority rights but was also about individual protection from majority tyranny—in other words, if Amar is wrong about popular sovereignty and its relationship to the Bill of Rights—then his argument for refined incorporation also collapses. If Amar is wrong, individual rights existed prior to the enactment of the Fourteenth Amendment, and the Fourteenth Amendment could not have "individualized" them further. Thus, like the rest of his conclusions, his doctrine of refined incorporation rests on his interpretation of popular sovereignty. In addition, "refined incorporation" leaves unclear which rights to incorporate. Since he often refuses to commit himself as to which rights are in fact incorporated, we must illustrate the malleability of refined incorporation by suggesting arguments that *could* be made using the theory of refined incorporation.

Criminal procedure provides an example. When it comes to the criminal procedure amendments, Amar has so far not considered the question of whether they have been "refined" by the Fourteenth Amendment into individual protections. That is, he assumes without argument that those amendments protect the community rather than the individual criminal defendants—although he applies them to the states anyway—and then simply interprets them narrowly.[76] But one might easily argue that because the criminal procedure amendments were originally designed to protect the public at large rather than individual citizens, they were not incorporated against the states (or at least not in the form that applies to the federal government). The seeds of this argument are already present in Amar's description of the repeated occurrence of "the people" in much of the Bill of Rights.

Amar's rare uses of refined incorporation also show just how malleable a doctrine it is. Recall that the first half of his theory requires him to prove that virtually all of the Bill of Rights refers to collective rights of "the public at large" rather than to individual rights. He nevertheless concludes that ordinary free speech rights are indeed individual:

> Of course, federalism played an important role in the unreconstructed First Amendment, but not in a way that impedes incorporation of its explicit rights and freedoms. Even if we assume that freedom of speech in state legislatures enjoyed special First Amendment status above and beyond the freedom extended to ordinary citizens, nothing about incorporation takes away state legislatures' freedom of speech; incorporation simply limits their freedom to use state law to silence ordinary citizens, and *that* freedom is not in any way protected by the First Amendment.[77]

We may well agree with Amar that the First Amendment was not primarily designed to protect the speech of state legislators. (Who ever thought this was the primary purpose?) But none of the first eight amendments refers directly to the rights of state officials. As the reader may notice, while Amar's observation may explain how even his First Amendment is not a "right of states," it does not explain how it is not a right of "the public at large." It is simply unclear how any provision of the Bill of Rights can begin life as a collective right but be transformed into an individual right—and whatever alchemy is at work should work equally well on all the rights.

Amar's combination of intratextualism and popular sovereignty, then, is no more successful at restraining judicial discretion than the other theories we have examined. If willful judges are intent on reading their own values into the Constitution, adopting Amar's theories will not prevent them from doing so—any more than it has prevented Amar himself from reading the Constitution in light of his own preferences.

OUR PERFECT CONSTITUTION

Like our other scholars, Amar tends to use his interpretive approach to reach results he likes. For example, he says that a textual analysis must include "the study of enactment history." But when it comes to interpreting the Equal Protection Clause, whose legislative history clearly shows no intent to prohibit segregation, he argues that we should ignore that history in favor of the text.[78] And, like the other scholars, he is willing to jettison his own theories completely when necessary to reach favored results. For example, he argues that the Sixth Amendment, which explicitly protects the right of the *defendant* to a public jury trial, accords the same rights to the government: "A sensible Sixth Amendment jurisprudence must begin with the plain meaning, but it must not end there. Though the rules of the amendment make sense as rules, deeper principles lurk beneath the rules. The amendment does mean what it says; but sometimes it means even more."[79] A clause that says that "the accused" "shall enjoy" a trial by jury suddenly means that a jury trial can be *forced* on an unwilling defendant—and that any state that tried to protect such defendants by limiting the government's right to demand a jury trial would be violating the Sixth Amendment!

Amar also engages in some questionable logic to avoid the implications of his theory. He admits that the Establishment Clause, because it protects not individual rights but collective ones, is not incorporated against the states, apparently leaving them free to favor any or all religious denominations.[80] He argues, however, that the Equal Protection Clause would take up the slack, prohibiting a state from, for example, proclaiming itself "the Mormon state."[81] But as a former student of his has persuasively shown, most Establishment Clause violations—including a proclamation of this sort—do not raise equal protection questions, because they do not denigrate or discriminate against persons but rather advocate a particular way of life.[82] For Utah to declare itself the Mormon state no more discriminates personally against non-Mormons than does the Minnesota statute designating blueberry as the official state muffin. The problem with the Mormon case, in the conventional view, is not that the law discriminates against non-Mormons, but that government is entitled to express official views about muffins but not about religious doctrine.

Sometimes his attempt to reconcile his theory with his desired results is even less plausible. For example, in defending affirmative action in education, he says that examining the question from "a practical and structural perspective" is appropriate because "the text and history of the Fourteenth Amendment seem rather open on the question of affirmative action."[83] Treating one race more favorably than another might still be according "equal protection" of the law, he suggests. But despite his intratextualism, he ignores another occurrence of the word "equal" in the Constitution: Article

II, § 1 requires the House to choose a president if two or more candidates receive an "equal" number of electoral votes.[84] That use of "equal" obviously means "the same," and could not be interpreted to permit preferences for any candidate. Why not interpret the Equal Protection Clause similarly? So it seems that neither text nor history is actually necessary for an accurate interpretation of the Constitution.

Like Scalia and Epstein, Amar importantly points out ideas that too often have been overlooked. His attention to text and context is commendable, and a good reminder that it is useful to start there. In particular, judges—and scholars—have had a tendency to focus on single clauses out of context, and Amar reminds us that the Constitution is a single document that should be read and interpreted as a unit. And, as Amar suggests, the founding generation itself thought of the document as a whole, viewing the structural and rights portions as complementary rather than in tension. It is also true, although we think Amar takes the point too far, that eighteenth-century Americans did not distinguish between individual rights and community prerogatives as clearly as we do today.

But Amar shares with the conservative scholars a distaste for precedent and a distrust of judges. His focus on popular sovereignty and his peculiar reading of the text puts juries at the center of protecting rights, and judges at the periphery. "The careful reader," he tells us at the end of his book on the Bill of Rights, "will no doubt notice that judges are not exactly the heroes and heroines of my tale."[85] Frequently, he says, "the citizens seem wiser than the Justices."[86] He reserves special scorn for federal judges, accusing them of "betray[ing]" the Bill of Rights and "strangl[ing] . . . in its crib" the Fourteenth Amendment.[87] And even judges who concur with his own views aren't good enough: he describes his purpose in the book as an attempt "to explain how today's judges and lawyers have often gotten it right without quite realizing why."[88] He adopts a cavalier view of precedent, suggesting only that it "seems permissible" to give past decisions "a rebuttable presumption of correctness." Any stronger theory of precedent, he argues, would allow judges too much power to "erase" the Constitution.[89]

Amar's distrust of judges is puzzling. First, one wonders how he expects those same judges (let alone politicians or ordinary citizens) to apply his subtle intratextualism correctly. As we have seen, intratextualism leaves much room for manipulation and hardly constrains judicial discretion. If Amar can use intratextualism to reach the results he prefers, aren't judges likely to do the same? Moreover, as others have pointed out, intratextualism at least triples the opportunities for error: it "requir[es] judges to select the proper second text, construe it correctly, and draw the right inferences concerning its relation to the first text."[90]

In chapter 8 we examine in detail why so many smart and capable scholars, with interesting ideas and insights, seem to have ended up making similar mistakes. But for now it is enough to reiterate a theme that has run through this chapter as well as the preceding ones: the problem is not the theory—textualism, originalism, or populism—but the way in which it is used. For Amar, the mistake is not in focusing on text and history, but in focusing *exclusively* on text and history.

Recognizing that foundationalist theories like Amar's are bound to run into trouble still leaves questions, of course. Why Amar seems so determined to embrace intratextualism is puzzling enough. An even deeper question concerns Amar's preference for popular sovereignty over judicial decisionmaking. It may be understandable that conservatives like Epstein, Bork, and Scalia, having seen the power of the Warren Court, would seek to cabin the power of the federal judiciary and to reverse the great precedents of that Court (and, in Epstein's case, of the New Deal Court as well). But why, in a conservative political era, would a self-described liberal like Amar reject the judicial empire built by the liberal Warren Court? And why would he and some other liberal academics turn to popular sovereignty, under whose banner opponents of the Warren Court—as well as current conservatives—have crusaded?

One explanation for the turn toward popular sovereignty might be simple fear. Twelve years of ideologically driven conservative Republican appointments to the bench were followed by eight years of moderate—not Warren era—Democrats, and now we are back to conservative Republicans. Liberals may plausibly fear a judicial turn against liberalism. Perhaps the populace is now more liberal than the federal bench, so popular sovereignty offers an alternative to a conservative judicial revolution. Or perhaps liberal enthusiasm for judicial activism was simply an aberration, brought on by the unusually liberal activities of the federal judiciary in the 1950s and 1960s.

In the next chapter, we turn to another liberal scholar who pursues an analogous goal through different means. Bruce Ackerman—like Amar, a Yale-educated professor who has spent much of his professional career there—attempts to use originalism to entrench Warren Court precedents and to protect them against a potential Republican revolution.

CHAPTER 6

BRUCE ACKERMAN'S
MAGIC AMENDMENT MACHINE

Yale law professor Bruce Ackerman, like his younger colleague Akhil Amar, is a liberal on most social issues. Like Amar, he is also committed to a somewhat abstract concept of popular sovereignty, and tends to venerate the nineteenth-century founders over the eighteenth-century ones. And, as we hope to show in this chapter, he is also a foundationalist whose structure is built on a weak foundation. But Ackerman's knowledge of history is both broad and deep, and he less often loses sight of the forest for the trees. His constitutional theories are nuanced and sophisticated—and for that reason we can learn much from them despite their ultimate implausibility. Nevertheless, he succumbs in the end to the same defects as the other scholars we have examined. His attempt to fit all of constitutional law into a single structure both fails to do justice to history and radically alters present constitutional understandings. And, as with the other scholars, his tunnel vision blinds him to potentially negative consequences of his theory.

CONSTITUTIONAL DUALISM

Ackerman calls himself a constitutional dualist. By this he means that the Constitution contemplates two types of politics: normal or ordinary politics and higher lawmaking or constitutional politics. Normal politics is what goes on in Washington—and at the polls—year in and year out. Busy private citizens muster just enough civic virtue to vote, but not enough to take their votes especially seriously. The politicians so elected are thus stand-ins for the populace but cannot truly speak in the name of We the People. There are no electoral mandates here. Higher lawmaking, in contrast, has occurred only three times in our history: during the founding period, during Reconstruction, and during the New Deal. It is a process of extended and thought-ful deliberation by a significant portion of the people, in which *private* citi-zens temporarily become private *citizens*. In this process, the people make a truly considered choice about the direction in which they wish the nation to go, and politicians implementing their choice *do* speak in the name of We the People. Thereafter, the people return to their civic slumber and the na-tion returns to ordinary politics, but the Supreme Court has a mandate to protect the results of the people's higher lawmaking from future ordinary politicians.[1]

Ackerman thus views himself as a committed and unwavering democrat who ultimately justifies his entire thesis in terms of the knowing and delib-erate consent of the people. Constitutional moments of higher lawmaking represent the purest form of popular consent, and are therefore superior to the mere unthinking acquiescence of ordinary politics. In other words, Ack-erman justifies judicial review—the courts' invalidation of popularly en-acted laws—by recourse to the Constitution's status as an expression of the will of the people in their most deliberative moments. He, like Amar and Bork, seeks a theory that will constrain judges so that they cannot stray from the people's will.

But like the other scholars who are the subject of this book, Ackerman's theory leads him to disturbing places. In some ways, Ackerman provides a contrast to the other scholars: rather than seeking to overturn much existing precedent, he seeks to enshrine it and make it untouchable by future Courts. Nevertheless, he also reaches some radical conclusions about cur-rent constitutional law. And—perhaps most distressing of all—Ackerman believes that our last constitutional moment occurred before the middle of the last century, so that most of us have lived our lives in the tawdry shad-ows, outside the luminous glow of true democracy.

His most radical break with our constitutional traditions is to argue that the people's consent need not be formalized into a written constitutional amendment to be binding on later generations. Although Article V of the Constitution specifies the various ways in which amendments can be added, Ackerman argues that these methods are not exclusive. Not only may We the People adopt constitutional amendments by national referendum, we may also change the Constitution without either a referendum or a particu-lar written amendment if we signal our considered assent to constitutional change.[2] To limit methods of constitutional change to the provisions of Ar-ticle V, Ackerman suggests, is to engage in unjustifiable "hypertextualism" or "formalism." As Richard Posner has commented, the thesis that the Consti-

tution can be amended informally is "startling," and "to legal professionals
. . . incredible."[3]

This move from formal to informal amendments, however, is crucial to
Ackerman's thesis, because it allows him to count the transformative judicial opinions of the New Deal era—which did not rest on any changes in the
written Constitution—as amending the Constitution. Ackerman is in this
sense almost a mirror image of Richard Epstein, who regards the New Deal
as the twilight of American constitutionalism. Ackerman even suggests that
formal adoption of a constitutional amendment is *neither* a necessary *nor* a
sufficient condition for successful constitutional change: he tells us that the
Twenty-Seventh Amendment, which was ultimately ratified two centuries
after it was proposed, "should be treated as a bad joke by sensible citizens"[4]
and not counted among the amendments to the Constitution. (The amendment prohibits Congress from making a pay raise to itself effective until after an intervening election.)

The keys to Ackerman's theory lie in two propositions about American
history: that the founders of the 1787 Constitution both contemplated and
implemented a particular mode of constitutional politics, and that later innovators altered the details but followed the general framework of higher
lawmaking. In particular, he sets out to prove that the recurring pattern of
American higher lawmaking involves "revolutionary" reformers who rejected existing methods of constitutional change in favor of winning the assent of We the People. Thus Madison and his Federalist friends peddled a
Constitution that was illegal under the then-governing Articles of Confederation; John Bingham and his Reconstruction colleagues successfully in-
serted into the Constitution written amendments that were not properly
ratified according to the strictures of Article V; and the New Dealers transformed the Constitution without adding even a single word to the document itself. To illustrate his point, Ackerman labels the illegally ratified
Reconstruction amendments "amendment-simulacra" and the New Deal
judicial opinions "amendment-analogues."[5]

The basic story that Ackerman tells about the Constitution's time-scattered
origins is well crafted and insightful, and worth reading for its own sake. Unfortunately, the history does not ultimately offer much support for his thesis. And so, like the other scholars who read history not for its own sake but
for the support it offers to their own agenda, Ackerman massages both the
historical evidence and his own framework to make the two fit. The result is
a structure that sometimes seems too clever by half and a conclusion that is
seemingly driven by ideology.

What he wants to accomplish is unobjectionable; the problem is in *how* he does it. To argue that actual practice and changing contexts can legitimize—or, for that matter, delegitimize—acts that might otherwise seem unconstitutional (or constitutional) when compared to the text is to take a quintessentially pragmatist approach. Thus we agree with Ackerman's general condemnation of what he calls, interchangeably, "hypertextualism" and "formalism." But Ackerman is not content to condemn formalism; he wants to beat the formalists at their own game. And so he turns to history, attempting to argue that his vision of a dualist constitution and the operation of constitutional politics were intended by the various framers themselves. He thus tries to use originalism, the paradigmatic formalist gambit, in support of his liberal constitutional agenda. His appeal is ultimately conservative: we *must* retain the legacy of the New Deal—as interpreted and implemented by the Warren Court—not because it is right or because we agree with it, but because the depression generation told us to.

DUALISM AT THE CREATION

The first flaw in Ackerman's theory is that he cannot support his contention that the eighteenth-century framers were constitutional dualists in the way he uses the term. He does a nice job in showing how the Federalists integrated existing institutions (like state legislatures) with innovative or even illegal assemblies, such as the Philadelphia Convention itself—in other words, of showing that they did not follow to the letter the then-governing procedures for constitutional change. That history, of course, is well known to historians,[6] although Ackerman's emphasis on the Federalists' use of "official confirmations" to catapult their enterprise from one "illegal initiative" to the next adds an interesting dimension. As he puts it: "Success depended heavily on the Federalists' unconventional use of existing institutional authority. In each state, the revolutionaries sought to persuade the legislature to ignore the legalist quibbling of their opponents and get on the institutional bandwagon by calling for a ratifying convention. They then used these legislative anchors to respond to charges of illegality down the road."[7]

But the fact that the Federalists themselves failed to play by the rules does not necessarily mean that they contemplated imitative successors. Demonstrating that the Federalists *acted* as dualists does not prove that they incorporated Ackerman's particular dualist theory into the Constitution. To support his theory, Ackerman must show that the founders did not expect their own handiwork in Article V to bind later generations—that they wanted future reformers to do as they did rather than as they said. This he fails to do.

Ackerman's attempt to show that the founders were dualists rests primarily on the Federalist Papers, the collection of essays defending the proposed Constitution by the pseudonymous Publius. Publius was in fact James Madison and Alexander Hamilton, with assistance from John Jay.[8] Relying on the Federalist Papers presents the usual problems of originalism, including raising questions about how widely they were read when they were originally published in New York newspapers, how representative they were (Madison and Hamilton were two of the strongest nationalists at the Convention), and whether any of the ratifiers relied on them (they were published after many states had already ratified the Constitution).[9] As one of Ackerman's critics has noted, Ackerman "takes Publius's statements at face value, rather than treating them as the political rhetoric of three committed Federalist statesmen who were endeavoring to influence public opinion in a state where defeat of the Constitution was widely anticipated."[10]

Even leaving those problems aside, the Federalist Papers do not support Ackerman's contentions. Ackerman begins with Publius's defense of the Philadelphia Convention's "illegal" act of ignoring both the Articles of Confederation and the delegates' own instructions from their respective states. According to Publius, in many circumstances the people's inherent right of revolution can be exercised only through essentially illegal conventions whose proposals are eventually ratified by the people.[11] The illegality of the founders' own act and their recognition that illegal constitutional change is necessary in some times and places, however, do not mean that the founders thought future illegal changes would be necessary.

Publius recognized—as Ackerman notes—that revolution is a dangerous business, whether conducted by armies or by convention delegates. As Charles Pinckney of South Carolina noted at the end of the Philadelphia Convention, "Conventions are serious things, and ought not to be repeated."[12] The trick is to structure a constitution that will allow for reform without necessitating revolution. The founders did so by including in Article V provisions that would make amending the Constitution difficult but not impossible—including a provision that would legitimate any repetition of their own arguably illegal Convention. Thus they created a document that allows the people to exercise their right of revolution without resorting to illegality.

Ackerman also overstates the "illegality" of the founders' actions. As historian Jack Rakove has argued, American thinking on constitutions and constitutionalism was in flux between 1776 and 1789. The original state constitutions were legislative enactments, not submitted to the people for ratification: the Revolutionary generation did not fully understand constitutions as higher law distinguishable from ordinary legislation. By 1787, relying in part on the innovative example of the popularly ratified Massachusetts constitution of 1780, Americans had begun to regard constitutions as fundamental law and hence to reject as defective constitutions, like the Articles of Confederation, that had not been ratified by the people. Rakove thus concludes that the ratification of the Constitution was more "superlegal" than "illegal."[13] Indeed, the main historical source, Madison's notes of the proceedings of the Philadelphia Convention that drafted the Constitution, suggests that it was only over the course of that Convention that the delegates themselves came to understand the relationship between the higher-law nature of a constitution and the need for popular ratification.[14]

In any case, noting the inconsistency between the amendment provisions of the Articles of Confederation and the Constitution's actual ratification process is not particularly new. Nor does it prove Ackerman's thesis that the founders self-consciously intended that future constitutional amendments might be enacted through processes other than those listed in Article V. For that proposition, he relies on a more complicated model of the interactions among theories of representation, judicial review, and the possibility of constitutional change.

Ackerman nicely argues that the filtered or mediated Constitution—which is overlooked by Amar, as we noted earlier—means that the people's elected representatives do not ordinarily speak directly for We the People, but instead use their own judgment to translate and moderate what Madison called the "transient impressions" of the voting public. But showing that the founders viewed ordinary politics as not fully representative does not establish Ackerman's dualist thesis that the founders contemplated higher lawmaking outside Article V. To prove this further point, Ackerman attempts to provide evidence that the Constitution contemplates one extra-constitutional method for exercising higher lawmaking and another for preserving it. It is at this crucial point that Ackerman's history and analysis are at their weakest.

Ackerman spins his dualist theory from only two passages in the Federalist Papers. First, he cites Publius's recommendation "that a constitutional road to the decision of the people ought to be marked out and kept open, for certain great and extraordinary occasions."[15] From this he concludes that Publius hoped that "the People [would], in their irregular way, prove equal to the challenge" of constitutional politics.[16] In the quoted passage, however, Publius was simply rejecting Thomas Jefferson's suggestion of regularly scheduled conventions for revising the Constitution, in favor of Article V's alternatives. There is absolutely no evidence that Publius was speaking of what Ackerman calls "irregular" constitutional politics rather than the formal methods of amending the Constitution.

Similarly, Ackerman reproduces a long passage from Hamilton's Federalist No. 78, the heart of which is that although the people have a right to alter or abolish the established Constitution,

> yet it is not to be inferred from this principle that the representatives of the people, whenever a momentary inclination happens to lay hold of a majority of their constituents incompatible with the provisions in the existing constitution, would, on that account, be justifiable in a violation of those provisions; or that the courts would be under a greater obligation to connive at infractions in this shape than when they had proceeded wholly from the cabals of the representative body. Until the people *by some solemn and authoritative act*, annulled or changed the established form, it is binding upon themselves collectively, as well as individually.[17]

Ackerman explains that "[t]his passage provides a wonderful summary of all the themes we have rehearsed: Publius's dualistic understanding of the People, his semiotic concept of representation, and his complex analysis of faction interact to yield a distinctive view of the Court's responsibilities."[18] Again, however, Ackerman provides no evidence that Publius's reference to "some solemn and authoritative act" describes anything other than the formal amendment process set out in Article V. The more natural reading of the language—absent historical evidence to the contrary—is that Publius was specifically referring to the authoritative acts contemplated by Article V.[19]

Indeed, Ackerman ignores quite significant contrary evidence. Another Federalist passage shows that Madison, at least, specifically *rejected* the idea of appealing to the people for constitutional change because he feared that they would not be up to the task of deliberative decisionmaking. Thus, in addition to his comments on Jefferson's proposal, Madison wrote in Federalist 49 that in debates about constitutional amendments, "the public decision . . . could never be expected to turn on the true merits of the question," because "[t]he *passions*, . . . not the *reason*, of the public, would sit in judgment."[20] Madison expressed similar sentiments in a private letter to

Edmund Randolph. Randolph had suggested convening a second constitutional convention, which Madison opposed on the ground that "there can be no doubt that there are subjects to which the capacities of the bulk of mankind are unequal, and on which they must and will be governed by those with whom they happen to have acquaintance and confidence."[21] One leading historian of the founding period concludes that Madison believed "that *no* extraordinary appeal to public opinion to resolve constitutional disputes should ever be attempted."[22] Like Amar, Ackerman tends to confuse the rather elitist founders with modern democrats, overstating their faith in the common people.

What, then, does Ackerman's historical survey prove? It proves only a set of uncontroversial propositions about the founders' beliefs: that ordinary laws are subordinate to the Constitution, that one function of the Supreme Court is to preserve that venerable document from the onslaughts of a temporarily impassioned majority, and that it takes an extraordinary process to change the Constitution. None of this requires a "dualist" view of the Constitution except in the most trivial sense, under which ordinary legislative enactments are distinguished from formal constitutional amendments.

But Ackerman means something much more significant: he argues that, following the intent of the original framers, the Constitution can be altered whenever We the People engage in constitutional politics, whether by means of a formal constitutional amendment or not. His historical evidence does not come close to supporting that proposition.

Thus, to the extent that Ackerman justifies his framework for constitutional politics outside Article V by reference to the original intent, it fails. We may or may not be dualists now, in Ackerman's meaning of the term, but those who wrote and ratified the Constitution in the late eighteenth century clearly were not.

HISTORY REPEATS ITSELF

If Ackerman does not show that the Federalists were dualists, he is no more successful at pigeonholing later momentous constitutional changes into the dualist framework. From Ackerman's perspective, it would not matter if later generations of constitutional innovators practiced his brand of constitutional politics—he is determined to ground his theory of constitutional change in the eighteenth century, and once he fails at that the game is lost. But a less committed originalist might be satisfied with evidence that longstanding historical practice supports Ackerman's dualist framework, even if the framers did not understand the Constitution to legitimate use of this practice. Nevertheless, Ackerman does not successfully show that We the People have engaged in a recognizable pattern of constitutional politics. Here the primary problem is not with Ackerman's historical account but with the conclusions he draws from it.

Ackerman sets up a framework for constitutional change by identifying five stages of constitutional politics. First, would-be reformers must somehow *signal* to the public that there is an important constitutional issue at stake. Then they make a *proposal* for change. The proposal is necessarily linked to the third stage, which Ackerman calls *"triggering"*: because the proposal is unlikely to succeed under the existing rules of constitutional change, the reformers must trigger a change in those rules. The fourth and fifth stages distinguish successful from unsuccessful constitutional reforms, and consist of *ratification* by the public and *consolidation* to bring in the dissenting voices.

The basic picture is one of constitutional reformers prodding a normally sluggish electorate into sending a message, and then using that message— backed by whatever institutional powers the reformers have—to bludgeon supporters of the status quo into submission. Ackerman suggests that this process occurred during both Reconstruction and the New Deal.

Thus, after signaling to the American public that the future of the Constitution was at stake, the Reconstruction Republicans took comfort from their (triggering) electoral victory in 1866. That confidence allowed them to push through the Fourteenth Amendment by unconventional means (nicely, but not newly, described by Ackerman). It also allowed them to attack the two remaining impediments to reform: they impeached President Johnson and stripped the Supreme Court of jurisdiction to avoid a constitutional challenge to Reconstruction. As Ackerman puts it:

> In contrast to the parliamentary system, the institutional protagonists in Washington D.C. could not call a special election at their convenience, but had to return to the voters on a fixed schedule. This meant . . . that if the President and [the] Court wished to obstruct Reconstruction, there was only one way the [Congress] could respond before 1868—threaten the more conservative branches with dire institutional consequences unless they called off their campaign of resistance.[23]

The Republicans at this point were taking a risk—if they lacked a popular mandate, they would be courting defeat. But Ackerman's story has a happy ending: the election of 1868 served to ratify the Reconstruction program, and the Supreme Court's acquiescence, in 1873, in the arguably illegal ratification procedures for the Fourteenth Amendment consolidated the Republican victory.[24]

The New Dealers followed much the same pattern, according to Ackerman. Franklin D. Roosevelt's victory over Herbert Hoover in 1932 served the signaling function, the New Deal itself was a proposal for an activist state, and the battles over the constitutionality of New Deal legislation were battles for the hearts and minds of the deliberative American public. This time, unlike the Reconstruction era, the president and the Congress were both in the reform camp, so it was only the Supreme Court that needed threatening. And threaten the reformers did: Ackerman describes FDR's court-packing plan as "functionally equivalent" to the Reconstruction Republicans' impeachment of Andrew Johnson. This time, however, the obdurantist conservatives backed down early enough—in the famous 1937 "switch in time" in which the Court showed itself finally willing to uphold key New Deal legislation—so that the reformers had no need to push through written constitutional amendments. "Only if the Justices refuse to recognize the legitimacy of a transformation do the President and Congress have an incentive to take the Article Five path." The Court's capitulation in 1937 eliminated that need: instead, the Supreme Court's "transformative opinions of the early 1940's . . . served as the functional equivalents of Article Five amendments, establishing fixed points for legal reasoning during the next era."[25]

Ackerman illustrates the parallels between the two eras by pointing out that it was largely the difference between Andrew Johnson's opposition and FDR's support that necessitated the resort to written amendments. He asks us to imagine what would have happened had Lincoln survived the assassination attempt and Roosevelt had not. Ackerman speculates that Reconstruction ideals might have been memorialized only in transformative judicial opinions, but the New Deal would have been codified in accordance with Article V.

> If this is right, the hypertextualist's worship of Article Five appears in a most peculiar light, as it gives decisive weight to the tragic accidents of American history. After all, Roosevelt was also the object of assassination, only narrowly missing the fatal bullet. If his attacker had been a better marksman, and Lincoln's a worse one, modern hypertextualism would have had a very different spin. It would have urged modern interpreters to focus intently on the text of the New Deal Amendments, while

casting a skeptical glance at the Chase Court's invocations of equal protection. But surely American lawyers owe more to their fellow citizens than such a heavy-handed formalism.[26]

Surely they do. But has Ackerman offered a viable alternative by propounding the five-stage process of constitutional politics? After a brief digression on Ackerman's historical accuracy, we turn to that question.

BUT DID IT HAPPEN THAT WAY?

Ackerman's history of Reconstruction and the New Deal is significantly more sophisticated than his history of the founding. Even so, he has to work a bit to squeeze the events into his organizational framework. For example, the New Dealers' brush with judicial defeat might have made them leery of relying on even the new Supreme Court for future enforcement of the new paradigm; moreover, future Congresses or future presidents could easily undo what had been done by mere legislation. Thus Ackerman's explanation of the vanishing incentive to memorialize the changes by constitutional amendment is too facile.

Ackerman also silently takes sides in several active debates among historians without sufficiently explaining why he reaches the conclusions he does. Leading historians disagree about the extent to which either Reconstruction or the New Deal were truly "revolutionary." At the risk of oversimplification, one might say that Michael Les Benedict views the leaders of Reconstruction as conservatives wishing to preserve as much of the existing order as possible, and Eric Foner sees them as thoroughgoing radicals.[27] Ackerman takes the "revolutionary" position, but does not pay enough attention to the counterarguments.[28] Similarly, Ackerman appears unaware of various disputes about the historiography of the New Deal, as Laura Kalman points out: "Ackerman acknowledges neither that the idea of First and Second New Deals evokes different meanings for historians, nor that historians have challenged the suggestion of two separate New Deals."[29] Moreover, she writes,

> Ackerman's celebration of the New Deal is sharply at odds with the historiography. . . . [F]ew consider the New Deal as revolutionary as Ackerman maintains . . . . "[M]ost historians in the last two decades have accepted some variation of Leuchtenburg's stance of muted praise." Ackerman's description of the New Deal makes Leuchtenburg's sound positively sour in comparison.[30]

Another historian suggests that "Ackerman has relied on a limited, and largely discredited, fragment of the historical literature," "ignor[ing] patterns of economic power and influence, and the ways in which economic interests shaped and reshaped the New Deal."[31] And Ackerman's description of the populace and its role in the New Deal is bland and unrealistic. Other historians have shown how We the People had "ethnic, class, regional, and other identities." They were "not passive consumers of political debates," but rather actively responded to the politicians' agenda in sometimes unexpected ways.[32]

Ackerman's view of the three periods is also unduly time limited. The founding period did not spring full-blown from the minds of Madison, Hamilton, and the others in 1786 or 1787—nor did it end with the ratification of the Constitution (or even with the ratification of the Bill of Rights). It began even before independence, as colonists began to develop the ideas of popular sovereignty, representation, and governance that would influence the political events of the next few decades. And it continued through at least the election of 1800, as one crisis after another forced "the founders" to shape and reshape the regime established by the Constitution.[33] Similarly, Eric Foner documents how developments in the antebellum period shaped Reconstruction, suggesting that it is artificial for Ackerman to begin the story with the Thirteenth Amendment.[34] And decades before FDR was first elected to the presidency, the early-nineteenth-century Progressives laid the groundwork for the New Deal transformation—which arguably continued into World War II and even into Lyndon Johnson's Great Society.[35]

Ackerman also sometimes seems blinded by his own insights. For example, he suggests that formal amendments do not even enjoy a superiority over informal ones in the eyes of the modern judiciary:

Today's Justices of the Supreme Court are *far* more ready to ignore some of the greatest texts left by Reconstruction than they are to ignore the New Deal charge of *Lochnerism*. For example, all legal historians recognize that the Reconstruction Republicans—both in and out of Congress—placed their highest hopes on the Fourteenth Amendment's solemn guarantee that no state shall "abridge the privileges or immunities of citizens of the United States." And yet the courts have never seriously redeemed the promise of this text. While judges are constantly on the lookout for the least signs of the *Lochnerian* heresy, most go to their graves without giving an hour's thought to the provision of the Fourteenth Amendment that the Republicans supposed would serve as the central memorial of their achievement.[36]

Ackerman is correct, but only if one takes a formalist approach. It may be true that judges do not cite the Privileges or Immunities Clause, but they are nevertheless keenly aware of the privileges and immunities—the natural rights, as it were—of American citizens. What does it matter that the Privileges or Immunities Clause is a dead letter if the Court can find a right to privacy, including a right of reproductive choice, in the Due Process Clause?[37] And while the charge of *Lochnerizing* does indeed strike terror into the hearts of judges, it does not seem to stop them from engaging in it while simultaneously denying that they are doing so. They still manage to find all sorts of unenumerated rights protected by various clauses of the Constitution. Indeed, they still sometimes protect property rights in ways that essentially ensure some remaining constitutional space for the laissez-faire economics protected by the *Lochner* Court.[38]

These lapses should remind us that history does not come in the neat packages that theories like Ackerman's would suggest. He seems to have an explanation for every unruly fact, but sometimes those explanations strain credulity. Nevertheless, most of Ackerman's description of Reconstruction and the New Deal is roughly accurate.

More troubling, however, is Ackerman's view of history as inevitably progressive. Other scholars have noticed his Whiggish tendency to see only good in American history, and to ignore the possibility that constitutional moments might produce bad results.[39] Ackerman's optimism combines with the fuzziness of his description of constitutional moments to yield a serious problem: he cannot distinguish the New Deal from other, potentially more disturbing, eras of constitutional change.

MISSING CONSTITUTIONAL MOMENTS

Using Ackerman's technique to distinguish constitutional politics from ordinary politics has led other scholars to identify some rather less flattering instances of American higher lawmaking. Michael McConnell shows persuasively that the end of Reconstruction, culminating in the Compromise of 1877 that awarded the presidency to Republican Rutherford Hayes in exchange for the Republicans' promise to end all attempts to enforce their Reconstruction enactments, fits perfectly as an example of Ackerman's constitutional politics.

McConnell suggests that the signaling and proposal that mark the beginning of constitutional politics had occurred by the time of the 1874 election, which he describes as "a referendum on the nation's continued commitment to civil rights, much as the elections of 1934, 1936, and 1938 were referenda on the New Deal."[40] And the election of 1876 certainly served to ratify a mobilized People's decision to change constitutional course:

> The election of 1876 may have been the most violent, fraud-ridden, and tumultuous in history; . . . No one doubted that these elections were fought over the future character of the constitutional regime in the southern states. There was no dearth of passion or participation. There was violence aplenty. In the tense months following the election of 1876, Democratic newspapers proclaimed, "Tilden or War" and Democratic governors prepared their militias for armed resistance to a usurpatious Republican administration. According to one participant in the events, "it seemed as if the terrors of civil war were again to be renewed." He observed that more people expected fighting to break out in 1877 than had expected it in 1861. And whatever one may think of the political morality of the participants, there can be no doubt that a substantial portion of the deliberation was at the level of principle: the Democrats' attack on centralized government and defense of states' rights versus the Republicans' waning but still powerful commitment to Reconstruction.[41]

After the 1877 Compromise signaled the People's ratification, the losers gracefully capitulated, consolidating the victory of the anti-Reconstruction "reformers."[42] The Supreme Court then issued a series of "transformative" opinions essentially nullifying the recently enacted Fourteenth Amendment, invalidating important Reconstruction legislation, and generally codifying the constitutionality of states' rights and Jim Crow.[43] We the People had spoken once again.

If McConnell is right—and Eric Foner, one of the leading scholars of Reconstruction, thinks he is[44]—then endorsing Ackerman's antiformalist approach to constitutional amendment is more than a little problematic. While uncodified higher lawmaking might yield a New Deal, it might also yield less salutary changes. Ackerman has responded that McConnell's portrayal is inaccurate, largely because the Jim Crow "reformers" never successfully repealed the Fourteenth Amendment nor enacted any national legislation.[45] This response is hardly satisfactory. First, of course, if we can have unwritten constitutional amendments, we can also have unwritten repeals, and the not-so-benign neglect with which all branches—to say nothing of the southern states—treated the Fourteenth Amendment and the major Reconstruction statutes seems to qualify as such. The absence of national legislation seems trivial in the face of the discriminatory legislation passed in northern as well as southern legislatures.[46]

Regardless of whether McConnell or Ackerman has the better of the historical argument, moreover, the plausibility of McConnell's argument—well supported by historical evidence—suggests that Ackerman's theory is not self-executing. As long as we must make *judgments* about whether to treat a particular era as an example of constitutional politics, there will be reasonable differences of opinion.[47] Those legitimate differences of opinion then serve to undermine the certainty of Ackerman's defense of the New Deal as an unquestioned and unquestionable part of the Constitution.

The uncertainty is magnified when one turns to the modern era. Ackerman is at great pains to distinguish the New Deal from what has been called the "Reagan Revolution." He admits that Ronald Reagan's election in 1980 served a signaling function, but maintains that Reagan ultimately failed to convince the American people to alter the constitutional course set by the New Deal.

This is where Ackerman reveals his political agenda. Ackerman's foundationalist attachment to constitutional dualism stems from his strong desire to protect the New Deal—and, more significantly, the Warren Court—from possible judicial retrenchment. To do so, he must somehow elevate the New Deal Court precedent to constitutional status, while simultaneously denying that the current, more conservative, Court has a similar popular mandate. In a candid moment, he essentially admitted this goal:

> I write as a member of a generation that, over the last twenty years, has conspicuously failed to gain broad and deep popular support for any major constitutional initiative. During times such as these, our principal task is to keep alive the American tradition of popular sovereignty by preserving, as best we can, the memory of previous achievements. Rather than throwing the New Deal out of the court of constitutional opinion on a formalism, the higher calling is to understand its profound contribution to the sense that Americans still live under government *by the People*.[48]

Indeed, Ackerman has been unabashedly working toward constructing a constitutional justification for entrenching the Warren Court for years. In 1985, he published an article arguing that the then-existing intellectual justifications for Warren Court precedents were—and would soon be broadly exposed as—hopelessly inadequate. He explained that existing protections for racial equality and religious freedom were based largely on "bad political science" that concentrated on the Court's role in rectifying the unjustified political powerlessness of certain groups. But, as he noted, "political reality" was quickly demonstrating that many such groups—most prominently racial minorities—did in fact possess a great deal of electoral power. Hence those "who look upon our tradition of civil liberties as one of the greatest achievements of American law" face formidable challenges: "we must explain to our fellow Americans that there are constitutional values in our scheme of government even more fundamental than perfected pluralism," lest constitutional law become "a transparent apologia for the status quo."[49] He apparently thinks he has found a way to do this with constitutional dualism.

But Ackerman's weak dismissal of the changes wrought by conservative Republicans since 1980 merely illustrates the depth of the ideological motivation behind his theory of constitutional politics. He rests his case against a modern constitutional moment primarily on four failures: the failure of Republicans to capture the House during the Reagan presidency; Reagan's failed attempt to place Robert Bork on the Supreme Court; the reaffirmation, despite fierce Republican opposition, of abortion rights in *Planned Parenthood of Pennsylvania v. Casey*;[50] and the election of Bill Clinton in 1992.[51] But interpreting those events as negating the possibility that Americans have repudiated the New Deal illustrates the subjectivity of his analysis, and shows how often he must distort either the facts or the theory to reach his preferred conclusions.

Start with *Casey*, which he seems to view as the would-be conservative reformers' most momentous failure.[52] Ackerman describes the object of the Reagan "reform" movement as a challenge to "the continuing validity of New Deal liberalism." And he labels the battle over *Roe v. Wade* "a crucial arena" for testing whether Americans retained their commitment to the New Deal or, on the other hand, thoughtfully rejected it in favor of Reagan's morning in America. On that view, the Court's unwillingness to overturn *Roe*, despite the presence of five Reagan-Bush appointees (six if you count Chief Justice Rehnquist, who was appointed to the Court by Nixon but elevated by Reagan), clearly represents a dismal failure of the reformers' agenda.[53]

There are two fatal problems with Ackerman's analysis: *Roe* is not part of the New Deal, and Reagan's primary attack on the New Deal centered on federalism and activist government—on getting the federal government off the backs of the people—not on overturning *Roe*. While Reagan did campaign against *Roe*, in light of both his prior political stance and his failure to even try to do much about *Roe*, abortion was not his primary concern. And although Ackerman links reproductive rights to the New Deal through a complicated—and ultimately unsuccessful—intellectual maneuver,[54] most voting Americans in and out of Congress probably would not consider limits on abortion laws to be a vital part of the New Deal's activist and redistributionist state. While the attack by social conservatives on *Roe* failed, the attack by libertarians on the New Deal's economic regulation was much more successful.

Thus although the conservative Republican attack on *Roe* failed, judged as a repudiation of an activist and redistributionist federal government rather than as a crusade against abortion, the Reagan Revolution was arguably much more successful. The tax cuts of the early 1980s have remained largely in effect, welfare "as we know it" is ending, and block grants have allowed states much more control over the distribution of federal largesse. Indeed, the gap between rich and poor has increased to a size not seen since the New Deal—or even earlier.[55] And the victories have been consolidated by the same Supreme Court that refused to overturn *Roe:* the Court has embarked on a determined course of reining in the authority of the federal government and protecting the states from encroachments on their sovereignty.[56]

Ackerman's reliance on the Bork nomination and on Clinton's election is similarly flawed. Viewed through the narrow lens of abortion rights, both events might indicate a failure for Republican reformers. But in terms of a reappraisal of the New Deal itself, neither event bears the weight Ackerman puts on it. Bork, after all, never challenged the New Deal or an activist government, but only an "activist" Supreme Court. What he wanted to change was not the principles of the New Deal but the subsequent Warren Court interpretations of the Constitution—which Ackerman has *not* suggested were an instance of popular higher lawmaking. (He would be hard pressed to do so, given popular opposition to so many of that Court's rulings.) Other, more successful nominations also minimize the significance of the Bork rejection: Justices Scalia and Thomas are if anything *more* conservative, and clearly more willing to attack the New Deal, than Bork was at the time.[57] And Bill Clinton is hardly a model New Deal Democrat: his most important domestic policy initiative was the end of "welfare as we know it," and his New Deal–inspired universal health care programs never got out of the starting blocks.

Indeed, a number of political scientists have concluded that American political views between 1965 and 1980 went through exactly the sort of change that Ackerman calls a constitutional moment. Disillusioned with the New Deal Democrats' slide from a party of the people to a party of the disadvantaged, many left the party—to return only when Clinton heralded a "new" and much more conservative Democratic vision.[58]

Ultimately, then, Ackerman's dualist framework is merely a mechanism by which he can argue that the precedents of the New Deal and the Warren Court should not be overruled. A fine sentiment (with which we largely agree); but why undermine it by using such a weak foundationalist argument? Moreover, Ackerman's dualist theory suffers from flaws other than its blatantly political application.

WE, THE PEOPLE WHO THINK LIKE ACKERMAN

Ackerman's theory of constitutional politics hinges on the active participation of We the People. In order to distinguish periods of higher lawmaking from politics as usual, without resorting to the formal criteria that mark a written amendment, Ackerman must be able to point to a mobilized and deliberative electorate. Unfortunately, what he ends up pointing to are mobilized and deliberative *elites.*

The description Ackerman gives of the process of popular participation in constitutional politics clearly envisions the mobilization of the ordinary public and not just elites:

> For me, "the People" is not the name of a superhuman being, but the name of an extended process of interaction between political elites and ordinary citizens. It is a special process because, during constitutional moments, most ordinary Americans are spending extraordinary amounts of time and energy on the project of citizenship, paying attention to the goings-on in Washington with much greater concern than usual. If the higher lawmaking system operates successfully, it will channel this active citizenship engagement into a structured dialogue between political elites and ordinary Americans—first giving competing elites the chance to elaborate alternative constitutional meanings; then inviting citizens to share in the debate and cast their votes.[59]

But when it comes to demonstrating and measuring the "extraordinary" participation and "much greater concern than usual" that mark constitutional moments, Ackerman actually has little evidence that the New Deal generated such mobilization. Instead, he talks about the headlines on the front page of the *New York Times* and about the attention lavished on the Supreme Court's resistance by the president and Congress. He notes that the mass media also reported on the New Deal battles, even broadcasting speeches by various protagonists. But other than a single reference to the then-new Gallup Poll, which showed that at a crucial juncture only 10 percent of those surveyed had no opinion, Ackerman does not show that ordinary Americans paid much attention to the goings-on in Washington. He certainly offers no comparative data about whether they paid more attention than in other historic periods.[60] Despite what those living in New Haven might think, the *New York Times* is not the newspaper of choice for most ordinary Americans.

Recent events should make us especially wary of equating media coverage with popular interest. The scandal surrounding President Clinton's affair with Monica Lewinsky—and Clinton's subsequent impeachment and trial on charges of perjury and obstruction of justice—captured the media's attention at a virtually unprecedented level. But poll after poll showed that a majority of Americans followed it for its entertainment value, considering it high drama rather than high politics. And as one scholar notes, the Clinton impeachment should put to rest fantasies about deliberative American politics: "If the impeachment of Bill Clinton accomplished anything, surely it should have disabused constitutional theorists of the Panglossian ideal of democratic deliberation in America as a sober, cool, ratiocinative exercise in achieving consensus through reason-giving."[61] In short, as a leading historian has noted, "Ackerman asserts rather than demonstrates an equivalence between the outlooks of reform elites and those of popular movements."[62]

Ackerman makes a similar mistake, confusing elitism and populism, in his description of the goals of the original founders. He describes their invention of conventions as representing "a distinctive mix of popular will and elite deliberation—combining the popular involvement of 'direct democracy' with the enhanced deliberation of 'representative democracy.' " He thus tries to claim a populist mantle for what the founders did. But as we showed in chapter 5, many of the Federalists were wary of populism, and turned to conventions as a way of selling their new Constitution rather than as an integral part of government. Many Federalists wanted as little democratic participation as possible, which explains (among other things) the rather bizarre method they created for presidential elections. In fact, Ackerman himself admits that the founding was exclusionary and not very representative; even the turnout among the limited number of eligible voters was low.[63]

It may or may not be possible to identify periods of actual mobilized deliberation among nonelites, especially in the age before sophisticated polls and instant interactive surveys. But without such an identification, Ackerman's description of constitutional politics as an exercise of higher lawmaking of We the People degenerates into constitutional manipulation by members of the elite—like Ackerman himself.

THE CONSTITUTION IN CRISIS

Perhaps the most serious problem with Ackerman's thesis of dualism as justified by original intent is his choice of the three examples of constitutional politics. For them to be exemplary, he must show that their legitimacy rested on the fact of public mobilization rather than on the urgency of national crisis. But the founding, Reconstruction, and the New Deal were not ordinary times, and all the protagonists knew it. Each set of Ackerman's founders had what one historian calls a "crisis mentality."[64] Desperate times call for desperate measures, and the reformers whose handiwork successfully resolved the crises refused to be bound by preexisting rules that limited their flexibility. Another way to put it is that each generation recognized that the Constitution is not a suicide pact.

Ackerman provides an example of this recognition of crisis and consequent disregard for rules when he quotes Sidney George Fisher's essay of 1862: "The Constitution belongs to the people,—to the people of 1862, not to those of 1787. It must and will be modified to suit the wishes of the former, by their representatives in Congress, or it will be destroyed. . . . If the people cannot preserve the Constitution, it must perish, for it cannot be preserved by the Judiciary."[65]

A similar attitude prevailed at the 1787 Convention. Challenged to justify the Convention's power to propose a new Constitution, Edmund Randolph "was not scrupulous on the point of power."[66] According to James Madison's notes, Randolph replied: "When the salvation of the Republic was at stake, it would be treason to our trust, not to propose what we found necessary. . . . There are certainly seasons of a peculiar nature where the ordinary cautions must be dispensed with; and this is certainly one of them."[67] Robert Yates's notes of Randolph's speech are even more blunt: "There are great seasons when persons with limited powers are justified in exceeding them, and a person would be contemptible not to risk it. . . . I am certain that a national government must be established, and this is the only moment when it can be done."[68]

The New Dealers perceived no less a crisis, and had no less determination in the face of legal obstacles. In his first inaugural address, Roosevelt called "the national emergency" "critical," and said that if necessary he would ask Congress for "power to wage a war against the emergency, as great as the power that would be given to me if we were in fact invaded by a foreign foe."[69] Al Smith, the ex-governor of New York and FDR rival, said that the depression was "doing more damage at home to our own people than the great war of 1917 and 1918 ever did."[70] He urged Americans to follow the same course they did in the war: "we took our Constitution, wrapped it up and laid it on the shelf and left it there until it was over."[71]

Ackerman probably would not deny that all these reformers reasonably believed that they were fighting for the very continued existence of the United States and its Constitution. But that recognition undermines the power of his examples, simply because they are so extraordinary. All of the reformers believed that their circumvention of the rules was essential, but *none* of them believed that future generations should be permitted to circumvent the reformers' own changes at will. The problem for Ackerman is that averting disaster is a rare and unusual occurrence, and does not provide a good model for other circumstances. As Jack Rakove has put it, the circumstances of the founding and Reconstruction "are so extraordinary as to verge on the truly unique."[72]

Indeed, that is how many of the participants thought about what they were doing. The Reconstruction founders, for example, justified their program and its departures from previous rules as a legitimate consequence of the Civil War, and thus as an extraordinary one-time event. Ackerman rejects this argument—known as the "Grasp-of-War" doctrine—on the ground that it provides an insufficient justification. But as Michael Les Benedict points out, what matters is not whether the Grasp-of-War doctrine actually justifies Reconstruction, but whether Reconstruction Republicans *believed* that it did.[73] Because if they did—and Ackerman provides no evidence at all that they did not—then they did not expect future generations to repeat their actions or engage in unconventional higher lawmaking.

Dualism as a defense of constitutional change beyond Article V, then, is less a matter of the constitutional theories of the various framers and more a matter of felt necessity. They did what they had to. Why should we not do the same under our own different circumstances? A pragmatist would say that we should, but Ackerman worries that a pragmatist approach might legitimize (or at least not exclude) cutting back on the New Deal and the Warren Court. And so he makes the same mistake that most of our other scholars do: rather than attempting to persuade readers of the substantive correctness of his preferred interpretation of the Constitution, he tries to enshrine that interpretation as the *only* possible one by linking it to popular sovereignty.

How serious is Ackerman's mistake? Does he have the right idea but simply call it by the wrong name? As we suggest in the next section, the problem is more serious. Misled by his attachment to a magic constitutional moment, he proposes rather radical changes to the Constitution itself.

FROM CONSTITUTIONAL MOMENTS TO DIRECT DEMOCRACY

Ackerman's primary error stems from his foundationalism—his insistence that all constitutional interpretation be shoehorned into a single grand scheme. He seems not to recognize that constitutional change often occurs gradually and incrementally, not in momentous upheavals during which the People arise from their slumber. (Antietam and Gettysburg may represent an exception—but their origins, of course, lie in the gradual cumulation of earlier events.)

Ackerman's account of the New Deal, for example, fails to credit the work done by early-nineteenth-century Progressives, and by even earlier generations, in building an activist federal government. The New Deal was a significant expansion, but it was largely a quantitative rather than a qualitative leap.[74] The principles of the New Deal, then, grew incrementally rather than springing full-blown from the Roosevelt administration and the Congress. We the People had been fitfully giving their consent to the changes all along. As Larry Kramer has shown, even the Supreme Court had been acquiescing—in fits and starts, but with a clearly favorable trend—until it "panicked" in 1935 and 1936.[75] Indeed, one strain of New Deal scholarship argues that the Supreme Court's 1937 shift was the result of "internal" doctrinal developments, not a response to political pressure.[76] All these historical arguments, whether ultimately persuasive or not, undermine Ackerman's claim to be presenting the one true history of the Constitution, and Ackerman takes insufficient notice of them in his haste to construct a one-size-fits-all constitutional theory.

In particular, recognizing the usually incremental nature of constitutional change defeats Ackerman's political purpose by legitimating recent gradual changes away from the New Deal. It also undermines his theory of constitutional amendment outside Article V: if the New Deal was really not the sudden constitutional innovation he portrays, then it becomes harder to label it an "amendment" rather than another evolutionary development, and harder to distinguish Ackerman's constitutional moments from the pragmatist's constitutional drift.

But so what? Why isn't Ackerman just another pragmatist, seeking to distinguish himself by overselling his uniqueness? He differs from true pragmatists in two ways, one theoretical and one more practical. First, his very attempt to create a grand theory of constitutional moments—even if it shades into pragmatism—misleads him (and his readers) insofar as it implicitly asserts that theory can solve every constitutional conundrum. In other words, faith in foundationalism, in Ackerman no less than in our other scholars, blinds him to the messy realities of constitutional law and history.

More practically, Ackerman's theory of dualist democracy fosters such an attachment to instant popular control over the Constitution that it leads him to suggest radical constitutional amendments of his own. It also leads him to ignore other important aspects of constitutional interpretation, such as the text itself—indeed, as we have seen, part of Ackerman's Constitution is not textual at all.

He makes two proposals. First, to prevent transformative judicial appointments not backed by a mandate from We the People, confirmation of Supreme Court justices should require a two-thirds majority in the Senate.[77] This constitutional amendment is transparently designed to make it more difficult to undo the New Deal or the Warren Court, or to promote constitutional revolutions in new directions. But Ackerman overlooks the fact that this strategy might well backfire. Vesting the Senate alone with power to confirm judicial appointments already gives disproportionate power to sparsely populated—and generally conservative—states.[78] (We discuss this problem further in chapter 8.) A supermajority requirement would exacerbate this problem, and allow an even smaller percentage of the national population to veto changes supported by the rest of the nation. Since Ackerman appears to applaud the move toward nationalism that he labels the "leitmotiv" of his trio of constitutional moments,[79] he might not be pleased with the results of his suggested revision.

His second proposal is even more radical. He would add to Article V another method for amending the Constitution: a second-term president may propose a constitutional amendment "in the name of the American people," which, after approval by Congress, is put on the ballot at the next two presidential elections. If the people approve, the Constitution is successfully amended.[80]

The proposal's derivation in Ackerman's theory of dualist democracy is obvious. He contends that reelection of a president "is sometimes, [although] not invariably, accompanied by plausible claims that the People are up to something." Thus the reelection of the president and his constitutional proposal serve the signaling and proposing functions of Ackerman's five-stage process. And the fact that not every president will have the referendum-forcing power ensures that referenda are triggered "at constitutional moments and not at other times."[81] The popular referendum itself—because it takes place only in the context of a constitutional moment—guarantees the consent of a mobilized People before any constitutional changes are wrought. Thus are the weaknesses of the referendum process neutralized, according to Ackerman.

And weaknesses there are. Many have catalogued the states' questionable experience with popular referenda and with the political manipulation that invariably accompanies the appeal to the voters. As one scholar points out:

> In many cases, direct democracy has been used in a variety of ways that appeal to the worst of majorities: anti-gay-rights initiatives; anti-immigrant initiatives; English-only amendments; and, in the not-too-distant past, initiatives to prevent busing and the enactment of housing discrimination laws. While many of these provisions were either struck down by the Supreme Court or are being challenged there, the events leading up to their enactment were often marked by angry, divisive debates.[82]

Or as another scholar notes: "popular masses too quickly form preferences, fail adequately to consider the interests of others, and are overly susceptible to contagious passions and the deceit of eloquent and ambitious leaders."[83] And direct democracy only exacerbates the problems of judicial interpretation that drove Ackerman to propose constitutional dualism in the first place.[84]

It is especially surprising to find liberals supporting this type of direct democracy. Perhaps, like Amar, Ackerman has been too long steeped in the rarified atmosphere of the Yale Law School and too little exposed to what We the People have really been up to. Or maybe he is more savvy than he lets on, and that is why his dualism theory ends up depending on elites more than on ordinary Americans. But if he expects members of the elite—including law professors—to be able to exert a similar influence on the referendum process, he should take a closer look at what happened in California during the raucous battle over ending affirmative action. Predictably, most of the educated elite—including most law professors—opposed Proposition 209. Equally predictably, the People didn't listen.

If Ackerman's dualism is in part an instrument of his political agenda, the scholar we examine in the next chapter is even more transparent. Like Richard Epstein—but with a different substantive agenda—Ronald Dworkin seeks to base a grand constitutional interpretation on a foundational moral theory. Unfortunately, he is no more successful than the others.

CHAPTER 7

RONALD DWORKIN AND THE
CITY ON THE HILL

Ronald Dworkin is widely considered the most important American legal philosopher of recent times.[1] He first received wide attention for his analysis of legal reasoning in hard cases. Rejecting the view that judges must resort to nonlegal sources when no clear rule applies, he argued that the law itself provides the resources for filling gaps between rules. Imagining an ideal judge named Hercules, Dworkin explained how Hercules could derive broad principles by constructing a coherent vision of the legal system as a whole (an admittedly Herculean task).[2] In recent years, Dworkin has focused more intently on constitutional law. Although he has retained his interest in the interplay between law and moral principles, his theories have evolved in ways that are not always easy to pin down.[3] Our focus is primarily on the most fully developed version of his views, as presented in his recent book on constitutional interpretation, *Freedom's Law.*[4]

Conventional legal scholars are sometimes dismissive of Dworkin's constitutional views. Dworkin's conclusions track the agenda of liberal judges like William Brennan, opening Dworkin to the charge of being merely a clever rationalizer. (Of course, as we have seen throughout this book, this charge could with equal justice be applied to other constitutional theorists.) Moreover, he tends to resort to sweeping ethical precepts at the expense of close readings of legal texts, making him sound at times more like a moralist than a lawyer.

We are not unsympathetic to this dismissive response. But as with some of the other scholars discussed in this book, we found that as we examined Dworkin's views in greater depth, they proved unexpectedly nuanced and illuminating. This does not mean that we embrace his theory. But we do think his project can be understood in a way that constitutional lawyers should find appealing. At the same time, it also aptly illustrates the inevitable failings of grand theory. Moral value judgments are an essential judicial seasoning, but to make them the basis of jurisprudence is like making latkes using only onions.

Dworkin attacks originalism for confusing the framers' expectations with their intended meaning, and populism for misunderstanding the normative basis of democracy. Having disposed of these competing theories, he is then left with the task of constructing his own. We begin with his views about the nature of constitutionalism and then focus more specifically on how judges should decide constitutional issues.

DWORKIN AND THE SPIRIT OF LIBERTY

To understand a system of thought, it is often useful to begin not with the answers but with the problem: we understand Dworkin's contortions only when we find out what itch he is attempting to scratch. Much of his writing is obviously motivated either by technical problems of jurisprudence or by current political or legal controversies (notably, the Bork nomination). But much of it can also be read as part of an extended attack on the problem posed by Judge Learned Hand in writings such as *The Spirit of Liberty*.[5] That problem can be simply stated: in a world of moral uncertainty, how can judges justify overturning democratic decisions in the name of constitutional principle? As we have seen, resolving this problem is also at the heart of other current theories. In this section, we consider Hand's view and then examine Dworkin's objections to two common responses to that view, originalism and populism. The next section explores Dworkin's own approach to the problem.

LEARNED HAND'S CHALLENGE TO CONSTITUTIONALISM

Learned Hand is such a perfect name for a judge that it seems almost too pat that it should belong to one of the great judges of the past century.[6] Yet Hand was also a man of great, sometimes almost crippling humility, doubtful of his own ability and judgment.[7] Indeed, his judicial greatness may not be unrelated to his self-doubt and his struggles to reach closure on issues despite that doubt. Hand was particularly skeptical of the possibility of achieving moral certainty. Since we are primarily interested in Dworkin's understanding of Hand rather than in Hand himself, it is worth quoting Dworkin's appraisal:

Hand's skepticism consisted not in the philosophical view that no moral conviction can be objectively true, but in a disabling uncertainty that he—or anyone else—could discover which convictions were true: he thought moral matters were much too subtle and complex to allow anyone much confidence in his own opinions. He often said that he despised "absolutes." He meant, by that ambiguous phrase, that he distrusted any attempt to resolve the untidy complexity of a moral or legal or political issue in a neat and simple formula. . . . [H]e had come to the remarkable view that the spirit of liberty is essentially the spirit "that is not too sure that it is right," and . . . he recommended, as a "combination of tolerance and imagination that to me is the epitome of all good government," Benjamin Franklin's plea that people should on occasion "doubt a little of [their] own infallibility."[8]

Hand thus almost obsessively doubted himself and his own views, but such doubts never seem to plague Dworkin. As anyone with even a slight familiarity with his views will recognize, a defining trait is his rejection of the moral skepticism that he attributes to Hand. As opposed to Hand, Dworkin would find his credo in the Supreme Court's proclamation that "[l]iberty finds no refuge in a jurisprudence of doubt."[9]

As Dworkin explains, Hand's resistance to judicial review was based on his vision of democratic community as well as his skepticism of absolutes. Hand "believed passionately in the virtues of what is often called civic republicanism: he thought that a political community could not flourish, or its citizens develop and improve their own sense of moral responsibility, unless they participated in the community's deepest and most important decisions about justice."[10] Famously, Hand said that he would find it irksome to be ruled by Plato's philosopher kings. Even if he knew how to pick them, he said, he would "miss the stimulus of living in a society where I have, at least theoretically, some part in the direction of public affairs."[11]

Dworkin rejects Hand's answer but thinks that Hand posed exactly the right question: why should the moral views of judges sometimes prevail over legislative views in a democracy? The "great constitutional clauses set out extremely abstract moral principles that must be interpreted before they can be applied," and it is "therefore an inescapable question whether, in the end, the interpretations of the legislatures or those of the judges will prevail." Consequently, Dworkin finds the structure of Hand's argument— "his insistence on the need for a dramatic choice between constitutional philosophies, and his emphasis on the importance of that choice for self-government"—even more crucial today than when Hand wrote. Clearly, Hand's views posed a tremendous challenge for Dworkin, one that he felt unable to avoid because he agreed with Hand that "no logical space" exists between judicial and legislative supremacy.[12]

Beginning with the dilemma posed by Hand allows a coherent and appealing presentation of Dworkin's constitutional philosophy. Of course, he was not the first to reply to this dilemma, which we have already encountered under the rubric of the "countermajoritarian difficulty." As we have seen, much of modern constitutional scholarship can be understood as an effort to overcome this difficulty. Dworkin is unusual, however, in focusing so sharply on the moral nature of the dilemma. In the next subsections, we consider some responses to Hand's concerns, responses Dworkin finds wanting. In the process of developing his own views, he offers a powerful critique of many of the foundationalist theories we have examined.

AGAINST ORIGINALISM

One escape from Hand's dilemma is to insist that judges merely follow the instructions of the framers, who were themselves representatives of the populace. Thus, when the Court strikes down a statute, it may appear that unelected judges are overriding the will of the majority, but actually the Court is merely implementing the previous decision of an even more imperative supermajority. In this picture, the basic choice of principles is determined by the framers; the courts are faithful agents rather than independent actors, humble servants rather than Platonic guardians. This is of course a familiar picture of constitutionalism, one painted in most detail by Bork, Scalia, and Amar. Dworkin has devoted a great deal of energy to debunking this picture, prompted in part by Bork's controversial nomination to the Supreme Court.

In his critique of originalism, Dworkin distinguishes between two types of meaning. When the framers prohibited "cruel and unusual punishments," they may have meant this term as shorthand for a list of punishments commonly agreed to be unacceptable, such as drawing and quartering. Alternatively, they may have meant to invoke a general concept of cruelty. The difference can be seen by considering the death penalty. It clearly was not on the framers' list of unacceptable punishments. It was widely used in their day and is referred to elsewhere in the Constitution, including the Fourteenth Amendment (which requires due process for deprivations of life). But we might think today that the death penalty really is cruel. Given a conflict between the framers' specific applications of the term "cruelty" and the current understanding of the concept to which it refers, judges today must make a choice. This choice is not itself dictated by the intention of the framers.[13]

We believe that Bork himself would find little to quarrel with in this analysis of legal interpretation. (Recall his explanation of *Brown*, which we discussed in chapter 2, as involving a conflict between the framers' specific expectations about segregated schools and their more general mandate for racial equality.) Indeed, in some broad sense, Dworkin himself now seems to be an originalist. His recent work seems to accept that the meaning of a constitutional provision is fixed by the concept intended by the framers.[14] Why, then, is he so adamantly opposed to what he considers "originalism"?

The essence of the originalist program is to free judges from making controversial moral judgments by casting the choice of principles back to the framers. But Dworkin suggests that this program rests on confusion between the two types of meaning, so that the relative determinacy of the framers' specific examples lends a spurious air of certainty to the enterprise.[15] At least with respect to the most sweeping clauses of the Constitution, such as due process and equal protection, Dworkin does not believe that judges can avoid difficult moral judgments. Judges will have to pick an appropriate level of abstraction somewhere above the specific examples in the minds of the framers.[16]

For instance, the framers had a sweeping concept of equality, and according to Dworkin, we must be similarly broad today. If equal protection means anything more than evenhanded law enforcement, Dworkin maintains, the only alternative is a "principle of quite breathtaking scope and power: the principle that government must treat everyone as of equal status and with equal concern." (We later consider the substance of Dworkin's interpretation of equal protection.) Applying a principle of that breadth inevitably will require deeply controversial moral judgments by the Court. Originalism, Dworkin concludes, offers no escape from Hand's concern about the conflict between democracy and judicial review. A faithful effort to implement originalism will inevitably involve judges in controversial moral judgments about how to apply broad moral principles.[17]

Whether or not we buy the specifics of Dworkin's argument, it is hard to quarrel with his conclusion about originalism. Consideration of original intent simply does not eliminate the role played by the political and moral commitments of the interpreter. If we want proof, we need look no farther than the fact that Dworkin himself, Scalia, Bork, Epstein, Amar, and Ackerman all claim to base their constitutional interpretations on original intent.

Original intent, it would seem, is a launching point for many different journeys, not a travel itinerary.

AGAINST POPULISM

We have already seen how the countermajoritarian difficulty has shaped the thinking of constitutional scholars, some of whom respond with originalist arguments. Another response is populism. The simplest populist response is Hand's: jettison judicial review in favor of pure majority rule. Amar and Ackerman can be seen as providing more sophisticated populist responses. Amar argues that the Constitution can be changed by a nationwide referendum. If so, then judicial rulings are only provisional, a stopgap until the popular will on a subject can be directly expressed. (In this respect, Amar is really not so far from Hand.) Amar also wants to read the Constitution, to the greatest degree possible, as an endorsement of popular sovereignty rather than of individual rights. Ackerman's theory of constitutional change does not contemplate such frequent recourse to the popular will. Still, for Ackerman, the legitimacy of constitutional rulings such as the New Deal revolution ultimately rests on popular ratification. (For Ackerman, between constitutional moments there is no true popular will for the courts to frustrate, only the uninspiring operation of pluralism.) Thus, in their different ways, Amar and Ackerman try to reposition We the People as the authors of constitutional doctrine, rather than as victims of judicial review.

So far as we are aware, Dworkin has not commented directly on these neopopulist efforts. It is plain, however, that from his perspective they are profoundly misguided. Populists assume that democratic legitimacy rests on a purely majoritarian foundation—that is, that what genuinely makes a law binding is simply that it reflects some sufficiently focused expression of majority preferences. It is just this conception of democratic legitimacy that Dworkin rejects.

His critique of populism is based on a distinction between two kinds of collective action. (Note that this is a familiar argumentative move for Dworkin: a concept turns out to be available in two and only two varieties, and his opponents are stuck with the unacceptable one.) One form of collective action is statistical, in which the individual actions add up to a collective outcome but with no sense of acting *as* a group." Dworkin's example is the foreign currency market, in which the actions of individual traders result in shifts of exchange rates, but the traders have no sense of acting as a unified collectivity.[18]

The other form of collective action involves a sense of commitment to the group and joint responsibility for group decisions. A family decision might fit this mold. (We later consider what Dworkin means by this "communal" form of collective action, and how it relates to constitutionalism).

The crux of Dworkin's argument is that, when collective action is merely statistical, it has no moral standing. In making this claim, Dworkin considers several potential moral costs of overriding collective action. He finds that all the moral arguments for deferring to group decisions rest ultimately on the communal rather than the statistical vision of group action. Dworkin's arguments may be more understandable if we think of them as aimed at "government by public opinion poll." Populists believe that overriding the majority violates a form of liberty, the collective freedom of the people to rule themselves. (Here again, Dworkin refers to Hand's objection to being ruled by Platonic guardians.) But Dworkin says that we cannot consider an action of the government to be our own, and therefore a matter of *self*-rule, simply because we were allowed to vote on the subject. Even if the Jews had been allowed to vote against Nazi policies, they would have no reason to accept any responsibility for those policies or to view themselves as part of the community making those policies. To bring the "self" into self-rule, something more must be present than head counting. That missing ingredient, Dworkin maintains, is mutual respect.[19]

To understand this argument against the statistical view of collective action, recall the example of currency traders. Suppose the traders decide the dollar is going to decline and accordingly begin to move to other currencies. The Federal Reserve then steps in to support the dollar. (This may be either unwise or ultimately ineffectual, of course, but assume that it at least works temporarily.) Thus, although the traders "voted with their wallets" for a lower dollar, the dollar stays high because of a government response. It would be very odd to regard this as an infringement of the liberty of the traders to set currency levels. If anything, it would seem even more odd to view the government's intervention as a violation of their equality rights simply because a few people at the Fed had more impact on the dollar than the vast majority of traders.[20] The Fed has a kind of legitimacy, as an organ of democratic government, that does not attach to the statistical outcome of economic decisions by the populace. Thus merely statistical collective action does not involve either self-government or equality in any meaningful sense.[21]

Dworkin would insist that populists are wrong to claim that the Constitution's moral standing arises solely from popular consent. Suppose that We the People decided through the appropriate mechanism—Article V ratification, national referendum, transformative judicial decisions, or whatever—to disenfranchise a minority group We dislike. For Amar and Ackerman, such an amendment should be as much entitled to respect as any other part of the Constitution. But Dworkin would view the amendment as morally suspect. Rather than being an expression of the will of the democratic community, it would mark a tragic wound to that community. Again, for Ackerman and Amar, democracy would require enthusiastic enforcement of the amendment.[22] Not so for Dworkin. Indeed, if respectable legal arguments could be constructed for invalidating the amendment, he would applaud the ruling. For Dworkin, such a ruling could not be criticized as antidemocratic. Rather than acting as Platonic guardians, he would say, the judges would be vindicating self-rule by maintaining the integrity of the democratic community.[23]

We have dwelled on this argument at some length because we think that Dworkin has a valid point. As much as our society values self-rule, most people do not support the Constitution *purely* because it has a clear stamp of popular approval. Of course, popular adoption is important to our attitude toward the Constitution; we might feel differently if exactly the same legal text had been imposed by a conqueror after a war.[24] But we also believe in the Constitution in part because we think it *deserves* our support. To the extent this is true, we must have some norm beyond pure majoritarianism in mind.

THE "MORAL READING" OF THE CONSTITUTION

Dworkin provides a penetrating critique of efforts to banish the moral dimension from constitutional law through originalism or populism. But to answer Hand's challenge, he must do more than that. He must show how judges can appropriately exercise moral judgment without undermining democracy or the rule of law. Dworkin's vision of this judicial role is based on his "moral reading" of the Constitution, a reading that seeks to find (*contra* Hand) broad moral principles in the constitutional text, which judges must develop with as much integrity as possible. Dworkin insists that the moral reading is consistent with democracy even when it limits majority rule, and is also consonant with the nature of the judicial role.

INDIVIDUAL RIGHTS AND DEMOCRATIC LEGITIMACY

The major concern is that a moral reading of the Constitution by judges is antidemocratic. Dworkin thinks this fear is exaggerated because in many cases precedent and tradition will operate as an anchor, constraining decision. But "[v]ery different, even contrary, conceptions of a constitutional principle—of what treating men and women as equals really means, for example—will often fit language, precedent, and practice well enough to pass these tests, and thoughtful judges must then decide on their own which conception does most credit to the nation." The "constitutional sail is a broad one, and many people do fear that it is too big for a democratic boat."[25]

Dworkin thinks this fear is unfounded because the moral reading of the Constitution reinforces rather than undermines democracy. The argument turns on his concept of democracy. Recall that in criticizing the statistical interpretation of collective action, he contrasted it to the communal interpretation. Under the communal interpretation, action is truly collective only when individuals have reason to identify the action of the collectivity with themselves.[26] Dworkin identifies several conditions under which a collectivity can deserve this kind of individual support even when individuals disagree with a particular action of the group. First, he suggests, the group must have sufficient coherence, in terms of history and culture, to count as more than a random agglomeration of individuals. Second, every individual must have an equal right to participate in group decisions, not only through voting and officeholding but also through speech.[27] Third, the group must show some degree of respect for all of its members. As Dworkin says, "[m]oral membership involves reciprocity: a person is not a member unless he is treated as a member by others, which means that they treat the consequences of any collective decision for his life as equally significant a reason for or against that decision as are comparable consequences for the life of anyone else."[28]

The final and most subtle condition is what Dworkin calls "moral independence." In his view, the idea that self-government exemplifies a form of liberty assumes that "members of a political community can appropriately regard themselves as partners in a joint venture, like members of a football team or orchestra in whose work and fate all share, even when that venture is conducted in ways they do not endorse." But this idea is "nonsense unless it can be accepted by people with self-respect," and such people would never be willing to turn over to a collectivity control over the most fundamental issues regarding the meaning of their lives. For example, no one with any self-respect would turn over to a majority vote of strangers the power to control his sex life or his religious views.[29]

To understand what Dworkin is trying to do here, it may be useful to recall Epstein's view of legitimate government. Epstein takes as a baseline the rights that people have against other private individuals. He then asks why these other individuals should gain extra rights against us simply because they outnumber us.[30] He concludes we should be willing to cede power to these individuals collectively (in the form of government) only when doing so will make us better off than we were under the common law baseline. This leads him to the proposition that government is legitimate only when it creates public goods and distributes them to everyone alike. Dworkin would respond that Epstein goes wrong in viewing the government as an embodiment only of *other* individuals but not of ourselves. Under the right circumstances, Dworkin would argue, the government is *us;* we are merely exercising our own power as part of a collectivity rather than individually. If Dworkin is correct that under the right circumstances we should identify ourselves as the source even of laws that disadvantage us, then Epstein's argument against redistribution breaks down.[31]

In responding to the kind of view represented by Epstein, Dworkin integrates many of the normatively important dimensions of democratic society. We suspect that many people in modern Western societies would find this an appealing portrait of the essentials of liberal democracy. By asking when free individuals could legitimately be asked to commit themselves to group decisions, Dworkin provides a neat way of tying together the ideas of self-rule, democratic community, and individual rights. We agree that strengthening these conditions sometimes reinforces rather than undermines true self-rule, even when the impetus comes from outside. Thus, when the federal government forced Alabama to give blacks effective voting rights and to modify its libel laws so as to protect critics of state government, the effect was to strengthen self-rule and democracy in Alabama. (It is probably for this reason that the Supreme Court has not viewed the drastic incursions on state lawmaking accompanying the Voting Rights Act as a serious threat to local self-rule.) We might also think, although perhaps with less confidence, that a state with an established church was in some sense less democratic as well as less free.

This is all well and good. And when the Constitution contains relatively clear protections for these democratic conditions, Dworkin provides a good case for why judicial enforcement is not undemocratic. But when more controversial judgments must be made about the scope of the democratic conditions, it is not at all clear that such judgments should be made by courts. Indeed, Dworkin admits that a democracy might well assign the job of protecting the democratic conditions to some other agency. The moral reading arguably tells us how the broad clauses of the Constitution should be read, namely, as reinforcing democracy in Dworkin's sense of the term. But the moral reading does not tell us who should be the reader.[32] To answer that question, Dworkin must provide an explanation of how the moral reading fits with the conventional role of judges in our society.

MORAL REASONING AND THE RULE OF LAW

Dworkin offers a three-pronged defense of assigning the moral reading to judges. The first claim is based on convention. Dworkin argues that key portions of the Constitution, such as the Equal Protection Clause, require fundamental moral judgments. The task of interpreting these provisions has conventionally been assigned to judges. Thus, in asking judges to undertake the moral reading, Dworkin claims to be doing no more than making explicit what has previously been an implicit part of their role:

> [A]uthority is already distributed by history, and details of institutional responsibility are matters of interpretation, not of invention from nothing. . . . If the most straightforward interpretation of American constitutional practice shows that our judges have final interpretative authority, and that they largely understand the Bill of Rights as a constitution of principle—if that best explains the decisions judges actually make and the public largely accepts—we have no reason to resist that reading and to strain for one that seems more congenial to a majoritarian philosophy.[33]

The weak point in this argument is the assertion that these clauses and the Court's past practice actually do embody sweeping moral principles of the kind Dworkin favors.[34] We return to his argument on this point when considering his views of substantive constitutional issues.

Dworkin's second argument for allowing judges to read the Constitution morally is also in some sense based on convention. He has long argued that, at least in our society, judicial decisions generally have a moral dimension, requiring judges to apply broad principles in order to resolve hard cases where more specific rules give out. Putting judges in charge of the moral reading of the Constitution thus does not differ in kind, according to Dworkin, from the kind of work they do every day in resolving difficult legal issues. This is a controversial thesis. Judge Posner, for one, does not believe that moral reasoning plays any significant role in judicial decisions, although he admits that judges do make intuitive value judgments.[35] But to the extent that we already do expect judges to engage in moral reasoning on a regular basis, our comfort level with the moral reading ought to be improved.

Finally, Dworkin seems to connect these two claims with a third claim about the integrity of the legal system. His general jurisprudential theory requires judges to adopt interpretations that give the legal system as much integrity as possible. Roughly speaking, he views integrity as an obligation to provide the best possible story connecting past legal decisions (including both court rulings and political actions such as the adoption of constitutional provisions). The best story has to be coherent and faithful to history, but there may well be more than one internally consistent story that provides a good fit with authoritative past decisions. When this is true, the judge must pick the story that makes the legal system the best it can be, the most deserving of our respect and allegiance.[36] Dworkin clearly thinks that the best story we can tell about the Constitution portrays the Bill of Rights as a manifesto of high moral principle rather than a limited set of eighteenth-century precepts.

If the judges are the ones to make the most fundamental moral decisions about our society, what happens to the idea of self-rule? Hand would hardly be comforted by the thought of Platonic guardians who limited their role to upholding the concept of democratic community, as understood solely by them rather than by the community itself. Dworkin's answer is that the judges do not have the final word, because judicial decisions often spark widespread public debate, which in turns spills over into disputes about the appointment of new judges.[37] In the end, the judge's answers are only provisional.

This is in some respects a "heartening vision of our Constitution and the culture it is meant to sustain."[38] At some high level of generality, we suspect that many of Dworkin's critics would endorse elements of his ideas about constitutionalism and democratic community. The key question, however, is whether the vision can be brought sufficiently down to earth to be usable for deciding important constitutional disputes.

DOES IT WORK?

At one point in his essay on Learned Hand, Dworkin wonders whether Hand might be persuaded by his arguments.[39] We imagine that, after complimenting his former law clerk on his brilliance and his well-deserved professional eminence, Hand might reply that Dworkin offers little more than an argument for Platonic guardians—providing only that some constitu-

tional provision gives these guardians a textual toehold for their moral leg-
islating, that they are appointed by some group of elected officials to their
lifetime posts, and that they have been in the business for a long time. Besides finding these insufficient grounds for accepting rule by a moral elite,
Hand would also probably find it incongruous that a group of aging lawyers
would be assigned this task. If Dworkin can show that in performing this
task, judges look more like lawyers than they do like lay ministers, moral
philosophers, or legislators, Hand might say that Dworkin had a real argument. Unless Dworkinian decisions can be firmly grounded in specific legal
sources—such as a constitutional text or its legislative history, or precedent—judges seemingly have no more claim to be making those decisions
than the average person on the street. If, for example, it turns out that the
Democratic judicial appointees always vote one way and the Republicans
another, we might as well leave control over constitutional issues in the
hands of the Senate.[40]

As Michael McConnell points out, Dworkin seems equivocal about how
much judges are restrained by their need to remain faithful to governing legal sources.[41] But to answer Hand, Dworkin need not claim that constitutional decisions are completely determinate or wholly independent of the
judge's individual values. What he does have to show, however, is that the
Dworkinian judge would be doing something recognizable in our legal culture as "judging." Examining Dworkin's treatment of concrete constitutional issues suggests, on the contrary, that in practice the Dworkinian judge
is not very different from a Platonic guardian after all.

RACE AND EQUAL PROTECTION

Brown v. Board of Education[42] is perhaps the central case in today's constitutional canon, and it is not surprising that Dworkin returns to it repeatedly.
As we discussed in connection with Bork, the weight of the evidence suggests that the framers of the Fourteenth Amendment accepted school segregation.[43] This presents a serious problem for originalists. For Dworkin,
however, the framers' expectations about how the amendment would apply
to segregation are not relevant; what matters is the core concept of equality
that they endorsed.[44]

Identifying the framers' concept of equality is not straightforward.
Dworkin has suggested several possibilities, each of which would be sufficient to support *Brown:*

1. *Black equality.* Under this theory, equal protection requires only that
   blacks be treated as equal citizens. This interpretation supports *Brown* if

racial separation was a form of inequality and was sufficiently related to blacks' status as citizens.[45] On this interpretation, the clause provides no protection to other groups.

2. *Invidious motivation.* This theory holds that certain kinds of preferences (those rooted in prejudice against particular groups) cannot be counted in making societal decisions. Segregated schools were based on just that kind of prejudice, and therefore are unconstitutional.[46] This concept would extend the Equal Protection Clause to other historically disadvantaged groups as well.[47] On the other hand, it would not prohibit benignly motivated race discrimination—even against blacks.

3. *Banned categories.* This is the familiar theory of colorblindness: laws cannot classify citizens on the basis of race.[48] It is unclear whether any other classifications (such as gender) are also banned.

4. *Equal citizenship.* On this theory, the Equal Protection Clause requires "for all Americans what equal citizenship, properly understood, demands."[49] Southern segregation obviously violated this principle of equality. This concept is essentially the same as number 1 but broadened to include other groups.

How is a judge to choose between these possible conceptions? As critics point out, Dworkin seems to take two quite different tacks in answering this question. He sometimes stresses the constraints that face judges: the Constitution's language and structure; its historical context; and precedent.[50] But he sometimes describes the judge's task as picking the right moral theory. For instance, regarding the First Amendment, he says that judges "must decide whether the true ground of the moral principle that condemns censorship, in the form in which this principle has been incorporated into American law, extends to the case of pornography."[51]

Brown does not require Dworkin to choose among the conceptions of equal protection, since all four support the result in that case. But affirmative action presents a more difficult problem. In *Freedom's Law,* he explains his view on affirmative action:

> Of course racial classifications are inherently dangerous, and must be carefully scrutinized, because they may reflect prejudice or naked favoritism by people in control. But it seems perverse to insist that racial classifications are wrong not just in those circumstances, but inherently, when the effect of that special severity toward racial classification is to perpetuate structural discrimination, that is, the situation in which individuals' fates are so largely governed by their race that our society remains divided on collectivist racial lines.[52]

Apart from its reliance on controversial empirical assumptions about the role of race in contemporary society, this brief passage is notable for its apparent acceptance of the invidious motivation theory (number 2 in the list above). But the reasons for rejecting the colorblindness theory (theory 3) are not explained in this passage. The reference to structural discrimination seems to invoke some notion of *de facto* social equality, which would presumably involve theory 4. A stronger hint of theory 4 is provided by Dworkin's criticism of recent Supreme Court decisions for "denying that structural discrimination is inconsistent with the Constitution's vision of an acceptable society."[53]

An earlier discussion of *Bakke* contains a fuller explanation of Dworkin's rejection of colorblindness. The fact that the framers were particularly concerned about racial issues, Dworkin says, provides no justification for a colorblind approach. This fact relates to their expectations rather than the meaning of their words, and in any event they did not embrace full-scale colorblindness. Dworkin considers two other possible justifications for colorblindness. One is a moral principle: "people must never be treated differently in virtue of properties beyond their control." But this principle, he says, has been rejected decisively in American law and politics: "Statutes almost invariably draw lines along natural differences of geography and health and ability." The other possible reason is the pragmatic one that "admissions or hiring programs that use racial classifications in any way will exacerbate racial tension and so prolong discrimination, hatred, and violence." But this, he says, "is exactly the kind of complex, forward-looking calculation of policy" that must be left to elected officials. Having rejected colorblindness, he sees only one plausible argument against quotas, which is that they completely ignore the welfare of some citizens, like Allan Bakke, in the calculation of what makes the community as a whole better off. Although Dworkin rejects this view of quotas, he recognizes that a reasonable judge might think otherwise.[54] Other forms of affirmative action he seems to find unproblematic.

Although they certainly would not find universal acceptance, there is nothing wrong with these arguments, which follow more or less the standard liberal line on affirmative action. Dworkin is strikingly dismissive of the arguments on the other side. Such arguments against affirmative action might take a number of forms: stressing the language of colorblindness in pre-affirmative action cases such as *Loving v. Virginia*,[55] contesting Dworkin's empirical assumptions about societal discrimination,[56] providing additional arguments about why racial categories are different than other classifications,[57] arguing that the kinds of distinctions that Dworkin tries to draw are unworkable in practice, or attempting a detailed historical examination of the framers' concept of equality. His treatment of the subject is always that of an advocate presenting a brief for a preordained position.[58] Certainly, there is little here to dispel Hand's concern about distinguishing legal from political judgments: Dworkin's views are clearly agenda-driven rather than grounded in constitutional history, text, or precedent.

PRIVACY AND SUBSTANTIVE DUE PROCESS

If *Brown* is the great point of consensus in modern constitutional law, *Roe v. Wade* is the great dividing point. Dworkin devotes considerable attention to *Roe* and related issues involving the right to privacy.[59] He more or less takes for granted that procreative freedom ought to be considered a constitutionally protected right. For present purposes, we, like him, take this to be settled by *Griswold*.[60] But this leaves the toughest question in *Roe*: how to assess the state's interest in protecting the fetus.

Dworkin contends that the state has no inherent interest in protecting the fetus itself, at least before viability, but that it does have an interest in recognizing the moral gravity of the abortion decision. As to the fetus itself, Dworkin begins with the relatively uncontroversial point that the fetus is not itself a legal "person" with rights of its own under the Constitution. Before viability, at least, he thinks it plain that the fetus is also incapable of possessing moral interests of its own, having no consciousness or ability to feel pleasure or pain. The further question of whether the fetus has the moral status of a human being, Dworkin suggests, rests on unprovable, quasi-religious views about the meaning of life. Thus the fundamental issue about abortion is "whether a state can impose a canonical interpretation of the inherent value of life on everyone." In a liberal society, Dworkin contends, the state lacks the power to settle such profound moral questions by fiat, although it does have the power to ensure that women deciding about abortions are aware of the moral seriousness of their decisions.[61]

We have considerable sympathy with this view as a moral argument, and suspect that it well captures the somewhat ambivalent attitude of many Americans toward abortion.[62] But it is an argument that touches base with "the law" in only the most fleeting way. The Constitution itself appears in this argument only as a sort of exemplar of liberal democracy. Nor is there much attention to the Court's other privacy cases and how they might bear on *Roe*, or of the possible relevance of the Court's rulings on gender discrimination. Nor does Dworkin pay any attention to the kinds of conceptions of privacy that might have influenced the framers, apart from mentioning that their specific views about abortion are irrelevant. If he wants to convince us that Justice Dworkin would be in any respect different from Philosopher Dworkin—that what he advocates is not merely the reign of philosopher kings—his discussion of *Roe* fails to support him.[63]

Moving beyond *Roe*, Dworkin makes a similar argument about assisted suicide. Just as abortion involves fundamental personal values about the meaning and value of life, so does the decision to end a hopeless existence.[64] (It is by no means clear that the two situations are morally equivalent, though Dworkin sees little distinction.)[65] Again, Dworkin's discussion reads more like an article in a philosophy journal than like a legal brief.

The fundamental question about Dworkin's approach is raised by the Supreme Court's final observation in the assisted suicide case: "Throughout the Nation, Americans are engaged in an earnest and profound debate about the morality, legality, and practicality of physician-assisted suicide. Our holding permits this debate to continue, as it should in a democratic society."[66] The Court viewed the moral debate about assisted suicide as properly the business of legislators and voters, not judges. For Dworkin, this argument is virtually nonsense. As he sees it, the contrary logic is irrefutable: (1) the Constitution is a charter of democratic liberalism, (2) the Supreme Court is in charge of deciding constitutional issues, (3) banning assisted suicide violates democratic liberalism, rightly understood, ergo (4) the Supreme Court must recognize the right to assisted suicide.

The Dworkinian syllogism misunderstands the role of the courts in our system of governance. It is true that our society largely assigns the final decision on issues of constitutional law to the courts. But this assignment of power is acceptable in part because our legal culture defines constitutional law more narrowly than Dworkin, so as not to fully encompass the task of defining liberal democracy. The fundamental nature of liberal democracy is an issue for the polity as a whole, not just the courts. If, like Dworkin, we wish to define constitutional law more sweepingly than the conventional practice, we must recognize that the task of defining constitutional rights in this broader sense has *not* been wholly left to the courts. For instance, Congress has played a major role in defining the meaning of racial discrimination in many settings. Dworkin has no general theory about how the power to decide constitutional issues should be allocated, and so he cannot reject the established practice of leaving some issues, which he considers constitutional in nature, at least in part to other branches of government.

If we take constitutionalism in its broadest sense, as the development of a basic framework for protecting liberty, we must recognize that this task has not been left purely in the hands of the courts. It is Dworkin's effort to pre-empt this task on behalf of the justices that leaves him most open to Hand's gibe about rule by Platonic guardians.

Hand would also, we suspect, have been disturbed by another feature of Dworkin's thought, upon which others have remarked.[67] Dworkin is re-markably confident that difficult moral dilemmas have clear-cut answers, so that those who fail to accept his argument must be wrongheaded or perhaps a bit dense. He is not alone in this unqualified intellectual confidence. Each of the scholars on whom we focus in this book believes that he, and he alone, has uncovered the key to understanding the Constitution. Whatever else may be wrong with their theories, none can be accused of a lack of self-esteem.

For ourselves, we prefer Hand's admonition that the spirit of liberty is that spirit that is none too sure it is right. As we noted earlier, the Supreme Court has recently reminded us that "[l]iberty finds no refuge in a jurispru-dence of doubt."[68] True enough, and Dworkin is right to think Hand would have done well to remember this. But another observation must also be made: democracy finds no refuge in a jurisprudence of certainty. Between the two must be found our salvation.

CHAPTER 8

DETHRONING GRAND THEORY

Despite some differences, the six constitutional theorists we have discussed share a deep similarity. They seek a universal method of interpretation that will serve as a recipe for judges faced with any constitutional issue. All of them see such a theory as vital to the proper functioning of the constitutional system. Conventional scholars seek theories about particular aspects of constitutional law, such as free speech or separation of powers. What sets these six scholars apart is their search for a master theory to govern constitutional practice.[1] Each theory claims to be global (covering all of constitutional law), normative (justifying judicial review), and prescriptive (providing a recipe for judges). Each scholar also conveys an unmistakable sense of certainty that his own theory—and his own particular application of that theory—is the one correct method of constitutional interpretation.

The effort to find a single overarching theory is relatively new in constitutional law, at least in the modern era.[2] This search for foundations derives its plausibility from a nagging concern about the legitimacy of judicial review—a worry that constitutional law may, as Judge Hand feared, be merely a screen for judicial value judgments. By identifying a foundational theory, scholars seemingly hope to make judicial decisions more objective and to defuse the charge that constitutional law lacks legitimacy in a democracy. In short, they seek to constrain judicial discretion by specifying with particularity the rules that judges must follow.

We believe that this project is both fundamentally misguided and doomed to failure. Its appeal derives in large part from a sense of innate conflict between democracy and judicial review. Some grand theorists eliminate the conflict by elevating a populist concept of democracy, making constitu-

140

tional rights merely a remnant of some past mandate from We the People. In contrast, others elevate the concept of rights while eclipsing the idea of majority rule. We argue, however, that this was a falsely posed dilemma from the start: despite some unavoidable tension between them, both majority rule and individual rights are central to true democracy. (In this respect, we agree with Dworkin, though not in his effort to make judges into moral philosophers.) Placing one in the background and spotlighting the other leaves only a caricature of our constitutional system, which accounts for the startlingly distorted appearance of the theories we have discussed.

We suggest in this concluding chapter that American government does not correspond to any neat version of populism. Though majority rule is obviously a key feature, it is qualified by the heavily gerrymandered Senate, by the power of bureaucratic institutions such as the Federal Reserve, as well as by the role of the courts. The key question is not whether any single feature of the system is or is not "majoritarian," but whether the system as a whole fits our concept of democracy. So far, judicial review has served well enough. And not only is it an unquestioned aspect of our system, but it has been emulated by most other democracies.

Apart from their overblown anxiety about democratic legitimacy, grand theorists also believe that the rule of law will suffer if judges lack sure theoretical guidance. But this fear is no better grounded than the concerns about majoritarianism. On the contrary, the alternative to grand theory—the common law method that builds principles up from individual cases rather than down from abstract theories—has served the rule of law reasonably well. Grand theory would be no improvement. In practice, grand theory would be unlikely to bring greater order to legal doctrine, and collective deliberation over constitutional issues would be disrupted by the cacophony of conflicting theories.

We close with an assessment of the vices and virtues of grand theory. As a normative program, grand theory is worse than useless. It cannot effectively constrain judges, and it distorts our constitutional landscape by focusing attention on overly narrow conceptions of constitutional interpretation. On the other hand, as a daring attempt to find broad patterns in constitutional law, it has the potential to provide novel (if partial) perspectives. Examples here include Amar's insight into the partially communitarian basis of the Bill of Rights, and the revival of interest in constitutional history sparked by originalists like Bork and Scalia. Thus we would not rule grand theory completely out of the future of constitutional scholarship even if we had the power to do so. But we think the most fruitful lines of scholarly inquiry lie elsewhere: in doctrinal critique, empirical studies, comparative law, and historical research. Even though grand theory may provide one source of insights to scholars, it has little to offer judges and others in search of sound resolution of constitutional issues.

GRAND THEORY AND THE COUNTERMAJORITARIAN DIFFICULTY

Grand theorists are often clever, imaginative, and learned. Yet their conclusions cannot help but strike the conventional lawyer as decidedly odd. Bork and Scalia believe most of the constitutional decisions of the past sixty years were usurpations that flouted the true constitutional scheme. Epstein seems to think the Court has hardly decided a case correctly in the past century, and that most of the federal legislation on the books is unconstitutional. Amar thinks little of precedent and wants to reinterpret the original Bill of Rights as an exercise in federalism rather than individual rights. He also thinks we can amend the Constitution by referendum, an interpretation that somehow seems to have eluded anyone else for the past two centuries. Ackerman thinks that the American people unwittingly amended the Constitution when they reelected FDR over Landon. Dworkin often seems to confuse the hardworking lawyers on the Supreme Court with moral philosophers. In each instance, remarkable though the theories may be, their implications somehow turn out to fit their creators' widely varying policy preferences. And to top it all off, each claims to have the imprimatur of the framers of the Constitution.

Viewed close up, these theories are remarkably ingenious intellectual structures. But at a distance, they all seem badly misconceived. The creators of these theories are neither fools nor crackpots. So we have to ask what functions these structures were supposed to serve. In large part, we believe, the structures are peculiar because they are designed to combat an exaggerated anxiety about constitutional legitimacy. The perceived menace to the legitimacy of constitutional law is the conflict between judicial review and majority rule. In their different ways, various grand theories are meant to secure the citadel against this threat. Since the threat is exaggerated, it is not surprising that the fortresses have an eccentric appearance.

The perception of potential illegitimacy derives from a familiar puzzle about judicial review. We all believe in majority rule. In this, populists like Amar are on solid ground. When the Supreme Court declares a statute unconstitutional, it is overturning what appears to be the popular will, which seems to replace the rule of the majority with the rule of the judges. Yet

Americans also believe in judicial protection of individual rights. How are the two beliefs to be reconciled?

In protecting the legitimacy of judicial review, grand theories take two quite different tacks. Some theorists privilege majority rule and attempt to explain judicial review as derivative from popular rule. Judicial review is valid only when it faithfully enforces the popular impulse embodied in constitutional amendments. Other theorists privilege individual rights, as enforced by the judiciary. They view government actions that transgress those rights as illegitimate, even if supported by the majority. For them, there is no conflict between individual rights and majority rule, because the majority's right to rule ends when it collides with the individual's rights.

Bork, Scalia, Ackerman, and Amar are theorists of the first sort: majoritarians or populists. They view judicial review as justified only to the extent that it upholds the popular will—if not of today's majority, then at least of yesterday's supermajority. Because both the Constitution and ordinary legislation are products of the popular will, the Court must choose between them, and in doing so it must favor the superior enactment. The basis for this superiority receives more attention from some of these scholars than from others. Bork and Scalia have no particular answer to why yesterday's constitutional vote should trump today's legislation. They are seemingly content to rely on this as a given of American legal culture. Ackerman and Amar, however, provide novel arguments as to why ordinary statutes should not weigh as heavily as constitutional provisions. Ackerman views statutes as mere by-products of everyday pluralist politics, more heavily influenced by interest groups than by true public deliberation and consensus. Amar stresses the "agency" problem, arguing that legislators may be self-serving rather than faithful agents of the people. They both view constitutional provisions as representing a purer expression of popular will and therefore as entitled to greater respect. When engaging in judicial review, the Court is merely favoring the clarion call of We the People over the conversational muddle of ordinary politics.

In contrast, Epstein and Dworkin—an odd couple if ever there was one—give primacy to individual rights. Epstein views government action as legitimate only under limited circumstances. He distrusts legislatures, viewing them mostly as playgrounds for special interests. Dworkin is, in principle, friendlier toward the political process, but he views democratic legitimacy as resting on protection of individual rights. Only a legal order that protects the fundamental rights of its citizens can expect its authority to be acknowledged, even by those who lose out in the political process. Hence, for Dworkin, enforcement of individual rights can never conflict with democracy. Both Epstein and Dworkin wall off a space for individual rights and argue that legitimate legislation begins just outside that wall. As it turns out, for both of them, almost all important social issues are *inside* the wall, to be decided by courts rather than legislatures. When a court invalidates legislation that violates individual rights, they maintain, it is doing no damage to *legitimate* legislative power.

Thus, in different ways, these theorists are trying to reconcile judicial review and majority rule—and thereby responding in very different fashions to Learned Hand's fear that judicial review replaces democracy with the reign of philosopher kings. The centrality of this dilemma to constitutional theory can hardly be overstated. In 1962, Yale law professor Alexander Bickel began a quiet revolution with the publication of *The Least Dangerous Branch,* in which he reintroduced and renamed the perennial issue: how do we reconcile judicial review by unelected judges with the idea of majoritarianism? Bickel labeled this question the "countermajoritarian difficulty." He was not the first to focus on the countermajoritarianism of the Court, but his work revitalized the question for modern constitutional scholars, though his own measured response to it was unfortunately less influential.[3]

For the next three decades, legal scholars tried to resolve Bickel's paradox, but few questioned its underlying premise that our constitutional democracy is based solely on majoritarianism. Indeed, the countermajoritarian difficulty has become central enough to attract its own historian, who has carefully traced its origins and evolution as a jurisprudential preoccupation.[4] As one scholar has noted, however, the obsession with the countermajoritarian nature of judicial review did not lead legal scholars—or other Americans—to reject judicial review itself, but only to try to structure constitutional interpretation so as to constrain judicial discretion.[5]

Nowhere was the influence of the majoritarian premise more influential than at Yale itself, and perhaps it is no coincidence that three of our scholars have strong ties to Yale. Akhil Amar has spent most of his adult life there. Bruce Ackerman received his law degree from Yale and has taught there for most of the past twenty-five years, and Robert Bork held the Alexander M. Bickel Professorship there for many years before he was appointed to the bench.[6] In addition, two other eminent law professors whose scholarship has focused primarily on resolving the countermajoritarian difficulty have significant Yale connections: both Robert Burt and John Hart Ely received their law degrees from Yale; Ely taught there for five years early in his career, and Burt has taught there since 1976 and now holds the Bickel Profes-sorship. Neither Burt nor Ely makes the type of sweeping foundationalist claims that Amar, Ackerman, and Bork do. Nevertheless, it is noteworthy that two more scholars with significant Yale connections focus on the coun-termajoritarian difficulty.[7] Although scholars are beginning to question whether Bickel's countermajoritarianism is an accurate description of either judicial review or the workings of the political branches,[8] Yale still bears the imprint of Bickelian constitutionalism, now expressed in the form of des-perate searches to find just the right constraining theory.

We agree that majoritarianism is a crucial part of our constitutional regime, and thus that judges should never overturn legislation lightly or without persuasive grounds. This much of the countermajoritarian diffi-culty is real. But scholars seem to turn this genuine difficulty into crisis of le-gitimacy, as if a good faith but erroneous judicial decision was the equivalent of a coup. It is this obsession with judicial legitimacy we mean to challenge.

This preoccupation seems so natural that it takes a shift in perspective to realize that in some ways it is quite odd. Indeed, judicial review is now an es-tablished aspect of democratic regimes. When judicial review seemed to be a uniquely American institution, shared by no other democracy, perhaps it was natural to regard it as an anomaly in urgent need of justification. Today this impulse seems anachronistic. Democratic governments around the world have adopted judicially enforceable written constitutions featuring various protections for individual rights against majority action.[9] What calls out for justification and legitimization today is not so much judicial review as its absence in some legal systems.

Although the countermajoritarian difficulty has a core of truth, it has been blown out of proportion. Consider an analogy. One of the core tenets of the American legal system is the importance of the jury. We place partic-ular importance upon the jury in criminal cases; but even in civil cases, the jury's role is protected by the federal Constitution and many state constitu-tions. One key function of the jury is to bring community values and judg-ment to bear on a case, rather than leaving it merely to the elite opinion of a judge, although we need not go as far as Amar in celebrating the jury's dem-ocratic function to see the analogy with the democratic political process.[10] For this reason, as well as for more immediate practical reasons, everyone agrees that judges should not lightly overturn jury verdicts.[11] Still, not infrequently, judges do overturn a jury verdict that they consider clearly un-supported by the evidence. But no one obsesses about the "counterjuritar-ian" difficulty. No scholar finds it necessary to design a whole theory of civil procedure around the problem of explaining the legitimacy of this practice. Nor, so far as we are aware, has anyone accused judges of acting like Platonic guardians when judges reverse jury verdicts from time to time for lack of support in the evidence.

Overturning a statute is a far more serious step than overturning a verdict in a single lawsuit, leading scholars to seek ways to resolve or minimize the countermajoritarian difficulty. This legitimate concern can sometimes be blown far out of proportion, leading to increasingly frantic efforts to escape the difficulty. Admittedly, whenever the Supreme Court invalidates a statute as inconsistent with the Constitution, it is blocking the current majority in the name of a document adopted by a past majority. But, as Chief Justice Marshall pointed out almost two centuries ago, occasionally frustrating the legislative will is simply a corollary of the decision to have a binding constitution.[12] And, being self-proclaimed originalists, none of our six scholars is especially concerned with the problem of current majorities being bound by the dead hand of the constitutional text. There is nothing particularly suspect about the idea that a constitution, as properly interpreted, may block the will of the current majority. That is one of its functions.

One response to this conventional defense of judicial review questions the specific role of judges rather than the binding effect of constitutional rules on current majorities. On this view, legislators should not be presumed to have deliberately enacted unconstitutional statutes; and thus every judicial invalidation is an affront to the legislature's own interpretation of the Constitution. The problem is exacerbated because virtually all of the constitutional issues that arise today necessarily turn on ambiguous constitutional language. (After all, Congress is unlikely to enact a statute that allows the election of a thirty-year-old president—and if it did, even the staunchest majoritarians would be unlikely to complain when the Supreme Court struck it down as a violation of the Constitution's demand that the president be at least thirty-five.) Even assuming the Constitution is designed to restrain current majorities, why should its interpretation be left to the judges at the expense of legislators?

John Marshall had an answer to that problem, too. Deciding legal issues is the job that judges are paid for (and legislators are not). Moreover, several clauses of the Constitution itself seem to contemplate such authority for judges.[13] And if part of the function of a constitution is to block current majorities, judges seem more likely to carry out this mandate than legislators.

Judge Hand would probably respond that we (and Marshall) have cheated by assuming that what judges do in constitutional cases can be considered the exercise of legal judgment, that it is akin to deciding nonconstitutional cases. But, Hand might argue, constitutional cases are different: in striking down a statute, judges are essentially making a *legislative* judgment about whether a statute is good policy, not a *legal* judgment about the meaning of the Constitution. If so, judges are operating as an arguably illegitimate third branch of the legislature.

On this view, the countermajoritarian difficulty should lead us to reject judicial review, leaving entirely to the legislature the task of reconciling the limits of the Constitution and the wishes of the majority, thus minimizing the conflict. And indeed, Hand viewed judicial review as a necessary evil, to be used only as a last resort.[14]

Our various grand theorists, however, choose a different approach: rather than rejecting judicial review, each seeks to constrain it. And each seems to think that the Supreme Court can only be rescued from a dreaded quasi-legislative status by adopting his particular theory. We will return to both Hand and the theorists, arguing in later sections that the Supreme Court's decisions on constitutional issues are indeed recognizably legal and thus appropriately assigned to judges, and that in any event grand theory cannot constrain judges in a meaningful way. But first, we need to address a deeper problem with the countermajoritarian difficulty: it rests on an overly reductionist view of democratic legitimacy.

WHAT COUNTERMAJORITARIAN DIFFICULTY?

In the previous section, we suggested that the countermajoritarian difficulty masks concerns about the difference between legal judgment and constitutional judgment, concerns that we intend to argue are overblown. But for a moment, let us take as a given the wildest fears of our grand theorists: assume that the justices are in fact Platonic guardians, having changed their togas for black robes but otherwise acting as an unelected superlegislature. In that case, would judicial review be morally illegitimate, akin to some form of dictatorship?

In this scenario, the Court would be acting something like a superlegislature or, perhaps more accurately, exercising something like a veto over certain classes of state and federal legislation. This view exaggerates judicial discretion. More importantly, it also fails to explain why even broad discretion would be such an abomination. Policymaking by judges might be objectionable, but it is a far cry from authoritarian government. True, federal judges are not elected, but this does not seem to be a fatal objection to a policymaking role. Like the heads of many administrative agencies, who also exercise key interpretive authority over legislation, judges are chosen by a system based on a democratic process (nomination by the president and confirmation by the Senate). Unlike agency heads, however, the justices enjoy life tenure. Perhaps it is this lack of accountability, combined with a selection process one step removed from the populace, that gives judicial review the aura of being so uniquely undemocratic.

On balance, however, it is not clear that the Court is *radically* less "democratic" than other organs of government considered in isolation.[15] We currently have a countermajoritarian president who was elected despite coming in second in the national popular vote, admittedly an unusual (though not unprecedented) situation. But other organs of government are *designed* to be countermajoritarian. In particular, the Senate is elected from incredibly malapportioned districts. Fifty-one senators constitute a majority: are those fifty-one senators representing the smallest states—potentially accounting for just over 17 percent of the U.S. population—acting on behalf of the majority when they enact or block legislation (or when they ratify a treaty or confirm a judicial nomination, in which the House does not participate)?[16] Even the House of Representatives is not fully majoritarian, due to the details of the apportionment scheme.[17] In contrast, justices are nominated by the president, who normally represents a popular majority. As for accountability, the Court is not the only important national authority lacking direct political accountability: the Federal Reserve, for example, is nearly as free from accountability and arguably more important in setting national policy. Most Americans are more directly affected by inflation and unemployment rates than by whether flag-burning is legal or by whether the town hall can display a Christmas tree.

Thus, although it is certainly significant that the Court is less subject to electoral correction than the president or Congress, this obvious fact does not put the Court completely in a class of its own. And if this lack of electoral responsiveness is *really* what worries us, one solution might be to appoint older judges so as to ensure greater turnover and more institutional responsiveness to changes in public opinion. Another would be to politicize the nomination and confirmation process, which seems to be happening: presidents and senators more often measure candidates by ideology these days than in the past.[18]

Comparisons between the Supreme Court and other institutions, then, show that the Court is not the only "undemocratic" part of the government. Moreover, the judicial process has its own special forms of openness and accountability: unlike politicians, judges must consider and give reasoned responses to the claims of anyone who brings a case before them.[19] And there is another problem with obsessing about the countermajoritarian nature of the Court. We would not want to live under absolute rulers, even if they were initially picked through some democratic process. But judges are only part of the governance system; they are not our rulers. To assume that the whole system can be legitimate only if each part would be legitimate standing alone is to commit what economists call the "fallacy of composition."

The attack on judicial review assumes that the idea of democratic legitimacy applies to any particular organ of government or any specific governmental policy, as opposed to the government as a whole. But legitimacy may be better considered a holistic judgment about the entire governance system. Even markedly nonmajoritarian features, like the role of the House of Lords in nineteenth-century England, do not necessarily imperil overall democratic legitimacy, though they may or may not function desirably.

The Senate is again one of the best examples. In principle, no one can really justify having an equal number of representatives from Wyoming (the smallest state in the last census) and California (the largest) in one branch of the national legislature. If we had a parliamentary system in which full legislative power resided in the Senate, people who live in California and other populous states would be justified in revolting. In terms of democratic theory, the Senate is about as illegitimate as it could be. But the fact that the Senate has a "legitimacy deficit" seems to have no relevance to its operations. There seems to be little interest in reforming the Senate.[20] No one ever argues that the Senate ought simply to rubber-stamp legislation from the more democratically elected House. Nor does anyone object very strenuously to the Senate's malapportionment even in contexts where it has sole legislative authority, such as in confirming judges and ratifying treaties. The fact is that hardly anyone really cares, and no one thinks the democratic nature of our government is seriously compromised. Overall, whatever the theoretical flaws of the Senate, those flaws do not seem to skew the eventual outcomes of the legislative process enough to make a difference. In the meantime, the Senate sometimes seems to serve a useful role by providing a degree of deliberation that is missing in the House.

In other words, we accept the Senate without worrying about its democratic legitimacy, both because it would be hard to change and because the system as a whole seems legitimate. The senators also seem to be able to do their jobs satisfactorily without any grand theory that tells them how they should vote so as to maintain their tenuous grip on legitimacy.[21] Similarly, questioning the legitimacy of the Supreme Court may simply be a category mistake; perhaps the issue of legitimacy only applies to a government system taken as a whole.

One reason for applying the concept of legitimacy at the systemic level is that our conception of democracy is actually quite complex. Our constitutional scheme elaborately divides power among different organs of government, some (such as the Senate) being democratic in only a qualified sense. In their actual operations, the decisions of these institutions are shaped by extraconstitutional features such as political parties, government bureaucracies, and legislative committees—none of them directly representative of a majority of the public. The system as a whole operates reasonably democratically, but this does not mean that every individual component is majoritarian, or that we would want a wholly majoritarian form of government.

Another answer to the legitimacy issue is that judicial review (practiced without the benefit of grand theory) has withstood the test of time. It clearly enjoys unquestioned popular support. Indeed, even in the days when the work of the Court came in for the most stinging criticism, at the beginning of the Civil War and again early in the Great Depression, no important national figure proposed eliminating its ability to decide constitutional issues. Perhaps even more tellingly, so far as we are aware, no state has ever tried to take the power to enforce the state constitution away from the state supreme court (let alone try to do without a written constitution at all).

Earlier in this book, we recalled the story of the blind men and the elephant. What each of the blind men perceives is so different from the others that none of them can be blamed for failing to understand the overall design. Who could imagine an animal with parts like a snake, a horn, a broom, and a tree trunk? It sounds more like a modern sculpture than a living animal. Yet this hodgepodge assembly works just fine for the elephant. Our Constitution is a similarly odd conglomeration, with its majoritarian House and presidency, its less majoritarian courts and Senate, its separation of powers and federalism (which can frustrate the will of national popular majorities), and its guarantees of individual rights. This combination may make little sense in principle but seems to work acceptably in practice.

As an eighteenth-century English writer put it: "No Government ever was built at once or by the rules of architecture, but like an old house 20 times up & down and irregular." Thus, he added, "governments go *per hookum & crookum &* then we demonstrate it *per bookum.*"[22] Buildings constructed according to grand theories are not likely to meet practical human needs. Neither are constitutional schemes.

The moral legitimacy of the constitutional order is built on disparate elements. The Constitution enjoys legitimacy for a host of very different reasons: because it was adopted by great men at a great moment of our history; because it was approved through an unusually democratic process for its own time (though not for ours); because it has worked reasonably well most of the time; because it symbolizes our nation's traditions and identity; because we believe in the rule of law and (perhaps wrongly) honor the Supreme Court; and just because we are used to it. Judicial review must be attuned to many goals. Sound judgment, open-mindedness, and accumulated judicial experience provide better guides to achieving these multiple goals than could be found in any theory, no matter how brilliant. Like the elephant, constitutionalism is an odd creature but nonetheless a robust one. But we cannot expect to deduce any elegant theories from a social institution so variously constructed.

Thus grand theory is not merely flawed as a methodology. It also rests on a basic misunderstanding of constitutionalism. Grand theories attribute a degree of normative coherence to the constitutional regime that does not exist. Substantively, the Constitution is not based on an overarching vision of the division of powers, or sweeping philosophical theories about rights. The framers made use of their best theoretical understandings, but they were designing a practical instrument of government, not a class project for a political theory course. Nor can we deduce the proper method of constitutional interpretation from some axiom of political legitimacy such as populism, libertarianism, or egalitarianism. The legitimacy of the constitutional order does not rest on any such unitary basis. Grand theory embodies a reductionist vision of constitutionalism, which cannot do justice to the untidy grandeur of our constitutional regime.

GRAND THEORY AND THE RULE OF LAW

We are not advocates of judicial activism. We agree that the Court should not lightly overturn legislative decisions, just as a reviewing court should not hastily overturn a jury verdict. But as we have just argued, the institutional legitimacy of the courts is not at stake in either situation, provided that the court has a reasoned explanation for its decision. So, to the extent grand theory is intended to save judicial review from the threat of illegitimacy, it is fighting against a phantom menace.

But grand theory is only partly an effort to rescue the Supreme Court from the charge of democratic illegitimacy—an attempt to resolve the countermajoritarian difficulty. Another kind of argument can also be made for grand theory. The claim is that courts are supposed to engage in reasoned decisionmaking, and that articulating a general theory is the essence of reason. Thus it is claimed that without grand theory judicial decisions will be unprincipled. The problem is exacerbated in constitutional cases, which in turn leads back to Hand's fear: that in invalidating statutes, judges untethered by a grand theory are not engaging in principled judicial conduct. This claim seems particularly central to Scalia's views, though it figures in some other theories as well.

This claim, we contend, overlooks the plain reality that courts have made principled decisions—in constitutional law as well as other areas—for centuries without the benefit of grand theory. Nor do we accept the related claim that grand theory would lead to more coherent doctrinal rules. Any individual grand theory is likely to be too abstract to provide much specific guidance in dealing with complicated legal issues. Moreover, if judges did develop a taste for grand theory, the result would probably be chaos rather than consensus. Whatever coherence any individual judge might gain from his preferred theory would probably be lost in the clash of contending theories among judges. In short, we argue in this section, judges do not need a grand theory to rule on constitutional issues any more than they need a theory of epistemology to rule on the admissibility of evidence. Whatever conceptual theoretical merits a particular grand theory might have, such theories do not provide a practical decision tool for judges or public officials.

THE COMMON LAW ALTERNATIVE TO GRAND THEORY

Applying large scale theories is clearly not the primary way judges make decisions. Instead, they tend to proceed incrementally, moving case by case. Rather than attempting to articulate a general theory from the start, they try to develop and elaborate principles as they go along. In an exaggerated way, Dworkin's mythical judge Hercules embodies the common law method, though Dworkin himself seems to make little use of this method when he considers substantive constitutional issues. The common law method is familiar to every beginning American law student.[23] It is also, as David Strauss points out, a central feature of American constitutional law.[24] Even some writers with a strong originalist bent, like Michael McConnell, seem to acknowledge a role for common law evolution.[25]

At its best, this method can provide satisfyingly reasoned resolutions in difficult cases. Consider a recent, not particularly unusual, example. In *Brentwood Academy v. Tennessee Secondary Athletic Association*,[26] the issue was whether constitutional limitations such as the First Amendment applied to an athletic association, 85 percent of whose members were public schools.

Members of the state board of education were ex officio members of the group's board. Writing for the majority, Justice Souter's opinion first describes the various ways the association was "intertwined" with government, then compares those governmental connections with prior cases, and finally considers whether there are countervailing reasons why the group should be considered purely private. He reaches the unsurprising conclusion—anticipated by almost all of the lower courts to consider the issue—that the group is a state actor. Accusing the majority of a "fact-specific analysis," Justice Thomas' dissent calls for a more rule-oriented approach. Since the association failed to fit into any of three narrowly defined categories, he considers it private. Rules like Thomas's offer an alluring promise of predictability. It is hard to see, however, how any set of rules could encompass the myriad relationships that exist between government officials and other institutions. As *Brentwood Academy* illustrates, a rule-oriented approach would not even improve predictability. The lower courts had (with the sole exception of the decision under review) reached a consensus with little difficulty under the more flexible functional approach. It was Thomas's rule-based approach that would have produced unexpected results.

Grand theorists seem disdainful of this whole process. They yearn for certitude, for something more definite than the rather fuzzy process of reasoning by analogy and developing principles piecemeal. Their disdain, however, is a bit puzzling coming from American lawyers. Many important bodies of American law, including torts, contracts, and property, are dominated by the common law to this day. Others, such as criminal law, are rooted in concepts originally developed by the common law, or like antitrust rules, represent common law elaborations on open-ended statutes. If the common law process is so unprincipled and ad hoc, it is hard to see how it has been so successful.

In rejecting grand theory, we do not mean to endorse ad hoc or purely result-oriented decisionmaking. The Supreme Court's decisions in the 2000 presidential election illustrate the dangers of such decisionmaking.[27] Apparently motivated by a desire to bring closure to the election, the justices staked out novel positions regarding their ability to supervise the state court's interpretation of state election laws and their ability to use equal protection law to micromanage state election procedures. These innovations did not flow in any obvious way from recent rulings in allied areas, and indeed seemed at odds with the majority's general view of federalism. Nor did the justices seem to give any thought to how these rulings might operate as precedents; rather, they seemed anxious to forestall the precedential effects of the rulings. The remedial aspects of the rulings—the abrupt grant of a stay and the termination of any recount efforts at the eleventh hour—did not even pretend to provide reasoned explanation. All of this is light years away from the work of common law judges like Cardozo, who sought not only socially beneficial outcomes in particular cases, but also to build an evolving framework for future decisions.

At least since Karl Llewellyn—if not since Holmes—American legal pragmatists have defended true common law reasoning, as practiced by the great judges in our legal tradition. The fullest recent attempt to justify this process comes from Cass Sunstein. He argues that we often make the best decisions (particularly collectively) on the basis of what he calls incompletely theorized agreements. These agreements represent a consensus on the proper outcome in a given case, with only a partial attempt to work out a theoretical justification.[28] These incompletely theorized agreements are particularly prominent in law—enough so that for many lawyers, the only odd thing about the idea of an incompletely theorized agreement is that it seems to imagine the possibility of the other kind! (What lawyer has ever negotiated a completely theorized agreement or even seen one?) Life does not await theory. As Sunstein explains, agreement about legal issues often "involves a specific outcome and a set of reasons that do not venture far from the case at hand. High-level theories are rarely reflected explicitly in law."[29] One of the techniques used by judges, though not in good repute among grand theorists, is analogy, which Sunstein defends as a way of making incompletely theorized judgments about particular cases.[30]

This process is not without its flaws. Used badly, it can produce incoherent results or lose sight of deeper normative issues. But no one has yet offered a better way to decide hard cases. To paraphrase Churchill, common law reasoning may be the worst possible method of judicial decision, except for all the others.

Someone once defined an economist as someone who tries to prove that what is actually happening is theoretically possible. The efforts of legal philosophers to validate the common law method have something of this flavor. The fact is that English courts have been using this method since the Middle Ages, and our Supreme Court has been deciding cases without the benefit of a grand theory since it issued its first opinion. It seems a little late in the day to argue that the method does not work. Orville and Wilbur may not have known modern aeronautical theory, but the plane did get off the ground.

The real concern of the grand theorists is not that the process does not work, but that it gives judges too much leeway.[31] Judges do have leeway, which they sometimes exercise in ways that we may not like.* But this is a condition without a cure, other than simply killing the patient. Like their disdain for the common law process, the grand theorists' desire to restrain judicial discretion is an impossible dream based on an unwillingness to tolerate uncertainty.

None of the grand theories we have seen offers a solution to the problem of judicial discretion. As we saw earlier in the book, originalism places no significant constraint on the substantive legal conclusions reached by Bork and Scalia. (Don't forget that Amar and Ackerman, whose views could not be more different from Bork's and Scalia's, claim to find support in the same historical record.) Nor does the intratextualism touted by Amar offer much constraint. And all Ackerman's theory tells judges is to integrate post–New Deal law with the legacies of the founding and Reconstruction. This is not bad advice, but not exactly specific either. Dworkin's recourse to moral philosophy will seem constraining only by comparison with throwing darts. (If you doubt this, take a look at a current issue of a philosophy journal like *Ethics* to see the vast diversity of views expressed by modern moral philosophers.) Even Epstein's theory offers less than a specific roadmap for judges. Applying the theory requires a determination of whether a particular government action increases social wealth, combined with an estimate of how the gains are distributed. Both determinations involve often controversial economic judgments.

Our point is not that any of these methods is wholly indeterminate—or that any historical, textual, moral, or economic analysis is as good as any other. (We do not think this is true of common law arguments, either). The issue is not whether these methods can sometimes be used to find determinate solutions by disinterested, fair-minded thinkers. It is whether they are constraining enough to do so for the kind of judge who *needs* constraining. None of these methods is sufficiently determinate to stop willful judges from pursuing their own preferences. The solution is not to find some ironclad conceptual constraint but to avoid appointing willful judges.

If, as the grand theorists seem to hope, constitutional cases could be decided with simple recipes, the identity of the judges would be relatively unimportant. The judges would only need to be honest enough to follow

---

*For the benefit of those who believe we are simply apologists for the Supreme Court, we would be happy to supply a list—and not a short one—of cases with which each of us sharply disagrees.

the recipes, and bright enough to successfully move through each step. Under our view, far more judgment is involved in constitutional interpretation. Hence it is important that judges share the core values that we endorse as a society. This has been an increasing focus in confirmation hearings. It is also important that judges be open-minded, receptive to opposing views, and capable of balanced judgment. Unfortunately, the Senate has taken less interest in these critical characteristics, and presidents have sometimes seemed more interested in ideological predictability than sound judgment. But it is these traits of character, not adherence to a grand theory, that mark the difference between a principled judge and a willful one.

GRAND THEORY AND DOCTRINAL COHERENCE

Even if principled decisions in individual cases are as readily attainable without grand theory as with it, our scholars might still hope that grand theory would help judges reach greater consistency among cases.[32] A grand theory might lead to greater methodological consistency (although reading Scalia's opinions leaves some doubt on this score). But grand theories do not, in fact, particularly lend themselves to doctrinal consistency in difficult areas. They simply provide too little analytical leverage to help in drawing difficult lines.

To be fair on this score, let us consider an area where conventional legal reasoning has also led to what most observers consider a morass: the doctrine of standing, which we discussed briefly in chapter 3. Recall that Article III limits judges to deciding "cases and controversies," but does not define either term. Standing is one aspect of the case-or-controversy requirement, asking whether particular plaintiffs have the right to sue for particular kinds of injuries. While it is obvious that you can sue the government if it takes your property, what if it pollutes your air? Or if it fails to enforce the law requiring a private company to stop polluting your air? Or if it establishes a national church, but without either forcing anyone to attend or giving any financial subsidies—just a purely symbolic endorsement of a particular religion? Current doctrine gives complex, ambiguous, and often contradictory answers to these and similar questions. Would adopting a grand theory of constitutional interpretation help clarify this troubled area of the law?

The answer, in case you're holding your breath, is no. Let's run through our list of grand theories, beginning with originalism. An originalist judge would presumably ask what specific kinds of disputes judges were authorized to hear in 1789, since this would indicate what the Constitution means by the term "case or controversy." Since most modern causes of action did not exist at all in 1789, the next step is to ask whether they are sufficiently analogous to 1789 cases to be heard. (Or, if you prefer, whether the principle underlying 1789 practice encompasses these modern cases.) Notably, in his opinions on standing, Justice Scalia has never asked this question, but let us suppose he had. We can gauge the likelihood of success by looking at a similar issue which the courts and scholars have probed deeply. In apply-ing the Seventh Amendment, courts ask, not whether a case resembling a given modern claim would have been heard at all by the courts in 1789, but whether such an analogous claim would have been tried to a jury. The re-sulting area of law is charitably described as a doctrinal disaster area.[33] The potential for originalism to bring order out of the chaos of standing law seems similarly limited. Since the framers didn't really have any close paral-lels to modern administrative agencies, we can hardly imagine what kinds of judicial review of agency action they would have endorsed. So much for originalism.

Intratextualism also seems to offer very little assistance in line-drawing. True, we could scour the Constitution for other uses of relevant terms (such as "*cases* of Impeachment") or hope to find some guidance in the overall pat-tern of Article III. If anyone could come up with a useful intratextualist the-ory of standing, it would probably be Amar, given his impressive earlier work on federal jurisdiction.[34] But would such a theory provide specific guidance on when a potential injury becomes too speculative to serve as the basis for standing? Would it tell us when standing exists to make a facial challenge to a law, or to assert third-party rights? Not likely, is the answer.

The other theories can be treated more quickly. Ackerman's theory is helpful in pointing out that pre–New Deal ideas of standing need to be rethought in the age of the administrative state—but we knew that anyway. It is hard to see how his theory would help in drawing specific lines. As for Dworkin, what modern moral philosophy has to teach us about the law of standing seems deeply mysterious. We have no idea what Dworkin would say on the subject, let alone whether his theory would help draw lines. Fi-nally, Epstein's theory might seem with equal plausibility to mean that al-most no one has standing (unless they could have filed a common law writ against a similar private wrong), that everyone has standing (since bad gov-ernment regulations create systemic economic inefficiencies and pervasive rent-seeking incentives, which "take" everyone's property), or anything in between.

We should be plain here. We do not mean to say that our six theorists would have nothing of interest to say on the topic of standing, or even that they could not find useful insights in their general theories. On the contrary, they are all very bright people and undoubtedly each would find something innovative and interesting to say. We do, however, maintain two narrower propositions. First, their theories are sufficiently malleable to allow a number of different subthcorics to bc constructed about a topic like standing. So different judges who all agreed that Epstein or Dworkin or Amar were demigods could still come to quite different conclusions about the law of standing.

Second, grand constitutional theories (and even the subtheories that they generate) are likely only to give broad benchmarks. Almost any of these theories would tell us, we suppose, that you generally cannot file a federal lawsuit *simply* because you think that something you read about in the morning paper violates the law. Presumably, these theories would also tell us that the subject of a regulation has standing to challenge it, and probably also that other people who have some sufficient nexus with the dispute can do so as well. In other words, they will probably tell us that a line needs to be drawn somewhere between the extremes. (Of course, if they told us to embrace one extreme or another, they would make life much easier for judges, at the cost of creating havoc with our existing legal system.) But it is hard to imagine that the text, history, or normative theory of the Constitution is going to help much with the messy job of drawing these necessary lines. Perhaps recurring to first principles in standing cases would not prove any more confusing than the current case law, but there is no reason whatsoever to expect it to do better. Those who hope that grand theory will generate doctrinal coherence where conventional reasoning has failed to do so are wishing in vain.

GRAND THEORY AND COLLECTIVE DELIBERATION

In discussing incompletely theorized agreements, Sunstein stresses their utility in making *collective* decisions.[35] This is an important point, overlooked by grand theorists. Advocates of grand theory sometimes seem to assume that all judges will collectively adopt a single grand theory. But there is no reason to expect this to be true, unless a sufficiently long string of presidents agree on a theory and use it as a "litmus test." Nothing in our historical experience suggests that this is likely. So a turn to grand theory among judges would probably mean a turn to *multiple* grand theories. That would be fun for constitutional law scholars, but would not leave much of the Court as a deliberative institution.

Imagine arguing a case to the Court of Ultimate Constitutional Theory, a bench consisting of Justices Ackerman, Amar, Bork, Dworkin, Epstein, and

Scalia. The questions come from a dizzying number of directions. The originalists want to know what principle to extract from the writings of the framers and whether they had any specific practices bearing on the issue. Amar is interested in the detailed linguistic structure of the provision, how the same or related words are used elsewhere in the Constitution, and how some seemingly unrelated provision might be brought to bear through some dazzling reinterpretation. Ackerman wants you to relate the case to the New Deal revolution. Epstein wants an economic analysis (and most definitely does *not* want to hear about the New Deal). Dworkin wants to talk moral philosophy. None of them are interested in the others' questions.

Richard Fallon argues on behalf of grand theory that "affirmations of reasonable formal theories help to sustain conversation and to reinforce the sense that there is enough common ground to make reasoned debate possible."[36] But he also says that "reasonable commonality about argumentative premises and methodologies is necessary to maintain a sense of constitutional community within which disagreements can be experienced as reasonable, good-faith disputes about the proper application of principles that, at some level of abstraction, are broadly shared."[37] The trouble is that grand theorists don't share a "reasonable commonality" about their premises, so affirming their theories will do anything *but* help sustain conversation and a sense of common ground.

We fear that a Court composed of constitutional theorists, if they remained true to their creeds, would be less capable of collective deliberation and good-faith debate than a Court composed of ordinary judges. One reason is implicit in the story of the Court of Ultimate Constitutional Theory. There are significant benefits in having a shared language for debating constitutional issues. A Court containing multiple grand theorists would replace the current shared language of judges, that of conventional legal discourse, with a tower of Babel of conflicting tongues.

Grand theory would also undermine deliberation because it dramatically escalates the rhetorical stakes. The whole point of grand theory is that judges who fail to follow your theory are not just making mistakes in deciding cases. No, they are completely illegitimate, exercising raw power in a lawless way. This rhetorical escalation is reflected in the intemperate language of some of Justice Scalia's judicial opinions. But it is unfair to single out Scalia. Grand theorists generally seem to be condescending at best when discussing each other; constitutional law is apparently not big enough for more than one genius at a time. This is not an attitude conducive to judicial collegiality or constructive debate.

Conventional legal reasoning lacks the intellectual verve of grand theory. It is especially uninspiring when employed, as it sometimes is, in the hands of mediocrities. (But it is possible to imagine mediocre theorists as well as mediocre lawyers, and the picture is no more inspiring.) The common law process is more successful some times than others, and when it works poorly, the result is often a muddle. Thus the desire for cleaner, more consistent rulings is understandable. The problem is that grand theory will do nothing to get us there. Richard Posner observes that constitutional theory has relatively little utility for working judges "immersed in deciding cases as part of a committee."[38] As anyone who has ever served on a committee knows, nothing is worse than a fellow committee member who is in the grip of a Theory.

THE USES AND ABUSES OF GRAND THEORY

We have argued so far that grand theory is unnecessary to establish the legitimacy of our ongoing constitutional practices, which find their ultimate justification in producing a tolerably fair and workable society. We have also argued that grand theory is destructive of reasoned decisionmaking by courts. Thus, as we discuss below, we agree with part of Judge Posner's recent argument against grand theory. Like Posner, we think grand theory is often a dead end. But unlike Posner, we think that taken cautiously and in small doses, it might have some potential benefits.

Grand theory might be used in two ways: normatively, to tell us how our system ought to work (which is the way the theorists want to use it), or descriptively, to help us see larger patterns or connections in constitutional law. Again, we agree with Posner that *normative* use of grand theory is a virtual dead end, but grand theories may have some descriptive payoff. By giving us a picture of what constitutional law would look like if it were built on a single value or method, it can help us see things we might otherwise miss in the complex tapestry of constitutional doctrine and history.

GRAND THEORY AS NORMATIVE

Our theorists clearly want not only to understand constitutional law, but to remake it in their own image. We think this a profoundly bad idea, and not just because of our criticisms of each particular theory. We have already explained why grand theory would probably do little to clarify doctrine and would likely lower the quality of deliberation of appellate courts. But even if a majority of the Court could coalesce on a single grand theory, and even if that grand theory did have clear-cut doctrinal implications, the turn toward theory would still be a mistake.

To begin with, as Judge Easterbrook reminds us, "[s]tability in a political system is exceptionally valuable."[39] One of the central purposes of a constitution is to provide a stable framework for government. Easterbrook views this as an argument for "an inflexible system of interpretation" so that all of us know that our own rights will be respected in the future. But it is still more an argument that changes in systems of interpretation, if they are made at all, should be made slowly. If everyone has been evaluating the constitutionality of various measures on the basis of common law reasoning, a sudden shift to some grand theory can only be destabilizing (and still more so if the theory results in a marked substantive swerve). The constitutional regime by definition provides a background structure for all kinds of political decisions, and indirectly for many private decisions made in light of the legal framework. We have every reason to be leery of major surprises in constitutional law.

Moreover, we hope that our chapters on individual theorists have illustrated the need for an understanding of constitutional interpretation that includes a broad range of interpretive devices and substantive values. Epstein is right that we must attend to individual rights, but Amar and Ackerman are also correct to value majoritarianism. Scalia's and Bork's focus on history and tradition strengthens constitutional law's historical roots, but Ackerman's theory of constitutional change prevents it from stagnating. Scalia is on to something when he suggests that judges should have a healthy respect for their own limitations, but sometimes, as Dworkin's theory posits, they just have to do the right thing.

Furthermore, grand theory seems likely to be a malign influence on the individual judge quite apart from its effect on collegiality. If we were to compile a list of judicial virtues, somewhere fairly high on the list would come intellectual humility—not in the sense of diffidence but of an open-minded willingness to listen and learn.[40] Grand theory impairs this ability to learn, for the grand theorist is convinced that he (and perhaps he alone) has been smart enough to figure out the ultimate essence of constitutional law. (Besides, changing any part of the grand intellectual structure would require adjusting the whole edifice, which would be too much trouble.) Grand theorists, one suspects, do not generally make good listeners. If we want judges who will listen to each other as well as to the arguments of lawyers, scholars, and the public, we should hope they steer clear of grand theory. We also hope that our critiques have shown the pernicious effect of tunnel vision on judgment, another crucial attribute of good judges.

For the same reason, grand theory would hinder public deliberation about constitutional issues. The Court's current eclectic approach makes it possible for the justices to address concerns arising from many different perspectives: from those who care about text and history, those who care about evolving legal doctrine, and those who care about societal needs. To adopt a grand theory is to abandon the ability to address at least some of these concerns. For instance, the originalist gives up any reliance on current social needs, and minimizes reliance on evolving doctrine. Hence the originalist really has nothing at all to say to those segments of the public who think a decision is socially destructive or leads to bizarre legal inconsistencies—except to remark that their concerns are legally irrelevant. Unless not only all of the justices, but all important social groups, buy into a particular grand theory, the Court will simply lose its ability to respond to the concerns of parts of our citizenry.

What could an originalist Court have to say to members of minority groups who were excluded from the original understanding in the first place? What could the Epstein Court say to liberals who believe in redistribution, or an Ackerman Court to conservatives who are skeptical of the New Deal? What can Amar say to antipopulists or libertarians who are unwilling to place majority opinion above individual autonomy? What could Dworkin say to a religious believer who does not accept his moral arguments? The problem is not that these grand theories rely on controversial arguments— any important judicial decision is likely to rely on arguments that not everyone will accept. Rather, the problem is that each grand theorist has only one argument to offer, and thus nothing but a deaf ear toward everyone else.

A more eclectic approach can try to weave a justification that draws on many different perspectives, and thus can appeal to many portions of the public. The paradigm remains Chief Justice Marshall's opinion in *McCulloch v. Maryland*,[41] which weaves text, history, and policy into a brilliant defense of congressional power. The lasting legacy of *McCulloch* is not only Marshall's recognition that Congress has implied powers to legislate, but his comprehensive exposition of the sorts of arguments that the Court will find persuasive in interpreting the Constitution.

Marshall's opinion is an example of legal pragmatism at its best: he used an eclectic mix of sources in support of his ultimate conclusion that Congress has the power to establish a national bank.[42] He turned to history, text, usage, structure, congressional action and inaction, logic, common law reasoning, and practical considerations in his quest to interpret the Necessary and Proper Clause. The opinion begins with a discussion of the long history of the national bank statute, initially enacted by the first Congress. Marshall turns next to the structure and history of the Constitution itself, concluding that it established "a government of the people," not of the states, and that under the Constitution the federal government cannot be controlled by the states. Moving on to a textual analysis, he notes the absence of any express limit on congressional power, and compares the clause granting Congress the power to enact all "necessary and proper" laws with the nearby clause prohibiting the states from taxing imports except as "absolutely necessary." He even looks to the placement of the Necessary and Proper Clause, among the list of congressional powers rather than in the section providing other limits on Congress, to bolster his conclusion that it should be broadly interpreted. Most memorably, he reminds his readers that the text must be read with its important object—that of creating an effective national government—in mind: "[W]e must never forget," Marshall wrote, "that it is a *constitution* we are expounding." And the Constitution was written to "insure, as far as human prudence could insure, [the] beneficial execution"[43] of the powers granted to Congress, which could not be done by reading the Necessary and Proper Clause too narrowly. Moreover, to allow state restrictions on the Bank would permit a less-inclusive body to overrule a more inclusive one, in which its own interests were already represented. No grand theory, and no single principle, could establish the legitimacy of the national bank as persuasively as Marshall's broad-ranging analysis.[44]

Luckily, there seems little risk that grand theorists will suddenly sweep the judicial nomination process. Even if they do, as Posner says, there is reason to doubt whether their actual practice as judges would be as dogmatic as their theorizing.[45] But to the extent that grand theory actually does make inroads into judicial practice, little good is likely to come from the process.

GRAND THEORY AS DESCRIPTIVE

The conclusion might seem to be that grand theory is a complete waste of time. We do not go so far. Grand theory can be useful in helping us to understand overlooked aspects of constitutional law. For instance, despite all its faults, originalism has reminded legal scholars of the importance of history and has led to some valuable historical research. Writers like Bork and Scalia can take some credit for this effect, even if the resulting research is not always favorable to their views. Similarly, Amar has forced many of us to take a more serious look at the constitutional text, while Ackerman has highlighted the pivotal importance of the New Deal era in the development of current law. While Epstein and Dworkin are preoccupied with normative issues, their theories direct our attention to important matters: Epstein stresses the link between constitutionalism and the market system, while Dworkin highlights the pervasive influence of moral norms on judicial reasoning. Indeed, almost any grand theory, regardless of its overall utility, could provide some illumination.

As illustrations, consider two purely hypothetical grand theories. The first theory is substantive—that is, it relates to the content of constitutional law. One kind of substantive theory, like Epstein's, tries to specify a foundational goal for the constitutional order. More or less at random, let us assume that the core purpose of government (and not coincidentally, of the Constitution) is to achieve favorable relationships with foreigners—that is, protection against foreign invaders when necessary (national security) and beneficial cooperation when possible (foreign affairs). A smart, dedicated researcher who followed this theory would probably find some very interesting things. She would plumb the history of the founding period, looking for evidence that the Constitution as a whole was mostly designed to strengthen national security. She would also be alert for signs that clauses with no obvious connection to national security (say the religion clauses or the Contract Clause) were actually designed with an eye to foreign relations. She would make a similar investigation of the Reconstruction amendments. Looking forward, she would be alert for mentions of foreign relations or national security consideration in judicial opinions, and she would probe the historical context of important opinions for signs of such concerns. We would also learn much more than we now know about the views of various justices on foreign policy and defense issues, and about how their experiences with the military or their travels abroad influenced their general view of the world. Given her overarching theory, she might well tend to stretch the evidence in places. Even so, we would be likely to learn a lot of new and very interesting things about how international relations have shaped constitutional law.

The second hypothetical theory is methodological rather than substantive. It begins with the premise that the framers were not legal realists, instead believing that legal rules are discovered rather than invented. Given this epistemic theory of law, consensus among many judges is a more reliable sign than the views of a few prominent ones. Hence, except in unusual circumstances, the Court should defer to any strong consensus among the state courts or the lower federal courts. (A subsidiary argument is that such deference increases legal predictability and stability.) This research agenda could lead to some interesting research into how the Court conceptualizes its relationship with other courts, which other courts or judges it finds most persuasive, and what circumstances lead the Court to reject an existing consensus. It would also lead to renewed interest in lower court rulings, which tend to be ignored by constitutional scholars.

The chance that something interesting would come of such research is obviously increased when scholars have the abilities of the theorists we have discussed in this book. It is no surprise, as we have repeatedly pointed out in our discussions of their work, that even where their theories fall flat, these theorists often have novel and useful points to make along the way.

So even a misguided research agenda can have serendipitous benefits. Of course, someone could embark on one of these research programs out of sheer disinterested curiosity. But it seems more likely that the initial spark would come from someone who dramatically overestimated the ultimate importance of these neglected subjects—someone, in fact, in the grip of a grand theory. To return to the story with which we began the book, if you are looking for someone to collect every latke recipe in the world and compile a comprehensive cookbook, it probably helps to get someone who is just a bit obsessed with the dish. So long as they don't talk the rest of the world into their own unbalanced diet, they might actually write an interesting book.

You might also learn something interesting about the author. This brings us to what may be the most important descriptive value of grand theory: its description of the theorist and his worldview. Reading Bork and Scalia, others may gain a sense from their theories of their bitter longing for a world of stable values and social solidarity, a longing they project into the American past. Epstein shows us how contemporary American law and government look from the vantage of a brilliant economic libertarian. In different ways, Dworkin and Ackerman both reveal a longing for another lost world, that of the 1960s and the Warren Court. And Amar, while revealing something about our populist present, also shows us what it would be like to read the Constitution with the same veneration as a religious document—thus rejecting aspects of constitutionalism in favor of pure populism but also taking one aspect of constitutionalism to new heights. We need not desire to live in their worlds in order to profit from better understanding them.

THE MANY FUTURES OF CONSTITUTIONAL SCHOLARSHIP

Grand theory has been such a dominant feature of constitutional scholarship in the past few years that it has eclipsed other approaches. But several other intriguing avenues for research exist, at least some of which might have more practical payoff than grand theory.

On the normative side, traditional doctrinal scholarship has been a neglected field. Though it has continued to receive some attention from notable scholars, it has had less academic cachet than grand theory. Despite its relative eclipse, however, doctrinal scholarship remains important. One type of valuable doctrinal scholarship is careful critique of existing doctrines by showing their inconsistencies or unpalatable consequences—along the lines of our critiques of some judicial opinions in this book. Informed professional criticism is one of the few short-term checks on the federal judiciary. (Admittedly, this may not be a powerful check, but judges do not like to be considered stupid by members of their profession any more than most people do.)

Another form of doctrinal scholarship is simply sorting out an ever-increasing clutter of precedents, finding patterns, and seeing how to build for the future. For instance, there are now over three hundred Supreme Court decisions involving the First Amendment. Yet the bulk of scholarship in the area is less concerned with intelligent analysis of current law than with advocating the author's pet alternative. Courts could use help with synthesizing the precedents into a coherent and workable body of rules.

Another pressing need is for the application of social science findings to issues of constitutional law.[46] For instance, there has been a flood of legal scholarship about affirmative action, mostly discussing normative arguments that have long been familiar to most educated Americans. But until the past few years, there has been little effort to generate new information about the actual operation and effects of affirmative action programs, or to make use of what information had been gathered by social scientists. Books like *The Shape of the River*[47] surely will not settle the debate, but they present data that is far more useful than the usual rehash of platitudes.

So much for work with direct normative implications. Although legal scholars have a tendency to cast themselves as normativists (we all want our work to change the world), in some ways this is an unduly confining role. For instance, while originalism has rekindled interest in history, it tends toward a blinkered and intellectually vapid view of history. Constitutional scholars are constantly searching for nuggets that might be decisive to current legal disputes. As a result, we pass over all the intriguing ambiguities and oddities that add subtlety and interest to the study of the past. Freed from the need for an immediate normative payoff, constitutional history could be a lot more intellectually exciting—and might have unexpected normative implications.

Current scholarship has just begun to touch upon some other areas of interest. One is comparative law. Now that judicially enforceable constitutional and quasi-constitutional rules have gone into effect around the world, we have opportunities for all kinds of interesting comparisons with the American approach.[48] For instance, the dormant Commerce Clause has long been considered a strange, perhaps illegitimate doctrine, lacking in textual or historical support. But the use of tribunals to strike down taxes and regulations burdening commerce turns out to be a common feature of major free trade agreements.[49] This does not necessarily validate the American approach, but it now seems much less idiosyncratic. Another area of interest is sociological. We know a lot about Supreme Court rulings, but less about the social forces that helped shape the issues before the Court during different historical periods, or about the way that society responded to the Court's rulings. But judicial review is above all else a social institution, and we should know more than we do about how that institution fits into the social fabric.[50]

We need more doctrinal work, more social science, more comparative work, and more history. This may be enough to keep us all busy for the foreseeable future. As we said in the previous section, however, there may also be room for some grand theory in the mix, just to add a splash of spice. But grand theory should view itself as a garnish, not a main dish—and should take itself a lot less seriously than it does today.

In any event, the future of legal scholarship matters less than the future of constitutional law, though as scholars we hope the two are not entirely unrelated. The Supreme Court will face many difficult issues in the future, and inevitably it will decide some of them incorrectly. But grand theory offers no safeguard against the risk of error. What it does offer are the risks of intellectual rigidity and intolerance, a deteriorating climate of discourse, and an ever more frantic effort to defend judicial legitimacy from nonexistent threats. In short, it is a form of divisive dogmatism.

However noble the intentions of the grand theorists, and however great their talents, their theories could only cause harm if implemented seriously by judges. What is merely an intriguing thought experiment in the academy might have woeful side effects if we try to run the experiment in the real world. Of the theorists we have discussed, only Scalia is in a position to put his theories into practice. Perhaps we should count it as a blessing that his efforts in that direction are halting and inconsistent.

We would like to see grand theory play a smaller role in the academy and no role at all in the larger world. Moreover, as we have tried to make clear throughout this book, even as we disparage their enterprise, we see much to admire in the passion, intelligence, and creativity of the theorists themselves. Regrettably, we believe, their energies have been misdirected toward the wrong project: creating an unshakeable foundation for constitutionalism. Alas, their search for secure foundations is ultimately as quixotic as the quest for perpetual motion.

We began this book with a joke about a woman who was obsessed with latkes. We can all recognize the absurdity of filling closets with potato pancakes. But sometimes, as we have seen, even the most brilliant among us can lose their sense of proportion. In law, as in life, balance is everything.

SHIRLEY EDELMAN'S LATKES
> **5 large potatoes, peeled; I large onion; 2 eggs;**
> **1/4 to 1/3 cup matzo meal; I tsp salt; I/4 tsp pepper;**
> **I tsp baking powder; vegetable oil for frying**

Grate potatoes and onion. Traditionalists insist on grating by hand, noting that a little skin and blood gives latkes their unique flavor. Pragmatists—including the septuagenarian author of this recipe—have converted to using the shredder blade on a food processor. Add eggs and mix well. Add matzo meal, salt, pepper, and baking powder, and mix well. (There can be no certainty on the appropriate amount of matzo meal: every potato, every onion, and every egg is different. Cooking, like constitutional law, is a messy business.) Heat oil—again, judgment and experience must substitute for black-letter rules on amounts—in a frying pan. Add the potato mixture approximately one tablespoon at a time. Cook pancakes until golden brown; turn and cook until other side is golden.

Makes 30–40 latkes, enough for 2–10 people. Serve with applesauce, sour cream, or plain.

NOTE: Like the Constitution, latkes keep well with a few adjustments. To make them in advance: undercook the latkes very slightly. Drain, then cool on sheets of wax paper. Freeze *on the wax paper,* to keep latkes separate. When frozen, they can be thrown together in a plastic bag or container and replaced in the freezer. Reheat frozen latkes in a 350-degree oven for 10–15 minutes.

A LITTLE LIGHT ENTERTAINMENT ON A SERIOUS SUBJECT
How would our scholars deal with this recipe? In asking this question, we obviously don't mean to minimize the significance of the theories we discuss, merely to add a little seasoning to the discussion. If they religiously applied their own theories to cooking (which, of course, they all have too much common sense to do), the results might be as follows:

Bork, faced with the uncertain amount of oil, would conclude that the directions for frying were an "ink blot" and would serve the latkes raw or refuse to make them at all.

Scalia would conclude that latkes were a liberal distortion of the recipe as originally understood, so he would make matzo (the unleavened bread described in Exodus) instead.

Epstein would condemn the directions as an unwarranted infringement on his liberty. He would make up his own recipe on the basis of modern economic analysis (although unlike his own constitution, we suspect his recipe for latkes would be quite tasty).

Amar would carefully deconstruct the text. Noting that the recipe calls for "baking powder," he would cook the latkes in the oven. Since the potatoes are referred to as "peeled" but no similar instruction is given for the other ingredients, he might also include the onion peel and egg shells.

Ackerman would ask whether the Diaspora should be considered to have altered the recipe so that it should be based on cornmeal rather than potatoes. He would end up with quite serviceable tortillas, and call them latkes.

Dworkin would consult the great philosophers such as Maimonides, who, of course, would give little guidance on latkes. So, like Epstein, he would construct his own recipe—which, though also probably tasty, would not taste anything like Epstein's.

Of course, these are caricatures—but if you make allowances for exaggeration, they give you the flavor of the individual theories.

CHAPTER ONE

1. Susan R. Klein, *Enduring Principles and Current Crises in Constitutional Criminal Proce-dure*, 24 Law & Social Inquiry 533, 536 (1999).
2. Judge Richard Posner, one of the most prolific and respected federal judges and longtime member of the University of Chicago faculty, has condemned these and other constitutional theories *in toto*. See Richard A. Posner, The Problematics of Moral and Legal Theory (1999). As the text makes clear, we do not agree with Judge Posner's complete rejection of all constitutional theory.
3. Steven G. Calabresi, *We Are All Federalists, We Are All Republicans: Holism, Synthesis, and the Fourteenth Amendment*, 87 Geo. L.J. 2273, 2274 (1999). His list includes Bork's The Tempting of America, Amar's The Bill of Rights, and Ackerman's We the People. *Id.* at 2274 nn.13, 16–17. In light of the connections we draw (in chapter 5) between the flaws we identify in constitutional scholarship and the academic obsession with the "countermajoritarian difficulty," it is interesting to note that Calabresi also lists Alexander Bickel's The Least Dangerous Branch and John Ely's Democracy and Distrust among his six most valuable books. *Id.* at 2274 & nn.14–15. Calabresi's sixth book, which does not fit this pattern, was authored by one of his former colleagues: Michael Perry's The Constitution in the Courts: Law or Politics? *Id.* at 2274 n.18.
4. In a broad sense, this book is the second in a series pursuing this project. The first, Beyond All Reason: The Radical Assault on Truth in American Law (1997), criticized "outsider" scholarship for its own brand of foundationalism. In this book, we take on more mainstream scholars. A proposed third book will illustrate how a nonfoundationalist, or pragmatist, approach might work in practice.
5. Randy E. Barnett, *An Originalism for Nonoriginalists*, 45 Loyola L. Rev. 611, 617 (1999). See also Frank H. Easterbrook, *Alternatives to Originalism?* 19 Harv. J.L. & Pub. Pol'y 479, 485 (1995) ("Nothing beats originalism in court").
6. Examples include Harry Kalven, John Ely, and Herbert Wechsler. Alexander Bickel also fits this description. As we discuss later, he was a progenitor of the current crop of constitutional theorists, but as Anthony Kronman has shown, Bickel was in fact

much more nuanced than his successors. See Anthony T. Kronman, *Alexander Bickel's Philosophy of Prudence,* 94 Yale L.J. 1567 (1985).

7. In the words of one judicial commentator, describing Akhil Amar and his co-author: "Their engine is not a political agenda, but an academic one: two law professors searching so desperately for a 'new' way to look at the Constitution that they don't mind ignoring two hundred years of accumulated thought on the subject." Hon. Morris B. Hoffman, *Populist Pabulum,* 2 Green Bag 2d 97, 98 (1998).

8. One of us has been arguing against the current academic bias toward novelty for over a decade. See Daniel A. Farber, *The Case against Brilliance,* 70 Minn. L. Rev. 917 (1986); Daniel A. Farber, *Brilliance Revisited,* 72 Minn. L. Rev. 367 (1987); Daniel A. Farber, *Gresham's Law of Legal Scholarship,* 3 Const. Comm. 307 (1986).

9. For descriptions of classical legal thought, see, e.g., Lawrence Friedman, A History of American Law 333–35, 530–38 (1973); Morton Horwitz, The Transformation of America Law, 1870–1970, at 9–31 (1992); Thomas Grey, *Langdell's Orthodoxy,* 45 U. Pitt. L. Rev. 1 (1983); Duncan Kennedy, *Toward an Historical Understanding of Legal Consciousness: The Case of Classical Legal Thought in America, 1850–1940,* 3 Res. L. & Sociology 3 (1980); Roscoe Pound, *Mechanical Jurisprudence,* 8 Colum. L. Rev. 605 (1908).

10. M. H. Abrams, *The Transformation of English Studies, 1930–1995,* in Thomas Bender & Carl E. Schorske, eds., American Academic Culture in Transformation: Fifty Years, Four Disciplines 123, 134 (1997).

CHAPTER TWO

1. Gary Lawson, *On Reading Recipes . . . and Constitutions,* 85 Geo. L.J. 1823, 1834 (1997).

2. Frank H. Easterbrook, *Abstraction and Authority,* 59 U. Chi. L. Rev. 349, 359 (1992).

3. Steven G. Calabresi & Saikrishna B. Prakash, *The President's Power to Execute the Laws,* 104 Yale L.J. 541, 552 (1994).

4. Richard S. Kay, *Adherence to the Original Intentions in Constitutional Adjudication: Three Objections and Responses,* 82 Nw. U. L. Rev. 226, 234 (1988). This focus on the general understanding of the Constitution when it was enacted, rather than the subjective understanding of the drafters, is the trend among originalists. See Randy Barnett, *An Originalism for Nonoriginalists,* 45 Loyola L. Rev. 611 (1999).

5. Robert H. Bork, The Tempting of America: The Political Seduction of the Law 7 (1990).

6. *Id.* at 351–52.

7. See Kay, supra note 4, at 288.

8. Robert H. Bork, *Neutral Principles and Some First Amendment Problems,* 47 Ind. L.J. 1, 9 (1971).

9. Easterbrook, supra note 2, at 364.

10. Frank H. Easterbrook, *Alternatives to Originalism?* 19 Harv. J.L. & Pub. Pol'y 479, 485 (1996).

11. See, e.g., Easterbrook, supra note 2; Frank H. Easterbrook, *What's So Special about Judges?* 61 U. Colo. L. Rev. 773 (1990) [hereinafter *Judges*]; Frank H. Easterbrook, *Approaches to Judicial Review,* in Jack David & Robert B. McKay, eds., The Blessings of Liberty: An Enduring Constitution in a Changing World 147 (1989) [hereinafter *Approaches*].

12. Gary Lawson, *The Rise and Rise of the Administrative State,* 107 Harv. L. Rev. 1231, 1231 n.1, 1253 (1994).

13. Steven G. Calabresi, *Textualism and the Countermajoritarian Difficulty,* 66 Geo. Wash. L. Rev. 1373, 1376, 1378, 1383 (1998).

14. Steven G. Calabresi, *The Tradition of the Written Constitution: A Comment on Professor Lessig's Theory of Translation,* 65 Fordham L. Rev. 1435, 1438 (1997).

15. Steven G. Calabresi, *Caesarism, Departmentalism, and Professor Paulsen,* 83 Minn. L. Rev. 1421, 1429 (1999). See also Calabresi, supra note 13, at 1387–90.

16. Bork, supra note 5, at 257.

17. *Id.* at 144.

18. *Id.* at 144, 149.

19. See, e.g., Easterbrook, supra note 2, at 374–75; Easterbrook, *Approaches,* supra note 11, at 153; Gary Lawson, *A Farewell to Principles,* 82 Iowa L. Rev. 893 (1997).

20. Easterbrook, *Approaches,* supra note 11, at 154; accord, Easterbrook, supra note 10, at 486.

21. Easterbrook, *Judges,* supra note 11, at 782.

22. Calabresi, supra note 14, at 1446.

23. Calabresi & Prakash, supra note 3, at 664.

24. Lawson actually says that the Constitution is "a recipe for a particular form of government," which should be read in the same manner that we read a recipe for fried chicken. Lawson, supra note 1, at 1833–34.

25. Martha C. Nussbaum, *Skepticism about Practical Reason in Literature and the Law,* 107 Harv. L. Rev. 714, 730 (1994).

26. David A. Strauss, *Common Law Constitutional Interpretation,* 63 U. Chi. L. Rev. 877 (1996).

27. On the Establishment Clause, see, e.g., Robert L. Cord & Howard Ball, *The Separation of Church and State: A Debate,* 1987 Utah L. Rev. 895; Douglas Laycock, *"Nonpreferential" Aid to Religion: A False Claim about Original Intent,* 27 Wm. & Mary L. Rev. 875 (1986). On the Second Amendment, see, e.g., Randy E. Barnett & Don B. Kates, *Under Fire: The New Consensus on the Second Amendment,* 45 Emory L.J. 1139 (1996); Saul Cornell, *Commonplace or Anachronism: The Standard Model, the Second Amendment, and the Problem of History in Contemporary Constitutional Theory,* 16 Const. Comm. 221 (1999). On the Fourteenth Amendment and segregation, see, e.g., Michael W. McConnell, *Originalism and the Desegregation Decisions,* 81 Va. L. Rev. 947 (1995); Michael J. Klarman, Brown, *Originalism, and Constitutional Theory: A Response to Professor McConnell,* 81 Va. L. Rev. 1881 (1995). On the Fourteenth Amendment and incorporation, see, e.g., Michael Kent Curtis, No State Shall Abridge: The Fourteenth Amendment and the Bill of Rights (1986); Akhil Reed Amar, The Bill of Rights: Creation and Reconstruction (1998); Charles Fairman, *Does the Fourteenth Amendment Incorporate the Bill of Rights? The Original Understanding,* 2 Stan. L. Rev. 5 (1949). On the Eleventh Amendment, see, e.g., Martin H. Redish, Federal Jurisdiction: Tensions in the Allocation of Judicial Power 192–93 (2d ed. 1990); William P. Marshall, *The Diversity Theory of the Eleventh Amendment: A Critical Evaluation,* 102 Harv. L. Rev. 1372 (1989); Lawrence C. Marshall, *Fighting the Words of the Eleventh Amendment,* 102 Harv. L. Rev. 1342 (1989); Calvin R. Massey, *State Sovereignty and the Tenth and Eleventh Amendments,* 56 U. Chi. L. Rev. 61 (1989); Vicki C. Jackson, *The Supreme Court, the Eleventh Amendment, and State Sovereign Immunity,* 98 Yale L.J. 1 (1988); William A. Fletcher, *A Historical Interpretation of the Eleventh Amendment: A Narrow*

Construction of an Affirmative Grant of Jurisdiction Rather than a Prohibition against Jurisdiction, 35 Stan. L. Rev. 1033 (1983); Alden v. Maine, 527 U.S. 706 (1999).

28. James H. Hutson. *The Creation of the Constitution: The Integrity of the Documentary Record,* 65 Tex. L. Rev. 1, 33–34 (1986).

29. *Id.* at 22–24.

30. *Id.* at 36.

31. For an elaboration of this point, see Daniel A. Farber & Suzanna Sherry, A History of the American Constitution 378–81 (1990) and sources cited therein; Joseph M. Lynch, Negotiating the Constitution: The Earliest Debates over Original Intent (1999); H. Jefferson Powell, *The Original Understanding of Original Intent,* 98 Harv. L. Rev. 885 (1985).

32. Jack H. Rakove, *Two Foxes in the Forest of History,* 11 Yale J.L. & Humanities 191, 195 (1999) (book review).

33. Bruce Ackerman, *Robert Bork's Grand Inquisition,* 99 Yale L.J. 1419, 1423 (1990) (book review).

34. For Bork's account, see Bork, supra note 5, at 28–34. For a suggestion that Taney's analysis was originalist and accurate, see William Wiecek, The Sources of Antislavery Constitutionalism in America, 1760–1848, at 62–83 (1977). For an argument that *any* plausible theory of constitutional interpretation could have produced *Dred Scott,* and thus that Bork and others are wrong to use it to condemn nonoriginalist approaches, see Mark A. Graber, *Desperately Ducking Slavery:* Dred Scott *and Contemporary Constitutional Theory,* 14 Const. Comm. 271 (1997).

35. Bork, supra note 5, at 183.

36. *Id.* at 166.

37. The Nomination of Robert H. Bork to Be Associate Justice of the Supreme Court of the United States: Hearings Before the Senate Comm. on the Judiciary, 100th Cong., 1st Sess. 249 (1987) (Part I) (testimony of Robert Bork) (discussing Ninth Amendment); see also Bork, supra note 5, at 166 (discussing Privileges or Immunities Clause).

38. 1 Annals of Cong. 456 [439] (James Madison, June 8, 1789). The page numbers in the first volume of the Annals of Congress vary depending on the printing. The printing with the running page title "History of Congress" conforms with the remaining volumes in the series while the printing with the running page title "Gales & Seaton's History of Debates in Congress" is unique. Checklist of United States Public Documents 1789–1909, at 1463 (3d ed. 1911). The initial page citation is to the "Gales & Seaton" version, and the citation in brackets is to the "History of Congress" version.

39. 1 Annals of Cong. at 457.

40. See, e.g., Randy E. Barnett, ed., The Rights Retained by the People: The History and Meaning of the Ninth Amendment (1989, 1993) (2 vols.); Suzanna Sherry, *The Founders' Unwritten Constitution,* 54 U. Chi. L. Rev. 1127 (1987); Suzanna Sherry, *Natural Law in the States,* 61 U. Cincinnati L. Rev. 171 (1992); John Choon Yoo, *Our Declaratory Ninth Amendment,* 42 Emory L.J. 967 (1993).

41. See Michael Kent Curtis, No State Shall Abridge: The Fourteenth Amendment and the Bill of Rights (1986); Farber & Sherry, supra note 31, at 253–73; Michael Kent Curtis, *Historical Linguistics, Inkblots, and Life after Death: The Privileges or Immunities of Citizens of the United States,* 78 N.C. L. Rev. 1071 (2000) [hereinafter *Historical Linguis-*

tics]; Trisha Olson, *The Natural Law Foundation of the Privileges or Immunities Clause of the Fourteenth Amendment,* 48 Ark. L. Rev. 347 (1995).

42. See Curtis, *Historical Linguistics,* supra note 41; Earl M. Maltz, *The Concept of Incorporation,* 33 U. Richmond L. Rev. 525, 527 (1999), and sources cited therein.

43. Corfield v. Coryell, 6 F. Cas. 546, 551–52 (1823). For a few representative citations to *Corfield* during Reconstruction era congressional debates, see, e.g., Cong. Globe, 39th Cong., 1st Sess. 474–75 (Trumbull), 600 (Trumbull), 1118 (Wilson), 2764 (Howard) (1866).

44. Calabresi, supra note 14, at 1447. For Lessig's perspective, see, e.g., Lawrence Lessig, *Fidelity in Translation,* 71 Tex. L. Rev. 1165 (1993); Lawrence Lessig, *Understanding Changed Readings: Fidelity and Theory,* 47 Stan. L. Rev. 395 (1995); Lawrence Lessig, *Translating Federalism:* United States v. Lopez, 1995 Sup. Ct. Rev. 125; Lawrence Lessig, *Fidelity and Constraint,* 65 Fordham L. Rev. 1365 (1997).

45. Calabresi, supra note 14, at 1447–48.

46. John Hart Ely, Democracy and Distrust: A Theory of Judicial Review 38–39 (1980).

47. Bork, supra note 5, at 154–55.

48. Easterbrook has concluded that the Court's procedural due process doctrines are historically unsupportable, Frank H. Easterbrook, *Substance and Process,* 1982 Sup. Ct. Rev. 85, but has otherwise concentrated more on theory than on substance.

49. Bork, supra note 5, at 5, 352.

50. *Id.* at 97.

51. *Id.* at 62. The Oklahoma case is Skinner v. Oklahoma, 316 U.S. 535 (1942), which Bork discusses in The Tempting of America, supra note 5, at 62–67.

52. *Id.* at 62.

53. 347 U.S. 483 (1954).

54. Calabresi, supra note 13, at 1377.

55. He also cites the work of Michael McConnell, which is highly controversial. See supra note 27.

56. Bork, supra note 5, at 83.

57. Michael Klarman calls this point "well-established." Klarman, supra note 27, at 1894. Some of the voluminous sources in agreement include Alfred Avins, *The Fourteenth Amendment and Jury Discrimination: The Original Understanding,* 27 Fed. B.J. 257 (1967); Alfred Avins, *Anti-Miscegenation Laws and the Fourteenth Amendment: The Original Intent,* 52 Va. L. Rev. 1224 (1966); Alexander M. Bickel, *The Original Understanding and the Segregation Decision,* 69 Harv. L. Rev. 1 (1955); Earl M. Maltz, *The Civil Rights Act and the* Civil Rights Cases: *Congress, Court, and Constitution,* 44 Fla. L. Rev. 605 (1992); James E. Bond, *The Original Understanding of the Fourteenth Amendment in Illinois, Ohio, and Pennsylvania,* 18 Akron L. Rev. 435 (1985). But see McConnell, supra note 27.

58. 35th Congress, 2d session, Feb. 11, 1859 (in Alfred Avins, ed., The Reconstruction Amendments' Debates: The Legislative History and Contemporary Debates in Congress on the 13th, 14th, and 15th Amendments 18, 1st column (1967) [hereinafter *Reconstruction*]).

59. 36th Cong., 1st Session, April 12, 1860 (in Avins, *Reconstruction,* supra note 58, at 27, 3d column).

60. 37th Cong. 2d Session, April 3, 10, 1862 (in Avins, *Reconstruction,* supra note 58, at 35, 3d column).

61. Bork, supra note 5, at 82.

62. See Robert H. Bork, Slouching towards Gomorrah: Modern Liberalism and American Decline 231–43 (1996) (criticizing affirmative action).

63. United Steelworkers of America v. Weber, 443 U.S. 193, 213 (1979) (Blackmun, J., concurring).

64. 410 U.S. 113 (1973). For a suggestion that *Roe* is more justifiable under the Equal Protection Clause than under the Due Process Clause, see Ruth Bader Ginsburg, *Some Thoughts on Autonomy and Equality in Relation to* Roe v. Wade, 63 N.C. L. Rev. 375 (1985).

65. See, e.g., Steven G. Calabresi, *"A Government of Limited and Enumerated Powers": In Defense of* United States v. Lopez, 94 Mich. L. Rev. 752, 826–31 (1995); Frank H. Easterbrook, *Stability and Reliability in Judicial Decisions,* 73 Cornell L. Rev. 422, 429–32 (1988); Kay, supra note 4, at 229.

66. The case striking down segregated schools in the District of Columbia is Bolling v. Sharpe, 347 U.S. 497 (1954), which Bork criticizes in The Tempting of America, supra note 5, at 83–84. The case striking down racially restrictive covenants is Shelley v. Kraemer, 334 U.S. 1 (1948), which Bork criticizes in *id.*at 151–53.

67. Bork, supra note 5, at 56.

68. See Heart of Atlanta Motel v. United States, 379 U.S. 241 (1964); Katzenbach v. McClung, 379 U.S. 294 (1964).

69. Bork, supra note 8, at 20–35. Although Bork backed away from this position for a while, he now seems to have regained his distaste for free speech outside of electoral politics.

70. Bork, supra note 62, at 140.

71. *Id.* at 141.

72. Miller v. California, 413 U.S. 15, 23 (1973).

73. Bork, supra note 62, at 147.

74. *Id.*

75. For descriptions of this history, see, e.g., Michael Kent Curtis, Free Speech, "The People's Darling Privilege": Struggles for Freedom of Expression in American History (2000); David M. Rabban, Free Speech in its Forgotten Years (1997).

76. See Abrams v. United States, 250 U.S. 616, 630 (1919) (Holmes, J., dissenting); Whitney v. California, 274 U.S. 357, 375–76 (1927) (Brandeis, J., concurring).

77. Bork, supra note 62, at 102.

78. Abrams v. United States, 250 U.S. 616, 630 (1919) (Holmes, J., dissenting).

79. West Virginia State Bd. of Educ. v. Barnette, 319 U.S. 624, 642 (1943).

80. Brandenburg v. Ohio, 395 U.S. 444 (1969).

81. Bork, supra note 62, at 58.

82. *Id.* at 66.

83. *Id.* at 57.

84. *Id.* at 98.

85. Lawson, supra note 12, at 1231.

86. He also argues that a government subpoena for documents is a taking of property that sometimes requires compensation, Gary Lawson & Guy Seidman, *Taking Notes: Subpoenas and Just Compensation,* 66 U. Chi. L. Rev. 1081 (1999), an idea that has never occurred to any court or constitutional scholar in the past two hundred years and that could cripple our criminal justice system.

87. Easterbrook, supra note 2, at 378.

88. Lawson, supra note 1, at 1835.
89. Kay, supra note 4, at 256.

CHAPTER THREE

1. On the unresolved contradictions in Scalia's thought, see Michael W. McConnell, *Textualism and the Dead Hand of the Past*, 66 Geo. Wash. L. Rev. 1127, 1137 (1998).
2. See Antonin Scalia, A Matter of Interpretation: Federal Courts and the Law (1997) [hereinafter *Interpretation*] (essay by Scalia and commentary by other scholars).
3. On the failure of Scalia's methodology to constrain his decisions effectively, see David M. Zlotnick, *Justice Scalia and His Critics: An Exploration of Scalia's Fidelity to his Constitutional Methodology*, 48 Emory L.J. 1377, 1413–26 (1999).
4. 514 U.S. 549 (1995).
5. 521 U.S. 898, 904–23 (1997).
6. 18 U.S.C. § 922(s)(2) (1994).
7. *Printz*, 521 U.S. at 925.
8. *Id.* at 920 (quoting New York v. United States, 505 U.S. 144, 166 [1992]).
9. 505 U.S. 144 (1992).
10. *Id.* at 922 (quoting U.S. Const., Art. II, § 3).
11. 521 U.S. at 923.
12. Evan H. Caminker, Printz, *State Sovereignty, and the Limits of Formalism*, 1997 Sup. Ct. Rev. 199, 223 (1998).
13. Morrison v. Olson, 487 U.S. 654, 703, 734 (1988) (Scalia, J., dissenting).
14. 504 U.S. 555 (1992).
15. Of course, we would be the last to say that constitutional law can be reduced to a literalistic reading of individual clauses; while Scalia's reading of the clause may be ironic, it is not necessarily erroneous.
16. City of Richmond v. J.A. Croson Co., 488 U.S. 469, 520–28 (1989) (Scalia, J., concurring in the judgment) (affirmative action); Adarand Constructors, Inc. v. Pena, 515 U.S. 200, 239 (1995) (Scalia, J., concurring in part and concurring in the judgment) (affirmative action); Planned Parenthood v. Casey, 505 U.S. 833, 979–1002 (1992) (Scalia, J., concurring in the judgment in part and dissenting in part) (abortion); Lucas v. South Carolina Coastal Council, 505 U.S. 1003, 1006–32 (1992) (property rights); Nollan v. California Coastal Comm'n, 483 U.S. 825, 827–42 (1987) (property rights); R.A.V. v. City of St. Paul, 505 U.S. 377, 379–96 (1992) (cross-burning).
17. 494 U.S. 872, 888 (1990).
18. Planned Parenthood v. Casey, 505 U.S. 833, 1000–1 (1992) (Scalia, J., concurring in the judgment in part and dissenting in part) (emphasis in original). For similar reasons, Justice Scalia opposed any recognition of a right for dying patients to refuse unwanted medical care. He argued that the Court has no more knowledge of this area than any "nine people picked at random from the Kansas City telephone directory." Cruzan v. Director, Missouri Dep't of Health, 497 U.S. 261, 293 (1990) (Scalia, J., concurring). No matter how clearly a dying person indicates his desire to forgo extraordinary medical intervention, "it is up to the citizens of Missouri to decide, through their elected representatives, whether that wish will be honored." *Id.* To find "a constitutional right here we would have to create out of nothing (for it exists

neither in text nor tradition) some constitutional principle whereby, although the State may insist that an individual come in out of the cold and eat food, it may not insist that he take medicine; and although it may pump his stomach empty of poison he has ingested, it may not fill his stomach with food he has failed to ingest." *Id.* at 300.

19. Stenberg v. Carhart, 530 U.S. 914, 955 (2000).

20. Grant Gilmore, The Ages of American Law 62 (1977). For other discussions of formalism, see Richard Posner, *Legal Formalism, Legal Realism, and the Interpretation of Statutes and the Constitution,* 37 Case W. L. Rev. 179 (1986–87); Frederick Schauer, *Rules and the Rule of Law,* 14 Harv. J. L & Pub. Pol'y 645 (1991).

21. Gilmore, supra note 20, at 62–63.

22. For an overview of Scalia's jurisprudential thinking, combined with some speculation about its biographical origins, see George Kannar, *The Constitutional Catechism of Antonin Scalia,* 99 Yale L.J. 1297 (1990). For recent critiques of Scalia's jurisprudence, see Cass R. Sunstein, *Justice Scalia's Democratic Formalism,* 107 Yale L.J. 529 (1997) (book review); William Funk, *Review Essay: Faith in Texts—Justice Scalia's Interpretation of Statutes and the Constitution: Apostasy for the Rest of Us?* 49 Admin. L. Rev. 825 (1997); Eric J. Segall, *Justice Scalia, Critical Legal Studies, and the Rule of Law,* 62 Geo. Wash. L. Rev. 991 (1994); Symposium, *The Jurisprudence of Justice Antonin Scalia,* 12 Cardozo L. Rev. 1583 (1991). For a defense of his views, see Hadley Arkes, *Scalia Contra Mundum,* 21 Harv. J. L. & Pub. Pol'y 231 (1997).

23. Antonin Scalia, *Assorted Canards of Contemporary Legal Analysis,* 40 Case W. Res. L. Rev. 581, 588 (1989–90).

24. Id. at 588–89. So powerful is Scalia's impulse for consistency that (at least in theory) it overrules even his belief in the primacy of text and original understanding in legal interpretation. At the margins, the mandate for a consistent and logical conceptual structure trumps the duty to obey the text of democratically enacted legislation. If a judge cannot manage to reconcile the existing intellectual structure with the result he considers correct, then "his notions of fairness or textual fidelity are simply out of whack, and he must subordinate them to the law." Even the Constitution and the texts of statutes, it seems, must bow before this imperative of intellectual consistency. *Id.* at 589.

25. Antonin Scalia, *The Rule of Law as a Law of Rules,* 56 U. Chi. L. Rev. 1175, 1177 (1989).

26. *Id.* at 1180–81. For Scalia's views regarding the importance of rules, see *id.* at 1176, 1178, 1181.

27. Frederick Schauer, Book Review, *Is the Common Law Law?,* 77 Cal. L. Rev. 455 (1989).

28. Scalia, *Common-Law Courts in a Civil-Law System: The Role of United States Federal Courts in Interpreting the Constitution and Laws,* in *Interpretation,* supra note 2, at 9.

29. Scalia, supra note 23, at 589 (in parentheses in original). This statement has an intriguing resonance with conservative philosopher Leo Strauss's views that texts by the wise conceal their true views. See Shadia B. Drury, Leo Strauss and the American Right 1 (1997). See also Richard A. Posner, *What Has Modern Literary Theory to Offer Law?,* 53 Stan. L. Rev. 195, 203 (2000).

30. Gordon S. Wood, *Comment,* in *Interpretation,* supra note 2, at 63.

31. *Id.*

32. Antonin Scalia, *Originalism: The Lesser Evil,* 57 U. Cin. L. Rev. 849, 861–62 (1989).

33. *Id.* at 862–63.

34. *Id.* at 864.
35. *Id.* Why Scalia regards flogging as unconstitutional but hanging as undeniably constitutional is a question he does not pursue.
36. Scalia, supra note 32, at 864.
37. Scalia, *Response,* in *Interpretation,* supra note 2, at 140.
38. Scalia, supra note 25, at 1186–87 (final emphasis added; other italics omitted).
39. Scalia, *Response,* in *Interpretation,* supra note 2, at 140 (on wilfulness); Scalia, supra note 25, at 1187.
40. Scalia, *Response,* in *Interpretation,* supra note 2, at 132 (emphasis in original); Wood, *Comment,* in Scalia, *Interpretation,* supra note 2, at 63.
41. Scalia, *Common-Law Courts,* in *Interpretation,* supra note 2, at 9, 12 (internal citation omitted).
42. Scalia, *Response,* in *Interpretation,* supra note 2, at 133; Scalia, supra note 32, at 864.
43. Scalia, *Response,* in *Interpretation,* supra note 2, at 149; Scalia, supra note 32, at 862.
44. Scalia, supra note 32, at 862; Scalia, *Interpretation,* supra note 2, at 134–36, 137, 139, 143–44. Scalia does not cite any historical evidence that guarding against changes in public values was the primary goal of the framers.
45. See generally, Scalia, *Interpretation,* supra note 2.
46. There are occasional deviations in cases involving procedural issues, particularly when Scalia is merely following Justice Thomas's lead. See, e.g., United States v. Hubbell, 530 U.S. 27 (2000) (Thomas, J., concurring) (arguing on historical grounds that right against self-incrimination extends to nontestimonial evidence, despite consistent contrary precedent) (joined by Scalia).
47. In Federalist No. 27, Hamilton made clear that the Constitution, "by extending the authority of the federal head to the individual citizens of the several States, will enable the government to employ the ordinary magistracy of each in the execution of its laws." Federalist No. 27 (Hamilton), in Clinton Rossiter, ed., The Federalist Papers 174, 176 (1961). He added that "this will tend to destroy, in the common apprehension, all distinction between the sources from which [government authority] might proceed; and will give the federal government the same advantage for securing a due obedience to its authority which is enjoyed by the government of each State." *Id.* at 176–77. In response to fears of a massive federal tax bureaucracy, Madison responded in Federalist No. 45 that the federal government's direct power to collect taxes would "not be resorted to, except for supplemental purposes of revenue . . . and that the eventual collection, under the immediate authority of the Union, will generally be made by the officers . . . appointed by the several States." Federalist No. 45 (Madison), in Rossiter, ed., The Federalist Papers 288, 292. For historical evidence that the framers intended Congress to commandeer the states as tax collectors, see Erik M. Jensen & Jonathan L. Entin, *Commandeering, the Tenth Amendment, and the Federal Requisition Power:* New York v. United States *Revisited,* 15 Const. Comm. 355 (1998).
48. Printz v. United States, 521 U.S. 898, 971, 939–76 (1977) (Stevens, J., dissenting, and Souter, J., dissenting).
49. Caminker, supra note 12, at 211 ("all of this interpretative work . . . ."). As affirmative evidence, all that Scalia could point to was the uncontested fact that conscription of state government had been found to be troublesome and ineffective under the Articles of Confederation, leading the framers to provide the government with the power to regulate individuals directly. But the addition of this new regulatory

power for the federal government, combined with qualms about the utility of the older commandeering power, falls short of any affirmative showing that the framers meant to deprive the government of the older power entirely.

50. Scalia, supra note 32, at 859–60.

51. *Id.* at 858.

52. Henry Paul Monaghan, *Stare Decisis and Constitutional Adjudication,* 88 Colum. L. Rev. 723, 736 (1988). See also James Roger Sharp, American Politics in the Early Republic: The New Nation in Crisis 78 (1993). For recent debate about the correct reading of the historical record, see Lawrence Lessig & Cass R. Sunstein, *The President and the Administration,* 94 Colum. L. Rev. 1 (1994); Steven G. Calabresi & Saikrishna B. Prakash, *The President's Power to Execute the Laws,* 104 Yale L.J. 541 (1994).

53. Boerne v. Flores, 521 U.S. 507, 553–54 (1997) (O'Connor, J., dissenting) (see sources cited therein).

54. *Id.* at 556 (quoting Madison), 557, 560–61, 562. For example, Quakers were often exempted from the duty to swear an oath of allegiance, and most legislatures exempted conscientious objectors from conscription. In addition, O'Connor noted, "North Carolina and Maryland excused Quakers from the requirement of removing their hats in court; Rhode Island exempted Jews from the requirements of the state marriage laws; and Georgia allowed groups of European immigrants to organize whole towns according to their own faith." For an in-depth exploration of the complex and somewhat ambiguous historical record, see Michael W. McConnell, *The Origins and Historical Understanding of Free Exercise of Religion,* 103 Harv. L. Rev. 1410 (1990).

55. *Boerne,* 521 U.S. at 538, 539, 541 (Scalia, J., concurring in part).

56. Scalia, *Response,* in *Interpretation,* supra note 2, at 138.

57. *Id.* at 138–39.

58. *Id.* at 139 (internal citations omitted). His use of these examples is criticized in Jeffrey Rosen, *Originalist Sin: The Achievement of Antonin Scalia, and Its Intellectual Incoherence,* 216 New Republic 26 (May 5, 1997).

59. R.A.V. v. City of St. Paul, 505 U.S. 377, 379–96 (1992). On the general difficulties of identifying when a Supreme Court decision creates "new" law, see Barbara E. Armacost, *Qualified Immunity: Ignorance Excused,* 51 Vand. L. Rev. 583 (1998). It should be noted that some of Justice Scalia's fellow originalists reject stare decisis. See Gary Lawson, *The Constitutional Case against Precedent,* 17 Harv. J. L. & Pol'y 23 (1994); Charles J. Cooper, *Stare Decisis: Precedent and Principle in Constitutional Adjudication,* 73 Cornell L. Rev. 401, 410 (1988) (judges should follow erroneous precedents only when failure to do so would "pitch the country into the abyss"); Michael Stokes Paulsen, *Abrogating* Stare Decisis *by Statute: May Congress Remove the Precedential Effect of* Roe *and* Casey, 109 Yale L.J. 1535 (2000).

60. For some notable examples of Justice Scalia's use of tradition, see Michael H. v. Gerald D., 491 U.S. 110, 124–28 (1989) (plurality opinion); Burnham v. Superior Court, 495 U.S. 604 (1990); Rutan v. Republican Party, 497 U.S. 62 (1990) (Scalia, J., dissenting). For an insightful critique of Scalian traditionalism, see David A. Strauss, *Tradition, Precedent, and Justice Scalia,* 12 Cardozo L. Rev. 1699 (1991). For discussion of traditionalism as an alternative to originalism, see Michael W. McConnell, *Tradition and Constitutionalism before the Constitution,* 1998 U. Ill. L. Rev. 173.

61. O'Hare Truck Serv. Inc. v. City of Northlake, 518 U.S. 712 (1996); Board of County Comm'rs v. Umbehr, 518 U.S. 668 (1996).

62. *Umbehr*, 518 U.S. at 668–69 (emphasis in original).

63. *Id.* 669–90 (emphasis in original).

64. *Id.* at 687, quoting Rutan v. Republican Party, 497 U.S. 62, 95–96 (1980) (Scalia, J., dissenting).

65. *Umbehr*, 518 U.S. at 711.

66. On the pervasive fear of corruption, see Daniel Farber & Suzanna Sherry, A History of the American Constitution 7–9 (1990) (quoting one 1776 writer as complaining that the king controlled parliament "by places, pensions, honours and promises"). The failure of the framers to anticipate the party system is a staple among historians. Sharp, supra note 52, presents a comprehensive recent discussion of the confusion and disruption caused in the early Republic by the inability to grasp the concept of the two-party system.

67. For instance, some intriguing recent efforts have been made to revive Burkeanism as an approach to constitutional law. See Ernest Young, *Rediscovering Conservatism: Burkean Political Theory and Constitutional Interpretation,* 72 N.C. L. Rev. 619 (1994).

68. One might imagine at least eight grounds for considering tradition in constitutional interpretation: (1) Perhaps the framers so understood the process of legal interpretation (or perhaps not). (2) The rule might derive from the conventional nature of language—the reason the word "cat" cannot apply to a Scottish terrier is simply that no one uses the word that way, and for the same reason the term "abridge the freedom of speech" cannot apply to patronage hiring because no one ever used the term that way. (3) Maybe the rule is based on judicial modesty—if everyone else in the world adopts a given interpretation, it would be arrogant for the justices to disagree. (4) Perhaps the point is to avoid destabilizing social arrangements, just as the Court follows its own precedents for that reason. (5) Maybe a long history of uniform interpretation is simply very strong evidence of the pre-1790 understanding. (6) Perhaps, it might be argued, such uniform interpretations represent the judgment of We the People about the Constitution, which must trump that of the Court or even that of the framers. (7) It might be unfair to "surprise" the current population with unexpected constitutional interpretations, because if anticipated such interpretations might have been dealt with by an amendment. (8) Reliance on universally shared views is the only acceptably restrained form of the "living Constitution."

69. On libel law, see Daniel A. Farber, The First Amendment 79–101 (1998).

70. *Umbehr*, 518 U.S. at 686 (Scalia, J., dissenting); *id.* at 701 (quoting LaFalce v. Houston, 712 F.2d 292, 294 [7th Cir. 1983] [Posner, J.]).

71. Compare David Strauss's observation that Scalia's traditionalism "takes the form not of a cool counsel of restraint and humility but of an urgent sense that something has gone awry and that the world should be returned to its older, more solid, traditional foundations. Certain recent developments are," Strauss adds, "for Justice Scalia, what the French Revolution was for Burke: a source not of new traditions to be accepted but of innovations to be overthrown, in the name of deeper traditions, as soon as possible." Strauss, supra note 60, at 1713–14.

CHAPTER FOUR

1. Epstein's views on the Commerce Clause are found in Richard Epstein, *The Proper Scope of the Commerce Power,* 73 Va. L. Rev. 1387 (1987), 1442 (Ford Motor Co.), 1454

(affirmative scope) [hereinafter *Proper Scope*]. His views on the Takings Clause are found in Richard Epstein, Takings: Private Property and the Power of Eminent Domain (1985) [hereinafter *Takings*]. For a sympathetic introduction to his thought, see Larry Alexander & Maimon Schwartzchild, *Subversive Thoughts on Freedom and the Common Good*, 97 Mich. L. Rev. 1813 (1999).

2. Richard Epstein, *Fidelity without Translation*, 1 Green Bag (2d) 21, 27 (1997).

3. Richard Epstein, Forbidden Grounds: The Case against Employment Discrimination Laws 135–43 (1992).

4. See Richard Epstein, *Lest We Forget:* Buchanan v. Warley *and Constitutional Jurisprudence of the "Progressive Era,"* 51 Vand. L. Rev. 787, 795 (1998).

5. See Gary Lawson, *The Constitutional Case against Precedent*, 17 Harv. J. L. & Pub. Pol'y 23 (1994); Gary Lawson, *The "Proper" Scope of Federal Power: A Jurisdictional Interpretation of the Sweeping Clause*, 43 Duke L.J. 267 (1993); Bernard H. Siegan, Economic Liberties and the Constitution (1980); Bernard H. Siegan, ed., Government, Regulation, and the Economy (1977).

6. See Epstein, supra note 4, at 795.

7. Richard Epstein, *Life Boats, Desert Islands, and the Poverty of Modern Jurisprudence*, 68 Miss. L.J. 861, 887 (1999).

8. 260 U.S. 393 (1922).

9. Kaiser Aetna v. United States, 444 U.S. 164 (1979).

10. Loretto v. Teleprompter Manhattan CATV Corp., 458 U.S. 419 (1982).

11. 505 U.S. 1003 (1992). Other notable recent cases include Nollan v. California Coastal Comm'n, 483 U.S. 825 (1987) (requirement that beach owner allow certain types of public access is a taking); Dolan v. City of Tigard, 512 U.S. 374 (1994) (requiring store owner to agree to bike path as a condition of an expansion project is a taking). The views of individual justices are probed in Richard Lazarus, *Counting Votes and Discounting Holdings in the Supreme Court's Takings Cases*, 38 Wm. & Mary L. Rev. 1099 (1997). For an overview of takings scholarship, see Barton Thompson, *Judicial Takings*, 76 Va. L. Rev. 1449, 1472–98 (1990).

12. John Hart, *Takings and Compensation in Early America: The Colonial Highway Acts in Social Context*, 40 Am. J. Leg. Hist. 253, 304–5 (1996).

13. The material in this and the succeeding paragraph is taken from William Michael Treanor, *The Original Understanding of the Takings Clause and the Political Process*, 95 Colum. L. Rev. 782 (1995).

14. On Madison's views, see *id.* at 836–55.

15. See Kris W. Kobach, *The Origins of Regulatory Takings: Setting the Record Straight*, 1996 Utah L. Rev. 1211, 1291–92.

16. Epstein provides a succinct summary of his theory in Richard Epstein, *An Outline of Takings*, 41 U. Miami L. Rev. 3 (1986), which provides the basis for this and the following two paragraphs. Epstein's views have given rise to a plethora of criticism. A useful discussion of the theory (and of takings theory more generally) can be found in William Fischel, Regulatory Takings: Law, Economics, and Politics 171–82 (1995). On the role of public choice theory in takings theory (on which Epstein relies heavily), see Daniel Farber, *Public Choice and Just Compensation*, 9 Const. Comm. 279 (1992).

17. Richard A. Epstein, *Introduction: The Harms and Benefits of* Nolan *and* Dolan, 15 N. Ill. U. L. Rev. 479, 489 (1995).

18. Epstein, supra note 16, at 18 (on transfer programs); Epstein, *Takings*, supra note 1, at 281 (on the New Deal). As a concession to the strong consensus in favor of pro-

viding some form of assistance to the poor, he now seems willing to consider allowing redistribution to the poor financed by flat taxes. See Richard Epstein, Simple Rules for a Complex World 144–48 (1995).

19. See Daniel A. Farber & Suzanna Sherry, A History of the American Constitution 3–9 (1990).

20. Epstein, *Takings,* supra note 1, at 20, 23–24.

21. *Id.* at 5, 16–17, 28, 31. See chapter 7 for a discussion of Dworkin. Epstein comes close to embracing Dworkin's analysis himself when he analogizes his view of the "internal logic" of the Takings Clause to the use of the "internal logic" of the Equal Protection Clause to outlaw gender discrimination. See Richard A. Epstein, *More Fidelity, Less Translation,* 1 Green Bag (2d) 177, 187 (1998).

22. See Richard A. Epstein, *The Static Conception of the Common Law,* 9 J. Leg. Studies 253, 254 (1980) ("it is wrong to suppose that the substantive principles of the legal system should change in response to new social conditions").

23. See Margaret Radin, *The Consequences of Conception,* 41 U. Miami L. Rev. 239 (1986).

24. Jonathan Hughes, American Economic History 123 (2d. ed. 1987); William J. Novak, The People's Welfare: Law & Religion in Nineteenth Century America (1996).

25. Epstein, *Takings,* supra note 1, at 28. For more on Epstein's view of the relevance of historical materials, see his contribution to the *Proceedings of the Conference on Takings of Property and the Constitution,* 41 U. Miami L. Rev. 49, 66, 81–82 (1986).

26. Treanor, supra note 13, at 789 (colonial practices), 842 (Madison).

27. Raoul Berger, Federalism: The Founder's Design (1987). Attacks on congressional power continue to attract conservatives. See Randy Barnett, *Necessary and Proper,* 44 UCLA L. Rev. 745 (1997).

28. Berger, supra note 27, at 32–34.

29. *Id.* at 125.

30. *Id.* at 166–70, 178–80. Notably, Berger does concede that it is probably impractical to root out all of the federal regulatory structure that has accumulated over the decades, but at least a freeze on further expansion, if not some pruning, is called for. *Id.* at 170–80.

31. Michael McConnell, *Federalism: Evaluating the Founders' Design,* 54 U. Chi. L. Rev. 1484 (1987). For more elaborate efforts to explore the normative arguments for state autonomy, see Thomas Ulen, *Economic and Public Choice Forces in Federalism,* 6 Geo. Mason L. Rev. 921 (1998); Barry Friedman, *Valuing Federalism,* 82 Minn. L. Rev. 317 (1997). For counterarguments, see Edward Rubin, *The Fundamentality and Irrelevance of Federalism,* 13 Geo. St. U. L. Rev. 1009 (1997). A useful overview can be found in David Shapiro, Federalism: A Dialogue (1995).

32. 514 U.S. 549 (1995).

33. See also Morrison v. United States, 529 U.S. 598 (2000) (striking down Violence against Women Act on federalism grounds).

34. 514 U.S. at 586.

35. *Id.* at 590–91.

36. McConnell, supra note 31, at 1490–91.

37. See Herbert Hovenkamp, *Judicial Restraint and Constitutional Federalism: The Supreme Court's Lopez and Seminole Tribe Decisions,* 96 Colum. L. Rev. 2213, 2231, 2233 (1996). Indeed, Congress went beyond a strict interpretation of its powers at an early date. See David Currie, *The Vaccine Agent,* 1 Green Bag 245 (Spring, 1998).

38. Richard Brandon Morris, The Forging of the Union 269 (1987).

39. Gordon Wood, The Creation of the American Republic 526 (1969).

40. Epstein, *Proper Scope,* supra note 1, at n.231.

41. The historical account is found in *id.* at 1389–96.

42. *Id.* at 1452 n.231.

43. 77 U.S. (10 Wall.) 557 (1870).

44. Epstein, *Proper Scope,* supra note 1, at 1411–12.

45. *Id.* at 1411–22.

46. *Id.* at 1422–32.

47. See Larry Kramer, *But When Exactly Was Judicially-Enforced Federalism "Born" In the First Place?* 22 Harv. J. L & Pub. Pol'y 125, 132–35 (1998).

48. 156 U.S. 1 (1895).

49. Epstein, *Proper Scope,* supra note 1, at 1432–39.

50. 301 U.S. 1 (1937).

51. Epstein, *Proper Scope,* supra note 1, at 1413.

52. Another example of this is found in his treatment of exit rights by monopolists in Richard Epstein, *Exit Rights and Insurance Regulation: From Federalism to Takings,* 7 Geo. Mason L. Rev. 293, 300–1 (1999).

53. Epstein, *Proper Scope,* supra note 1, at 1454.

54. *Id.* at 1454–55.

55. Epstein, supra note 3, at 143.

56. *Id.* at 143 (no political sentiment).

CHAPTER FIVE

1. See Akhil Reed Amar, *Justice Kennedy and the Ideal of Equality,* 28 Pac. L.J. 515 (1997) (affirmative action); Akhil Reed Amar & Neal Kumar Katyal, *Bakke's Fate,* 43 UCLA L. Rev. 1745 (1996) (affirmative action); Akhil Reed Amar, *The Case of the Missing Amendments*: R.A.V. v. City of St. Paul, 106 Harv. L. Rev. 124 (1992) (hate speech).

2. Akhil Reed Amar, The Constitution and Criminal Procedure: First Principles 1–45 (1997).

3. Akhil Reed Amar, *The Consent of the Governed: Constitutional Amendment Outside Article V,* 94 Colum. L. Rev. 457 (1994).

4. Amar, *The Case of the Missing Amendments,* supra note 1, (hate speech); Akhil Reed Amar & Daniel Widawsky, *Child Abuse as Slavery: A Thirteenth Amendment Response to DeShaney,* 105 Harv. L. Rev. 1359 (1992) (child abuse).

5. Akhil Reed Amar, *Attainder and Amendment 2:* Romer's *Rightness,* 95 Mich. L. Rev. 203 (1996). The Bill of Attainder Clause may well be related in interesting ways to the core meaning of the Equal Protection Clause, but Amar's argument here is a much more simplistic and straightforward one: enacting a statewide referendum that prohibits cities from protecting gays from discrimination violates the Attainder Clause itself, without more.

6. Akhil Reed Amar, *Intratextualism,* 112 Harv. L. Rev. 747, 789–92 (1999).

7. He uses the former term in *id.* at 1657, and the latter term in Akhil Reed Amar, *Foreword: The Document and the Doctrine,* 114 Harv. L. Rev. 26 (2000) [hereinafter *Foreword*]. They appear to describe a single method of constitutional interpretation, and we use them interchangeably.

8. Akhil Reed Amar, *A Few Thoughts on Constitutionalism, Textualism, and Populism,* 65 Fordham L. Rev. 1657, 1657 (1997).

9. *Id.*
10. Amar, supra notoe 5, at 203.
11. Akhil Reed Amar, *A Neo-Federalist View of Article III: Separating the Two Tiers of Federal Jurisdiction,* 65 B.U. L. Rev. 205, 207 n.7 (1985). In this footnote he particularly qualifies his adherence to textualism, but he never seems to say there is anything wrong with textualism. And in later work he both defends and uses it.
12. Akhil Reed Amar, The Bill of Rights: Creation and Reconstruction 296 (1998).
13. Amar, supra note 2, at 153.
14. Amar, *Foreword,* supra note 7, at 54–55.
15. Adrian Vermeule & Ernest A. Young, *Hercules, Herbert, and Amar: The Trouble with Intratextualism,* 113 Harv. L. Rev. 730, 734 (2000).
16. Amar, supra note 6, at 748.
17. 17 U.S. 316 (1819).
18. Amar, supra note 6, at 779–81.
19. *Id.*
20. Vermeule & Young, supra note 15, at 731–32.
21. Amar, *Foreword,* supra note 7, at 28.
22. Ira C. Lupu, *Time, The Supreme Court, and* The Federalist, 66 Geo. Wash. L. Rev. 1324, 1325 (1998).
23. Vermeule & Young, supra note 15, at 732.
24. Amar, supra note 6, at 812–16 (quotation at page 813). He does "qualify" these conclusions, but not in any significant—or useful—ways. See *id.* at 817. He reiterates his rejection of current doctrine in *Foreword,* supra note 7, at 59–60.
25. Amar, supra note 6, at 813, 816.
26. 424 U.S. 1 (1976).
27. See, e.g., J. Skelly Wright, *Politics and the Constitution: Is Money Speech?* 85 Yale L.J. 1001 (1976); J. Skelly Wright, *Money and the Pollution of Politics: Is the First Amendment an Obstacle to Political Equality?* 82 Colum. L. Rev. 609 (1982); Burt Neuborne, *Buckley's Analytical Flaw,* 6 J.L. & Pol'y 111 (1997); Owen Fiss, *Money and Politics,* 97 Colum. L. Rev. 2470 (1997); Ronald Dworkin, *The Curse of American Politics,* New York Review of Books, 17 October 1996, at 24.
28. See, e.g., Owen Fiss, The Irony of Free Speech (1996); Jamin Raskin & John Bonifaz, *Equal Protection and the Wealth Primary,* 11 Yale L. & Pol'y Rev. 273 (1993); Michael W. McConnell, *The Selective Funding Problem: Abortions and Religious Schools,* 104 Harv. L. Rev. 989 (1991); Laurence H. Tribe, *The Abortion Funding Conundrum: Inalienable Rights, Affirmative Duties, and the Dilemma of Dependence,* 99 Harv. L. Rev. 330 (1985); Frank Michelman, *Welfare Rights in a Constitutional Democracy,* 1979 Wash. U. L.Q. 659. See also Susan Bandes, *The Negative Constitution: A Critique,* 88 Mich. L. Rev. 2271 (1990).
29. Amar, supra note 6, at 773.
30. *Id.* at 817.
31. Daniel A. Farber, The First Amendment 21 (1998).
32. See Amar, *The Case of the Missing Amendments,* supra note 1.
33. 347 U.S. 497 (1954).
34. 347 U.S. 483 (1954).
35. For one example of the latter type of argument, see Daniel A. Farber & Suzanna Sherry, *The Pariah Principle,* 13 Const. Comm. 257 (1996).
36. Amar, supra note 6, at 747, 773, 789.

37. *Id.* at 785. This interpretation also seems dubious as a matter of policy. The federal government's powers and responsibilities were quite different in the territories than in the states. The tax base was also probably quite different. Why use the same tax laws for both?
38. Amar, supra note 12, at 67.
39. *Id.* at 166.
40. Amar, supra note 6, at 785, 799.
41. Amar, supra note 2, at 155.
42. This point is nicely elaborated in Susan Bandes, *"We The People" and Our Enduring Values,* 96 Mich. L. Rev. 1376 (1998).
43. Even within Amar's "agency cost" model, there are reasons to protect the guilty. Since routine monitoring of the fairness of the criminal justice system is difficult, enforcing procedural rules—even at the price of freeing some guilty defendants—sends a politically costly, and therefore reliable, signal that the rights of the innocent are rigorously protected. Also, the need to comply with procedural safeguards during enforcement may actually affect what substantive measures are enacted (and therefore who is "guilty"). For example, strict observance of strong limits on policing would make prosecution of "victimless" crimes difficult, thereby promoting libertarianism.
44. Amar, supra note 2, at 70–72, 153.
45. Akhil Reed Amar, *The Fifteenth Amendment and "Political Rights,"* 17 Cardozo L. Rev. 2225, 2225–26 (1996).
46. See Cristina M. Rodriguez, *Clearing the Smoke-Filled Room: Women Jurors and the Disruption of an Old-Boys' Network in Nineteenth Century America,* 108 Yale L.J. 1805 (1999).
47. We recognize that there is some intuitive connection, but it may run in the opposite direction: those who bear arms should be allowed to vote on the issues that may send them into battle. On the other hand, no one seems to have thought that the Nineteenth Amendment, giving women the right to vote, also required them to be drafted.
48. On historians' criticism of the legal "civic republicanism" scholarship, see, e.g., Joyce Appleby, Liberalism and Republicanism in the Historical Imagination (1992); Laura Kalman, The Strange Career of Legal Liberalism (1996); Daniel Rodgers, *Republicanism: The Career of a Concept,* 79 J. Am. Hist. 11 (1992); G. Edward White, *Reflections on the "Republican Revival": Interdisciplinary Scholarship in the Legal Academy,* 6 Yale J.L. & Humanities 1 (1994); Martin Flaherty, *History "Lite" in Modern American Constitutionalism,* 95 Colum. L. Rev. 523 (1995). On restricting arms-bearing, see Saul Cornell, *Commonplace or Anachronism: The Standard Model, the Second Amendment, and the Problem of History in Contemporary Constitutional Theory,* 16 Const. Comm. 221 (1999).
49. There is also a more mundane problem with Amar's voting theory: since appellate judges also vote—they sit on multimember panels and decide cases by majority vote—Amar's theory would suggest that every citizen has a constitutional right to sit as an appellate judge. Or, as another reviewer of Amar's work has pointed out, a right to sit on the Board of the Federal Reserve. Morris B. Hoffman, *Populist Pabulum,* 2 Green Bag 2d 97, 100 (1998).
50. Akhil Reed Amar, *The Central Meaning of Republican Government: Popular Sovereignty, Majority Rule, and the Denominator Problem,* 65 U. Colo. L. Rev. 749, 761 (1994).

51. Amar, supra note 12, at 21–22.
52. Akhil Reed Amar, *The Consent of the Governed: Constitutional Amendment outside Article V,* 94 Colum. L. Rev. 457, 503 (1994).
53. See generally Gordon S. Wood, The Creation of the American Republic 1776–1787 (1969); Forrest McDonald, Novus Ordo Seclorum: The Intellectual Origins of the Constitution (1985); Michael J. Klarman, *Constitutional Fact/Constitutional Fiction: A Critique of Bruce Ackerman's Theory of Constitutional Moments,* 44 Stan. L. Rev. 759, 781–85 (1992). This antipathy to populist government is briefly explored in the next few pages of text.
54. Roger Sherman, Thursday May 31, 1787, in James Madison, Notes of Debates in the Federal Convention of 1787, at 39 (Koch ed., 1966) [hereinafter *Madison's Notes*].
55. Elbridge Gerry, Thursday May 31, 1787, in *id.*
56. Edmund Randolph, Tuesday May 29, 1787, as reported by James McHenry, in 1 Records of the Federal Convention of 1787, at 26–27 (Max Farrand ed., 1911).
57. James Madison, Tuesday June 26, 1787, in *Madison's Notes,* supra note 54, at 193.
58. Madison to Jefferson, 24 October 1787.
59. Essay by Montezuma, *Philadelphia Independent Gazetteer,* 17 October 1787, reprinted in 3 The Complete Anti-Federalist 53–54 (Herbert Storing ed., 1981) [hereinafter *Complete Anti-Federalist*].
60. Letter of Agrippa, 4 February 1788, reprinted in 4 *Complete Anti-Federalist,* supra note 59, at 109, 111. Agrippa was probably James Winthrop, the librarian at Harvard who later became a Massachusetts judge. See *id.* at 68.
61. Essay by A Farmer, *Baltimore Maryland Gazette,* 15 February 1788, reprinted in 4 *Complete Anti-Federalist,* supra note 59, at 9, 15.
62. Letter of The Federal Farmer, 25 January 1788, reprinted in 2 *Complete Anti-Federalist,* supra note 59, at 339, 342. The Federal Farmer may have been New York merchant Melancton Smith. See Robert H. Webking, *Melancton Smith and the Letters from the Federal Farmer,* 44 Wm. & Mary Q. 510 (1987).
63. Amar, supra note 12, at 302.
64. G. Edward White, *Reading the Guarantee Clause,* 65 U. Colo. L. Rev. 787, 794–95 (1994). Martin Flaherty sums up historians' view of Wood's thesis by saying that "no one has seriously challenged the essentials of [its] central claims"—even "[Forrest] McDonald, who is quick to point out his disagreements with Wood, nonetheless agrees that the Constitutional Convention in large part arose as a response to perceived excesses of the state governments and that it produced a document reflecting a fundamental departure in political thought." Flaherty, supra note 48, at 540 & n.68. For other scholarship portraying the founders as less than democratic, see, e.g., Saul Cornell, The Other Founders: Anti-Federalism and the Dissenting Tradition in America, 1788–1828 (1999); McDonald, supra note 53; Saul Cornell, *Commonplace or Anachronism: The Standard Model, the Second Amendment, and the Problem of History in Contemporary Constitutional Theory,* 16 Const. Comm. 221 (1999); Joyce Appleby, *The American Heritage: The Heirs and the Disinherited,* 74 J. Am. Hist. 798 (1987).
65. For overviews, see generally McDonald, supra note 53, at 9–66; Scott Douglas Gerber, To Secure These Rights: The Declaration of Independence and Constitutional Interpretation (1995); Suzanna Sherry, *The Founders' Unwritten Constitution,* 54 U. Chi. L. Rev. 1127, 1132–34 (1987).
66. For discussions of many of these cases, see Sherry, supra note 65; Suzanna Sherry, *The Ninth Amendment: Righting an Unwritten Constitution,* 64 Chi.-Kent L. Rev. 1001

(1988); Suzanna Sherry, *Natural Law in the States,* 61 Cincinnati L. Rev. 171 (1992); Suzanna Sherry, *Foreword: State Constitutional Law: Doing the Right Thing,* 25 Rutgers L.J. 935 (1994); John Choon Yoo, *Our Declaratory Ninth Amendment,* 42 Emory L.J. 967 (1993).

67. Cass R. Sunstein, *Originalism for Liberals,* New Republic, 28 September 1998, at 15.
68. Amar, supra note 12, at 79 n.*.
69. *Id.* at 215.
70. Amar & Widawsky, supra note 4. The article discusses DeShaney v. Winnebago County Social Servs. Dept., 489 U.S. 189 (1989). When Joshua DeShaney's parents divorced, the state of Wisconsin awarded custody of the toddler to his father. State social workers became involved with the family after Joshua's father physically abused him, temporarily removing him from his father's custody but eventually re-turning him. When the social workers failed to protect four-year-old Joshua from a final beating that left him permanently disabled and institutionalized, his mother sued the state agency. The Supreme Court held that the Constitution was not violated by the state's failure to protect the child from his custodial parent.
71. Akhil Reed Amar & Alan Hirsch, For the People: What the Constitution Really Says about Your Rights 189–90 (1998). Since the language of the Amendment was taken directly from the Northwest Ordinance, it appears that citizens of some states have enjoyed a legal right to welfare since even before the Constitution itself.
72. Amar, supra note 12, at 293.
73. See, e.g., Eric Foner, Reconstruction: America's Unfinished Revolution 1863–1877 (1988); Michael Kent Curtis, No State Shall Abridge: The Fourteenth Amendment and the Bill of Rights (1986); Christopher L. Eisgruber, *The Fourteenth Amendment's Constitution,* 69 S. Cal. L. Rev. 47, 101 (1995); Michael Zuckert, *Completing the Constitution: The Thirteenth Amendment,* 4 Const. Comm. 259 (1987).
74. For an overview of the Court's struggles with the question of incorporation, see Michael Kent Curtis, *Historical Linguistics, Inkblots, and Life after Death: The Privileges or Immunities of Citizens of the United States,* 78 N.C. L. Rev. 1071, 1076–88 (2000). For an example of the Court's internal debate, compare the majority, concurring, and dis-senting opinions in Adamson v. California, 332 U.S. 46 (1947). The cases finally adopting the "selective incorporation" standard are Gideon v. Wainwright, 372 U.S. 335 (1963), and Malloy v. Hogan, 378 U.S. 1 (1964). The Court decided that states may use six-person juries in Williams v. Florida, 399 U.S. 78 (1970). See also John-son v. Louisiana, 406 U.S. 356 (1972) (less-than-unanimous jury verdicts in state court do not violate Sixth Amendment); Ballew v. Georgia, 435 U.S. 223 (1978) (five-person juries do violate Sixth Amendment).
75. Amar, supra note 12, at 221.
76. For a nice elaboration of this point, see Carol S. Steiker, *"First Principles" of Constitu-tional Criminal Procedure: A Mistake?* 112 Harv. L. Rev. 680, 689–90 (1999).
77. Amar, supra note 12, at 232.
78. Amar, *Foreword,* supra note 7, at 28, 63–64.
79. Amar, supra note 2, at 94.
80. Amar, supra note 12, at 34.
81. *Id.* at 252–54.
82. Andrew Koppelman, *Akhil Amar and the Establishment Clause,* 33 U. Rich. L. Rev. 393 (1999).
83. Amar & Katyal, supra note 1, at 1771.

84. This provision was later modified by the Twelfth Amendment, but it is still indicative of the meaning of the term "equal." Compare the Article V requirement that each state retain "equal Suffrage" in the Senate.
85. Amar, supra note 12, at 305.
86. Amar, *Foreword,* supra note 7, at 91.
87. Amar, supra note 12, at 305.
88. *Id.* at 307.
89. Amar, *Foreword,* supra note 7, at 81–83.
90. Vermeule & Young, supra note 15, at 767.

CHAPTER SIX

1. Ackerman's dualist framework is sketched out in the first two volumes of a projected three-volume series. The first volume, We the People: Foundations (1991) [hereinafter *Foundations*], lays the groundwork by explaining how the framers of the original constitution were dualists. The second volume, We the People: Transformations (1998) [hereinafter *Transformations*], examines Reconstruction and the New Deal.
2. On referenda, see Ackerman, *Foundations,* supra note 1, at 50–56; on unwritten amendments, see Ackerman, *Transformations,* supra note 1, at 255–382.
3. Richard A. Posner, Overcoming Law 215 (1995).
4. Ackerman, *Transformations,* supra note 1, at 491 n.1.
5. *Id.* at 269–70.
6. See, e.g., Jack N. Rakove, Original Meanings: Politics and Ideas in the Making of the Constitution 94–130 (1996); Richard S. Kay, *The Illegality of the Constitution,* 4 Const. Comm. 57 (1987).
7. Ackerman, *Transformations,* supra note 1, at 57–58.
8. Jay contributed only a handful of essays to the collection, which were not important for Ackerman's purposes.
9. For suggestions that the Federalist Papers had very little influence, see Stanley Elkins & Eric McKitrick, The Age of Federalism 22 (1993); Forrest McDonald, Alexander Hamilton, A Life 114–15 (1979); Linda Grant DePauw, The Eleventh Pillar: New York State and the Federal Constitution 114 (1966); Larry D. Kramer, *Putting the Politics Back into the Political Safeguards of Federalism,* 100 Colum. L. Rev. 215, 247–48 & nn.134–35 (2000); Elaine F. Crane, *Publius in the Provinces: Where Was "The Federalist" Published Outside New York City?* 21 Wm. & Mary Q. 589 (1964). Recently Kramer has concluded that Madison's fundamental political theories "played essentially no role in shaping the Constitution or its ratification." Larry Kramer, *Madison's Audience,* 112 Harv. L. Rev. 611, 616 (1999).
10. Michael J. Klarman, *Constitutional Fact/Constitutional Fiction: A Critique of Bruce Ackerman's Theory of Constitutional Moments,* 44 Stan. L. Rev. 759, 778 (1992).
11. Ackerman, *Foundations,* supra note 1, at 175–93.
12. James Madison, Notes of Debates in the Federal Convention of 1787, at 651 (Adrienne Koch ed., 1966) (Sept. 15) [hereinafter *Madison's Notes*].
13. Jack N. Rakove, *The Super-Legality of the Constitution, or, a Federalist Critique of Bruce Ackerman's Neo-Federalism,* 108 Yale L.J. 1931 (1999).
14. See Suzanna Sherry, *The Founders' Unwritten Constitution,* 54 U. Chi. L. Rev. 1127, 1146–55 (1987).

15. Ackerman, *Foundations,* supra note 1, at 179, quoting Federalist No. 49 (Madison), in Clinton Rossiter, ed., The Federalist Papers 314 (1961).
16. Ackerman, *Foundations,* supra note 1, at 179.
17. *Id.* at 193, quoting Federalist No. 78 (Hamilton), in Rossiter, supra note 15, at 469–70 (emphasis added).
18. *Id.* at 193. By "semiotic," Ackerman means only to restate the notion that the legislature is deliberative rather than acting as an unthinking obedient agent of its constituents.
19. Others have interpreted the language in this more natural way. See, e.g., Paul W. Kahn, *Reason and Will in the Origins of American Constitutionalism,* 98 Yale L.J. 449, 453 & n.13 (1989).
20. Federalist No. 49 (Madison), in Rossiter, supra note 15, at 313, 317.
21. Letter from James Madison to Edmund Randolph (Jan. 10, 1788), in 10 The Papers of Madison 355 (Robert A. Rutland et al. eds., 1977).
22. Rakove, supra note 13, at 1955.
23. Ackerman, *Transformations,* supra note 1, at 209.
24. The story is told in *id.*at 186–252.
25. *Id.* at 268, 315, 361.
26. *Id.* at 277.
27. See Michael Les Benedict, A Compromise of Principle: Congressional Republicans and Reconstruction, 1863–1869 (1974); Michael Les Benedict, *Preserving the Constitution, The Conservative Basis of Radical Reconstruction,* 61 J. Am. Hist. 65 (1974); Eric Foner, Reconstruction: America's Unfinished Revolution, 1863–1877 (1988).
28. He quotes from Michael Les Benedict's work on the Johnson impeachment, for example, but cites his work on Republicans only for uncontroversial facts—ignoring all of the conclusions Benedict draws from these facts. Eric Foner is cited only once (in the context of asking why legal historians have ignored the procedural irregularities in the ratification of the Reconstruction Amendments), and although Ackerman calls his work "outstanding," he draws nothing of substance from it. Compare Amar's treatment of Wood, discussed at page 88.
29. Laura Kalman, *Law, Politics, and the New Deal(s),* 108 Yale L.J. 2165, 2196 (1999).
30. *Id.* at 2199–2200.
31. Colin Gordon, *Rethinking the New Deal,* 98 Colum. L. Rev. 2029, 2032, 2036 (1998).
32. Daniel J. Hulsebosch, *Civics 2000: Process Constitutionalism at Yale,* 97 Mich. L. Rev. 1520, 1549 (1999).
33. See, e.g., Joanne B. Freeman, *The Election of 1800: A Study in the Logic of Political Change,* 108 Yale L.J. 1959 (1999).
34. Eric Foner, *The Strange Career of the Reconstruction Amendments,* 108 Yale L.J. 2003 (1999).
35. See, e.g., Larry Kramer, *What's a Constitution for Anyway? Of History and Theory, Bruce Ackerman and the New Deal,* 46 Case W. Res. L. Rev. 885 (1996), and the sources it cites. See also Stephen A. Siegel, Lochner *Era Jurisprudence and the American Constitutional Tradition,* 70 N.C. L. Rev. 1 (1991) (arguing that constitutional jurisprudence of pre–New Deal era was similar in some ways to New Deal jurisprudence).
36. Ackerman, *Transformations,* supra note 1, at 375–76. The term "*Lochnerizing*" derives from Lochner v. New York, 198 U.S. 45 (1905), in which the Supreme Court struck down a law regulating maximum hours of bakers. It is a derogatory term for judicial enforcement of rights not clearly enumerated in the Constitution.

37. See Planned Parenthood of Southeastern Pennsylvania v. Casey, 505 U.S. 833 (1992); Roe v. Wade, 410 U.S. 113 (1973). The Court has recently indicated that the Fourteenth Amendment privileges or immunities clause does retain significance. Saenz v. Roe, 526 U.S. 489 (1999).

38. See, e.g., Eastern Enterprises v. Apfel, 524 U.S. 498 (1998) (relying on due process as well as takings clause); Dolan v. City of Tigard, 512 U.S. 374 (1994); Lucas v. South Carolina Coastal Council, 505 U.S. 1003 (1992) (takings); Nollan v. California Coast Commission, 483 U.S.825 (1987) (takings). The Court also sometimes invokes laissez-faire economics in other settings, such as review of state regulations that burden interstate commerce.

39. See, e.g. William E. Forbath, *Constitutional Change and the Politics of History,* 108 Yale L.J. 1917, 1922 (1999); Joyce Appleby, *The Americans' Higher-Law Thinking behind Higher Lawmaking,* 108 Yale L.J. 1995, 1995 (1999); Foner, supra note 34, at 2009.

40. Michael W. McConnell, *The Forgotten Constitutional Moment,* 11 Const. Comm. 115, 124 (1994).

41. *Id.* at 127–28.

42. See, e.g., C. Vann Woodward, Reunion and Reaction: The Compromise of 1877 and the End of Reconstruction (1951).

43. McConnell, supra note 40, at 133–40.

44. See Foner, supra note 34, at 2007 ("Overall . . . Ackerman's attempt to refute McConnell persuades me that McConnell is correct").

45. See Ackerman, *Transformations,* supra note 1, at 471–74 n.126.

46. See, e.g., Leon Litwack, North of Slavery: The Negro in the Free States 1790–1860 (1961); Pauli Murray, ed., States' Laws on Race and Color (1997); Michael J. Klarman, *The Plessy Era,* 1998 Sup. Ct. Rev. 303; Michael J. Klarman, Brown, *Originalism, and Constitutional Theory: A Response to Professor McConnell,* 81 Va. L. Rev. 1881 (1995); Harold B. Hancock, *Reconstruction in Delaware,* in Richard O. Curry, ed., Radicalism, Racism, and Party Alignment: The Border States during Reconstruction 188 (1969); Edward J. Price Jr., *School Segregation in Nineteenth Century Pennsylvania,* 43 Pa. Hist. 121 (1976); Roger D. Bridges, *Equality Deferred: Civil Rights for Illinois Blacks 1865– 1885,* 74 J. Ill. Hist. Soc'y 83 (1981).

47. Other suggested constitutional moments, besides the two discussed in this section, include the Jeffersonian Republican triumph of 1800 and the later turn away from government regulation in favor of laissez-faire economics. See Freeman, supra note 33; Walter Dean Burnham, *Constitutional Moments and Punctuated Equilibria: A Political Scientist Confronts Bruce Ackerman's* We the People, 108 Yale L.J. 2237 (1999).

48. Ackerman, *Transformations,* supra note 1, at 344.

49. Bruce Ackerman, *Beyond* Carolene Products, 98 Harv. L. Rev. 713, 745–46 (1985).

50. 505 U.S. 833 (1992).

51. Ackerman, *Transformations,* supra note 1, at 389–403.

52. He labels it "the crucial decision" for testing the success of the Reagan revolution. Ackerman, *Transformations,* supra note 1, at 27. He also distinguishes it from some of the New Deal cases, explaining that *Casey* was not the sort of "landmark" decision that commits the Court "to the new constitutional order," *id.* at 408, and he devotes an entire section of one chapter to its significance. *Id.* at 397–403.

53. *Id.* at 390, 397–98.

54. He argues that reproductive rights are an example of the Supreme Court's synthesizing the principles of the founding era and those of the New Deal. The founding

era "link[ed] the constitutional commitment to individual liberty with the rhetoric of contract and private property," Ackerman, *Foundations,* supra note 1, at 152,
but the New Deal deprived constitutional liberty of its concrete basis in property
and contract by focusing on redistribution and governmental activism. The
Supreme Court made sense of this contradiction by linking individual liberty to
another value inherent in the Bill of Rights: privacy. See *id.* at 150–58. While
Ackerman's synthesis is very clever, it is not the only possible resolution of the
"contradiction" between the two eras of constitutional politics. And it is not the
sort of linkage that most Americans would be likely to make. For a critique of
Ackerman's attempt to link reproductive rights to the New Deal, see Klarman,
supra note 10, at 790–91.

55. See Paul S. Sarbanes, *Growing Inequality as an Issue for Economic Policy,* in Aspects of
Distribution of Wealth and Income 168 (Dimitri B. Papadimitriou ed., 1994) (in-
come gap largest since 1947); Morton Bahr, *Collective Bargaining Bridges the Income
Gap,* in The Inequality Paradox: Growth of Income Disparity 34 (James A. Auerbach
& Richard S. Belous eds., 1998) ("The rise in wage inequity is now the largest since
the Great Depression").

56. See, e.g., Alden v. Maine, 527 U.S. 706 (1999) (Congress cannot subject states to suit
in state court for violation of federal law); Printz v. United States, 521 U.S. 898
(1997) (Congress cannot require state law enforcement officers to perform background checks for gun purchases); City of Boerne v. Flores, 521 U.S. 507 (1997)
(Congress cannot require state and local governments to accommodate individual
religious beliefs); Seminole Tribe of Florida v. Florida, 517 U.S. 44 (1996) (Congress
cannot subject states to suit in federal court for violation of federal law); United
States v. Lopez, 514 U.S. 549 (1995) (Congress cannot prohibit possession of guns
near schools); New York v. United States, 505 U.S. 144 (1992) (Congress cannot require states to deal with nuclear waste).

57. Both Justice Thomas and Justice Scalia joined the majority in the cases cited in note
56 supra. Justice Thomas seems particularly willing to reconsider the New Deal
Court's view of congressional power. His concurrence in United States v. Lopez, 514
U.S. 549 (1995), would essentially take the Commerce Clause powers back to what
they were 1936. See also chapter 3 on Scalia's conservative views.

58. For accounts of the Democrats' long fall, see, e.g., Thomas B. Edsall & Mary D. Edsall, Chain Reaction: The Impact of Race, Rights, and Taxes on American Politics
(1991); Harvey C. Mansfield Jr., American's Constitutional Soul 21–69 (1991);
Kevin Phillips, The Politics of Rich and Poor: Wealth and the American Electorate in
the Reagan Aftermath (1990). For an account of how a new conservatism rescued
the Democrats, see, e.g., John F. Hale, *The Making of the New Democrats,* 110 Pol. Sci.
Q. 207 (1995). For an overview and critique of the current "constitutional order,"
which replaced the New Deal/Great Society regime, see Mark Tushnet, *Foreword:
The New Constitutional Order and the Closing of Constitutional Aspiration,* 113 Harv. L.
Rev. 29 (1999).

59. Ackerman, *Transformations,* supra note 1, at 187.

60. *Id.* at 316, 324–25.

61. Jeffrey Rosen, *The Age of Mixed Results,* New Republic, 28 June 1999, at 43, 49 (reviewing Cass Sunstein, One Case at a Time: The Age of Minimalism on the Supreme
Court [1999]).

62. Forbath, supra note 39, at 1923; see also Gerald N. Rosenberg, *The Unconventional*

Conventionalist, 2 Green Bag 2d 209, 215 (1999) (*"We the People* focuses almost entirely on elite behavior").

63. Ackerman, *Transformations,* supra note 1, at 83, 89–90.
64. Freeman, supra note 33.
65. Ackerman, *Transformations,* supra note 1, at 119, quoting Sidney George Fisher, Trial of the Constitution 96–97 (1862).
66. *Madison's Notes,* supra note 12, at 127 (June 16).
67. *Id.* at 127–28.
68. Notes of Robert Yates, June 16, in 1 The Records of the Federal Convention of 1787, at 262–63 (Max Farrand ed., 1911).
69. Franklin Delano Roosevelt, First Inaugural Address, March 4, 1933, reprinted in 2 The Public Papers and Addresses of Franklin D. Roosevelt 11, 15 (1938). His second inaugural is more hopeful, but catalogues the crisis in greater detail, listing the miseries of the American public (including the famous reference to the "one-third of a nation ill-housed, ill-clad, ill-nourished). Franklin Delano Roosevelt, Second Inaugural Address, January 20, 1937, reprinted in 6 *id.* 1, 4–5 (1941).
70. *Drastic Step Demanded,* New York Times, 8 February 1933, at 1.
71. *Id.*
72. Jack N. Rakove, *Two Foxes in the Forest of History,* 11 Yale J.L. & Humanities 191, 208 (1999). Rakove concludes that this undermines the analogy to the New Deal.
73. Michael Les Benedict, *Constitutional History and Constitutional Theory: Reflections on Ackerman, Reconstruction, and the Transformation of the American Constitution,* 108 Yale L.J. 2011 (1999).
74. For background on the pre–New Deal activist government, see Kramer, supra note 35, and the sources he cites; see also Gordon, supra note 31, at 2049–50.
75. Kramer, supra note 35, at 925–28.
76. See, e.g., Barry Cushman, Rethinking the New Deal Court: The Structure of a Constitutional Revolution (1998). For a description of the opposing, "externalist" school of thought, see, e.g., Kalman, supra note 29.
77. Ackerman, *Transformations,* supra note 1, at 407.
78. For elaborations of this point, see William N. Eskridge Jr., *The One Senator, One Vote Clauses,* in Constitutional Stupidities, Constitutional Tragedies 35 (William N. Eskridge & Sanford Levinson eds., 1998); Suzanna Sherry, *Our Unconstitutional Senate,* in *id.* at 95.
79. Ackerman, *Transformations,* supra note 1, at 13.
80. *Id.* at 410.
81. *Id.* at 411.
82. Brannon P. Denning, *Means to Amend: Theories of Constitutional Change,* 65 Tenn. L. Rev. 155, 184–85 (1997).
83. Julian N. Eule, *Judicial Review of Direct Democracy,* 99 Yale L.J. 1503, 1526–27 (1990). See also Elizabeth Garrett, *Money, Agenda-Setting, and Direct Democracy,* 77 Tex. L. Rev. 1845 (1999); Sherman J. Clark, *A Populist Critique of Direct Democracy,* 112 Harv. L. Rev. 434 (1998); Elizabeth Garrett, *Who Directs Direct Democracy?* 4 U. Chi. L. Sch. Roundtable 17 (1996–97).
84. See, e.g., Philip P. Frickey, *Interpretation on the Borderline: Constitution, Canons, Direct Democracy,* 1996 Ann. Surv. Am. L. 477; Sylvia R. Lazos Vargas, *Judicial Review of Initiatives and Referendums in Which Majorities Vote on Minorities' Democratic Citizenship,* 60 Ohio St. L.J. 399 (1999).

CHAPTER SEVEN

1. See Thomas D. Eisele, *Taking Our Actual Constitution Seriously,* 95 Mich. L. Rev. 1799, 1799 (1997) (book review).
2. See Ronald Dworkin, Taking Rights Seriously 105–30 (1977).
3. See Jeffrey Goldsworthy, *Dworkin as an Originalist,* 17 Const. Comm. 49 (2000); Silas Wasserstrom, *The Empire's New Clothes,* 75 Geo. L.J. 199, 200 n.8 (1986) (book review) ("[a] fastidious consistency has never been one of Dworkin's hobgoblins").
4. Ronald Dworkin, Freedom's Law: The Moral Reading of the American Constitution (1996).
5. Learned Hand, The Spirit of Liberty (1952). Hand's views are further developed in his The Bill of Rights (1958).
6. The definitive biography is Gerald Gunther, Learned Hand: The Man and the Judge (1994).
7. Dworkin, supra note 4, at 334–35.
8. *Id.* 341–42 (second bracket in original).
9. Planned Parenthood v. Casey, 505 U.S. 833, 844 (1992).
10. Dworkin, supra note 4, at 342.
11. Hand, *Bill of Rights,* supra note 5, at 73.
12. Dworkin, supra note 4, at 343, 347. It is easy to imagine why he might have found Hand's challenge irresistible. Dworkin was one of Hand's law clerks. For him, Hand was not merely a great judge but a revered figure. Going beyond the traditional veneration of law clerks for their judges, his gracious recent tribute to Hand even gives Hand some credit for his own marriage. *Id.* at 332. Dworkin's close relationship with Hand would in any event have made Hand's constitutional views a matter of great interest to him. But the interest may well have been heightened because, as he tells us, much of his clerkship year was spent discussing Hand's forthcoming lectures on constitutional theory. *Id.* at 347. It would not be surprising if, given the stark disagreement between Dworkin and the great judge whom he so much admired, the desire to answer Hand was a motivating force in his thought.
13. *Id.* at 291–94.
14. See Goldsworthy, supra note 3. See also Michael C. Dorf, *Truth, Justice, and the American Constitution,* 97 Col. L. Rev. 133, 138–43 (1997) (review essay), for a useful analysis of Dworkin's views.
15. Dworkin criticizes Scalia for confusing the two types of meaning in this way in *The Arduous Virtue of Fidelity: Originalism, Scalia, Tribe, and Nerve,* 65 Fordham L. Rev. 1249, 1250–57 (1997).
16. This choice of levels is itself a controversial moral decision. Dworkin believes, however, that provisions such as equal protection cannot legitimately be interpreted at a low level of abstraction, for to do so would be inconsistent with the deliberately broad constitutional language.
17. Dworkin, supra note 4, at 10, 14, 127, 293–302.
18. *Id.* at 19 (emphasis in original). We can also imagine a regime in which public opinion polls are routinely translated into law, but without producing any sense of collective community decision.
19. *Id.* at 21–26.
20. Of course, the traders themselves are only a subset of the population, but we have

no different reaction when the Fed adjusts the money supply, thereby changing the inflation and unemployment rates from those determined collectively by the private actions of everyone in the economy. Nor can we justify this on the ground that the Fed's action itself represents that of a majority, since the Fed is as a practical matter about as insulated from majoritarian influence as the Supreme Court.

21. Similarly, the government's failure to follow the latest shift in public opinion polls does not violate democratic principles. Public opinion polls and electoral results reflect everyone's views equally. Thus the public opinion poll is the paradigm of statistical equality because everyone has exactly the same chance of being randomly selected in the sample and everyone in the sample counts equally. But Dworkin argues that the statistical concept of collective political action can provide no basis for a norm of political equality. In the statistical conception, political equality must consist of everyone's preferences (the inputs) being equally likely to affect legal decisions (the outputs). But this kind of equality can provide no model of equal democratic citizenship, which must accommodate the reality that people have varying political connections, assets, and abilities. Moreover, some people have, by virtue of their offices, greater influence than others, and this is considered no threat to equality so long as those offices are in principle open to all candidates. Thus, Dworkin says, our concept of equality must mean something other than having a mathematically equal influence on outcomes. But equal influence is the only conception of equality possible within the statistical view of collective action. *Id.* at 26–29.

22. Ackerman has said so explicitly, noting that he would uphold as valid—if unwise— a constitutional amendment establishing Christianity as the state religion and proscribing all other religions. Bruce Ackerman, We the People: Foundations 14–15 & n.† (1991). Amar's view of the Constitution logically points to a similar result.

23. A helpful discussion of Dworkin's view of democracy can be found in Ara Lovitt, *Constitutional Confusion?* 50 Stan. L. Rev. 565, 586–88 (1998) (book note).

24. Although some white southerners might feel that the Civil War had this effect in their states, some blacks might well feel that their situation resembles colonialism, as might some Native Americans.

25. Dworkin, supra note 4, at 11, 12.

26. See Ronald Dworkin, *The Partnership Conception of Democracy*, 86 Cal. L. Rev. 453 (1998).

27. Because of this condition, McConnell is wrong in his otherwise perceptive review when he asserts that Dworkin would be content with a society in which a nondemocratic trustee showed equal respect and concern for all. See Michael W. McConnell, *The Importance of Humility in Judicial Review: A Comment on Ronald Dworkin's "Moral Reading" of the Constitution*, 65 Fordham L. Rev. 1269, 1291–92 (1997).

28. Dworkin, supra note 4, at 25. We ourselves have referred to a similar concept, preventing the government from branding any group as untouchables, as the "pariah principle." Daniel Farber & Suzanna Sherry, *The Pariah Principle*, 13 Const. Comm. 257 (1996).

29. Dworkin, supra note 4, at 25. Some might argue that no one with *true* self-respect would engage in certain sexual practices or adopt certain religious views—so Dworkin's argument would require some philosophical shoring up.

30. A similar argument is made in Gary Lawson, *On Reading Recipes . . . and Constitutions*, 85 Geo. L.J. 1823, 1835 (1997).

31. But Epstein would no doubt reply that this is an overly sentimental view of government, and that a more realistic understanding of government would prevent us from identifying it with our individual agency.

32. Dworkin, supra note 4, at 33–34.

33. *Id.* at 34-35. For Dworkin's defense of his reading of the Bill of Rights, see *id.* at 73–81.

34. See Dorf, supra note 14, at 167–68; McConnell, supra note 27, at 1278–86; Lovitt, supra note 23, at 576–84; Eisele, supra note 1, at 1811–13.

35. Richard A. Posner, The Problematics of Moral and Legal Theory 112–20 (1999).

36. This theory is developed in Ronald Dworkin, Law's Empire 284–312 (1986). For a recent critique, see Ken Kress, *Why No Judge Should Be a Dworkinian Coherentist*, 77 Texas L. Rev. 1375 (1999).

37. Dworkin, supra note 4, at 345–46.

38. Eisele, supra note 1, at 1810.

39. Dworkin, supra note 4, at 346–47.

40. Compared with other government institutions, the Senate has the advantage of slow turnover, so it could dampen ill-considered public enthusiasms, and although it is less representative than the House, it is presumably as representative as the Supreme Court. Admittedly, on more than one historic occasion, the Senate's capacity to make principled decisions might be questioned.

41. McConnell, supra note 27, at 1272–76.

42. 347 U.S. 483 (1954).

43. Since education of any kind had been denied southern blacks, separate schools were a big step up; perhaps it seemed unrealistic to carp over the form of schooling.

44. Dworkin, supra note 4, at 293–94.

45. *Id.* at 293. Chief Justice Warren's reliance on psychological studies to prove that segregated schools were unequal, and his effort to show the centrality of education to modern social functioning, provide support for this reading of *Brown* itself.

46. Dworkin, supra note 36, at 384.

47. The Court has extended some protections of the Fourteenth Amendment beyond racial discrimination to some historically disadvantaged groups, such as women. The now-famous footnote 4 in *Carolene Products* suggests a rationale for doing so. "There may be narrower scope for operation of the presumption of constitutionality when legislation appears on its face to be within a specific prohibition of the Constitution. . . . Nor need we enquire whether similar considerations enter into the review of statutes directed at particular religious, . . . , or national, . . . , or racial minorities . . . whether prejudice against discrete and insular minorities may be a special condition, which tends seriously to curtail the operation of those political processes ordinarily to be relied upon to protect minorities, and which may call for a correspondingly more searching judicial inquiry." United States v. Carolene Products Co., 304 U.S. 144, 152 n.4 (1938). "Discrete and insular" minorities might include, for example, people with disabilities and gay, lesbian, bisexual, and transgendered people. (The Supreme Court has not extended the amendment to apply to such groups however. See City of Cleburne v. Cleburne Living Center, 473 U.S. 432 [1985]; Romer v. Evans, 517 U.S. 620 [1996].)

48. Dworkin, supra note 36, at 385.

49. Dworkin, supra note 4, at 295.

50. *Id.* at 11.

51. *Id.* at 2. For commentary on these conflicting strains in Dworkin's thought, see McConnell, supra note 27, at 1271–78.
52. Dworkin, supra note 4, at 159.
53. *Id.* at 156.
54. Dworkin, supra note 36, at 394, 396, 397.
55. "In the case at bar, however, we deal with statutes containing racial classifications, and the fact of equal application does not immunize the statute from the very heavy burden of justification which the Fourteenth Amendment has traditionally required of state statutes drawn according to race." Loving v. Virginia, 388 U.S. 1, 9 (1967). "There can be no question but that Virginia's miscegenation statutes rest solely upon distinctions drawn according to race . . . . Over the years, this Court has consistently repudiated '[d]istinctions between citizens solely because of their ancestry' as being 'odious to a free people whose institutions are founded upon the doctrine of equality.'" *Id.* at 11 (quoting Hirabayashi v. United States, 320 U.S. 81, 100 [1943]). "At the very least, the Equal Protection Clause demands that racial classifications, especially suspect in criminal statutes, be subjected to the 'most rigid scrutiny,' . . . and, if they are ever to be upheld, they must be shown to be necessary to the accomplishment of some permissible state objective, independent of the racial discrimination which it was the object of the Fourteenth Amendment to eliminate." *Id.* (quoting Korematsu v. United States, 323 U.S. 214, 216 [1944]). See also Suzanna Sherry, *All the Supreme Court Really Needs to Know It Learned from the Warren Court,* 50 Vand. L. Rev. 459 (1997).
56. Epstein, for one, has much to say on this subject.
57. Apart from being immutable, racial traits also involve matters that would never be considered legally significant at all in a world without a history of discrimination. In the absence of a history in which racism held sway, who would possibly come up with the ideas of sorting schoolchildren by skin tone or favoring government contractors with dark pigmentation? Of course, all racial categorizations do not bear the same relationship with racism—some endorse it while others claim to get beyond it—but the entanglement of these categories with a racist past does give them a markedly different cultural meaning than categories based on geography or ability level.
58. This continues to be true in his most recent writing on the subject, Ronald Dworkin, Sovereign Virtues: The Theory and Practice of Equality (2000).
59. For a discussion of Dworkin's earlier (but basically similar) writing on the subject, see Abner Greene, *Uncommon Ground,* 62 Geo. Wash. L. Rev. 646, 653–57 (1994) (book review).
60. Griswold v. Connecticut, 381 U.S. 479 (1965). Dworkin also argues that the abortion decision is protected by the Free Exercise Clause, on the theory that it involves utterly fundamental views about the meaning and value of life. Dworkin, supra note 4, at 104–10.
61. Dworkin, supra note 4, at 88–89, 90–92, 104, 113–14.
62. Which is not to say that we consider the argument airtight. For one thing, his facts may be wrong: previability fetuses possibly *may* feel pain. For some criticisms of Dworkin's argument, see Dorf, supra note 14, at 152–59.
63. This is not to say that arguments of this kind have no place at all in constitutional law, but judges would be most unwise to allow such arguments to dominate their thought.

64. Dworkin, supra note 4, at 143–46. Dworkin reads the Supreme Court's decision on the subject in *Washington v. Glucksberg,* 521 U.S. 702 (1997), as accepting in principle the existence of such a right but viewing the associated risks as large enough to justify a state prohibition. See Ronald Dworkin, *Darwin's New Bulldog,* 111 Harv. L. Rev. 1718, 1729 (1998).
65. For a criticism of Dworkin's views, see Seth F. Kreimer, *Does Pro-Choice Mean Pro-Kevorkian? An Essay on* Roe, Casey, *and the Right to Die,* 44 Am. U. L. Rev. 803 (1995).
66. *Glucksberg,* 521 U.S. at 735.
67. See Lovitt, supra note 23, at 602; McConnell, supra note 27, at 1291–92.
68. Planned Parenthood v. Casey, 505 U.S. 833, 844 (1992).

CHAPTER EIGHT

1. See Richard A. Posner, *Against Constitutional Theory,* 73 N.Y.U. L. Rev. 1 (1998). Almost alone among our theorists, Justice Scalia seems to have had some occasional qualms about the validity of his public rhetoric, as we saw in chapter 3. But he now seems to have overcome these agnostic impulses about grand theory.
2. One scholar suggests that at least in its "countermajoritarian difficulty" form, the modern appeal of foundationalism derives from three factors. Barry Friedman, *An Academic Obsession: The History of the Countermajoritarian Difficulty, Part III* (forthcoming). First, the demise of formalism and the rise of legal realism conflicted with a continuing concern for the rule of law (as we have seen, Scalia is particularly concerned about this). Second, the "nearly heroic" stature of many of the early scholars concerned with the countermajoritarian difficulty "guaranteed transmission and growth" of its one-sided view of judicial review. Finally, liberals, who early in the twentieth century castigated the pre–New Deal Court for excessive interference with democratic governance, were hoist by their own petard when they were forced to defend the liberal Warren Court's invalidation of *conservative* legislation—leading them to focus on the countermajoritarian difficulty rather than on the substance of each Court's decisions. Obviously, these last two historical explanations for the obsession with the countermajoritarian difficulty do not provide any justification for foundationalism. Concern about the rule of law, however, is undoubtedly legitimate. We deal with this problem later in this chapter.
3. See Friedman, *An Academic Obsession,* supra note 2; Barry Friedman, *The History of the Countermajoritarian Difficulty: Part One: The Road to Judicial Supremacy,* 73 N.Y.U. L. Rev. 333 (1998) [hereinafter *The Road to Judicial Supremacy*]; Rebecca Brown, *Accountability, Liberty, and the Constitution,* 98 Colum. L. Rev. 531, 531–33 (1998).
4. See Friedman, *The Road to Judicial Supremacy,* supra note 3.
5. Steven L. Winter, *An Upside/Down View of the Countermajoritarian Difficulty,* 69 Tex. L. Rev. 1881, 1924–25 (1991).
6. At least one other scholar—a historian who has studied both the Yale Law School and legal liberalism—has noted the extent to which Ackerman follows Bickel. See Laura Kalman, *Law, Politics, and the New Deal(s),* 108 Yale L.J. 2165, 2207–13 (1999). Another scholar also characterizes Ackerman as trying to get around the countermajoritarian difficulty by denying its premises. Michael J. Klarman, *Constitutional Fact/Constitutional Fiction: A Critique of Bruce Ackerman's Theory of Constitutional Moments,* 44 Stan. L. Rev. 759 (1992).

Perhaps the best linkage of Amar, Ackerman, and Bickel is by Professor James Fleming:

> But Ackerman is hobbled by the question of "the possibility for popular sovereignty," just as Bickel was haunted by the "countermajoritarian difficulty." Accordingly, Ackerman develops a theory of democracy that reduces or recasts our Constitution and constitutional democracy into the mold of popular sovereignty, just as Bickel rejected as deviant any feature of our constitutional scheme that did not conform to a theory of majoritarian representative democracy. (Amar is either the synthetic culmination or the reductio ad absurdum of the Yale school, for he fundamentally conceives popular sovereignty as majoritarian representative democracy.)

James E. Fleming, *We the Unconventional American People*, 65 U. Chi. L. Rev. 1513, 1541 (1998). Like Fleming, we see connections among some of our scholars through Bickel's countermajoritarian difficulty (although we believe the fundamental flaws in their methodolgies run deeper).

7. See John Hart Ely, Democracy and Distrust: A Theory of Judicial Review (1980); Robert A. Burt, The Constitution in Conflict (1992). For a recent reappraisal of Ely's work, see Brian Boynton, *Democracy and Distrust after Twenty Years: Ely's Process Theory and Constitutional Law from 1990 to 2000*, 53 Stan. L. Rev. 397 (2000).

8. See, e.g., Friedman, *The Road to Judicial Supremacy,* supra note 3; Michael J. Klarman, *Rethinking the Civil Rights and Civil Liberties Revolutions*, 82 Va. L. Rev. 1 (1996); Steven P. Croley, *The Majoritarian Difficulty: Elective Judiciaries and the Rule of Law,* 62 U. Chi. L. Rev. 689 (1995); Barry Friedman, *Dialogue and Judicial Review,* 91 Mich. L. Rev. 577 (1993); Mark A. Graber, *The Nonmajoritarian Difficulty: Legislative Deference to the Judiciary,* 7 Stud. Am. Pol. Dev. 35 (1993); Winter, supra note 5, at 1924–25. One might call these scholars the anti-countermajoritarianists.

9. See, e.g., Anthony Lester, *The Overseas Trade in the American Bill of Rights,* 88 Colum. L. Rev. 537 (1988). Since Lord Lester wrote, the trend has continued apace.

10. Akhil Reed Amar, *Intratextualism,* 112 Harv. L. Rev. 747, 789–92 (1999).

11. Among the practical reasons are to reduce the number of appeals and retrials, to take advantage of the ability of group decisions to iron out individual idiosyncracies, and to avoid second-guessing the observations of the majority of the people who were in a position to observe the trial.

12. Marbury v. Madison, 5 U.S. 137, 176–77 (1803):

> The powers of the legislature are defined and limited; and that those limits may not be mistaken or forgotten, the constitution is written. . . . It is a proposition too plain to be contested, that the constitution controls any legislative act repugnant to it; or, that the legislature may alter the constitution by an ordinary act. Between these alternatives there is no middle ground. The constitution is either a superior, paramount law, unchangeable by ordinary means, or it is on a level with ordinary legislative acts, and like other acts, is alterable when the legislature shall please to alter it. If the former part of the alternative be true, then a legislative act contrary to the constitution is not law: if the latter part be true, then written constitutions are absurd attempts, on the part of the people, to limit a power in its own nature illimitable. Certainly all those who have framed written constitutions contemplate them as forming the fundamental and paramount law of the nation, and consequently the theory of every such government must be, that an act of the legislature repugnant to the constitution is void.

This theory is essentially attached to a written constitution, and is consequently to be considered by this court as one of the fundamental principles of our society.

13. Including the Supremacy Clause, which makes the Constitution specifically binding on state judges.

14. Learned Hand, The Spirit of Liberty 109–10 (1952); Learned Hand, The Bill of Rights 56 (1958). One of the earliest advocates of this "minimalist" theory of judicial review, James Bradley Thayer, urged that judges should only invalidate statutes if there was a very clear conflict with the Constitution. See James Bradley Thayer, *The Origin and Scope of the American Doctrine of Constitutional Law*, 7 Harv. L. Rev. 129 (1893).

15. For another version of this critique of the countermajoritarian difficulty, see Erwin Chemerinsky, *Foreword: The Vanishing Constitution*, 103 Harv. L. Rev. 43 (1989).

16. See Lynn A. Baker & Samuel H. Dinkin, *The Senate: An Institution Whose Time Has Gone?* 13 J.L. & Pol. 21 (1997).

17. See Paul Edelman & Suzanna Sherry, Pick a Number, Any Number: State Representation in Congress after the 2000 Census (forthcoming, Cal. L. Rev. [2002]).

18. See Stephen L. Carter, The Confirmation Mess: Cleaning up the Federal Appointments Process (1994).

19. See Christopher J. Peters, *Assessing the New Judicial Minimalizing*, 100 Colum. L. Rev. 1454, 1477–92 (2000).

20. It is true that Article V seems to limit the use of constitutional amendments to modify representation in the Senate, but there are various ways of getting around this prohibition. The Article V proviso may not protect itself from amendment, so a two-step process could be used with one amendment repealing the proviso and a second reapportioning the Senate. Or we could leave the Senate intact, but eliminate its lawmaking role, perhaps establishing another chamber elected by larger regional districts. Or we could even argue, as one of our colleagues has suggested in conversation, that the "Senate" contemplated in Article V no longer exists anyway, given the shift from selection of senators by the state governments to popular election.

21. One can easily imagine a theory deducing from the original nature of senators as state rather popular representatives the conclusion that they can vote against legislation only if it violates states' rights.

22. See Jack N. Rakove & Elizabeth Beaumont, *Rights Talk in the Past Tense*, 52 Stan. L. Rev. 1865, 1894 (2000) (quoting a letter of Sir George Saville, written in 1768).

23. In our view, the common law method need not be introspectively focused on past decisions and can effectively respond to changing social conditions and improved information—though admittedly the courts could do better in this regard. See Michael C. Dorf, *Foreword: The Limits of Socratic Deliberation*, 112 Harv. L. Rev. 4 (1998).

24. See David A. Strauss, *Common Law Constitutional Interpretation*, 63 U. Chi. L. Rev. 877 (1996).

25. Michael W. McConnell, *The Importance of Humility in Judicial Review: A Comment on Ronald Dworkin's "Moral Reading" of the Constitution*, 65 Fordham L. Rev. 1269, 1292 (1997).

26. 531 U.S. 288 (2000).

27. See Bush v. Gore, 531 U.S. 98 (2000); Bush v. Palm Beach County Canvassing Board, 531 U.S. 70 (2000).

28. Cass Sunstein, Legal Reasoning and Political Conflict 9 (1996). Sunstein is far from alone in advocating this pragmatic approach. For other prominent examples, see Richard A. Posner, The Problems of Jurisprudence (1990); Karl N. Llewellyn, Jurisprudence: Realism in Theory and Practice (1962).

29. Sunstein, supra note 28, at 37.

30. *Id.* at 67. For another thoughtful recent appraisal of common law constitutionalism, see Peters, supra note 19, at 1504–13, 1523–29.

31. See Lillian R. BeVier, *The Moment and the Millennium: A Question of Time, or Law?* 66 Geo. Wash. U. L. Rev. 1112, 1117 (1998) (textualists are "tenaciously devoted to an ideal of legitimacy that requires judicial decision making to be constrained by objective standards and criteria external to the judges themselves").

32. Richard H. Fallon Jr., *How to Choose a Constitutional Theory,* 87 Cal. L. Rev. 535 (1999).

33. Lawyers and judges during the eighteenth century were not oriented toward articulating broad principles; the historical record is fragmentary, and various colonies (as well as England) had differing practices. It is also often quite hard to determine the most analogous eighteenth-century cause of action to some statutory claim created two centuries later.

34. See Akhil Reed Amar, *A Neo-Federalist View of Article III: Separating the Two Tiers of Federal Jurisdiction,* 65 B.U. L. Rev. 205 (1985); Akhil Reed Amar, *The Two-Tiered Structure of the Judiciary Act of 1789,* 138 U. Pa. L. Rev. 1499 (1990).

35. Sunstein, supra note 28, at 39.

36. Fallon, supra note 32, at 565–66.

37. *Id.* at 22.

38. Posner, supra note 28, at 10.

39. Frank H. Easterbrook, *Textualism and the Dead Hand,* 66 Geo. Wash. L. Rev. 1119, 1122 (1998).

40. Anthony T. Kronman, The Lost Lawyer: Failing Ideals of the Legal Profession (1993). See also McConnell, supra note 25, at 1292 (criticizing Dworkin on this basis).

41. 17 U.S. 316 (1819). Amar claims *McCulloch* as an example of his documentarian method because the opinion "cites no cases by name." Akhil Reed Amar, *Foreword: The Document and the Doctrine,* 114 Harv. L. Rev. 26, 32 (2000). But Marshall differs from Amar in the breadth of his interpretative tools, his lack of interest in forcing cases into a preexisting global framework, and the unerring sense of statesmanship that drives his analysis.

42. For discussions of legal pragmatism, see, e.g., The Revival of Pragmatism: New Essays on Social Thought, Law, and Culture (Morris Dickstein ed., 1998); Pragmatism in Law and Society (Michael Brint & William Weaver eds., 1991); Posner, supra note 28; Daniel A. Farber, *Reinventing Brandeis: Legal Pragmatism for the Twenty-First Century,* 1995 U. Ill. L. Rev. 163; Thomas C. Grey, *Holmes and Legal Pragmatism,* 41 Stan. L. Rev. 787 (1989); Daniel A. Farber, *Legal Pragmatism and the Constitution,* 72 Minn. L. Rev. 1331 (1988).

43. 17 U.S. at 407; *id.* at 415.

44. For a similarly pragmatic—and very perceptive—analysis of another famous case, *Missouri v. Holland,* 252 U.S. 346 (1920), see Philip Bobbitt, Constitutional Interpretation 43–108 (1991).

45. Indeed, a study in the area of statutory interpretation suggests that theoretical views about methodology may have little impact on judges' votes. See Daniel Farber, *Do Theories of Statutory Interpretation Matter? A Case Study,* 94 Nw. L. Rev. 1409 (2000).

46. See Posner, supra note 28, at 11–22.
47. William G. Bowen & Derek Bok, The Shape of the River: Long-Term Consequences of Considering Race in College and University Admissions (1998); for a critique, see Stephan Thernstrom & Abigail Thernstrom, Book Review, *Reflections on the Shape of the River*, 46 UCLA L. Rev. 1583 (1999).
48. See Vicki C. Jackson & Mark Tushnet, Comparative Constitutional Law (1999).
49. See Robert E. Hudec & Daniel A. Farber, *Free Trade and the Regulatory State: A GATT's Eye View of the Dormant Commerce Clause*, 47 Vand. L. Rev. 1401 (1994).
50. Some of the work in this area includes Michael J. Klarman, *Majoritarian Judicial Review: The Entrenchment Problem*, 85 Geo. L.J. 491 (1997); Lawrence M. Friedman, A History of American Law (2d ed. 1985). See also Malcolm M. Feeley & Edward L. Rubin, Judicial Policy Making and the Modern State: How the Courts Reformed America's Prisons (1998).